m

10/04 DATE DUE FOR RETURN

DEVASTATING EDEN

DEVASTATING EDEN

The Search for Utopia
in America

BRIAN THOMPSON

HarperCollins*Publishers*

HarperCollins*Publishers*
77−85 Fulham Palace Road,
Hammersmith, London, w6 8JB

www.harpercollins.co.uk

Published by HarperCollins*Publishers* 2004
I

Copyright © Brian Thompson 2004

Brian Thompson asserts the moral right to
be identified as the author of this work

A catalogue record for this book
is available from the British Library

ISBN 0-00-713738-9

Set in PostScript Monotype Apollo with Castellar display
by Rowland Phototypesetting Ltd, Bury St Edmunds, Suffolk

Printed and bound in Great Britain by
Clays Ltd, St Ives plc

For Bill Greaves

CONTENTS

ILLUSTRATIONS

Harmony, 24 January, 1826, (41 124) by Charles Alexander Lesueur, Museum of Natural History, Le Havre, France.

PAGE 5:

Top: Pencil Portrait of Frances Wright d'Arusmont and William Phiquepal d'Arusmont accompanying Frances Wright, ILS 11 Oct. 1835, The Pierpont Morgan Library, New York. MA 1950.

Bottom: Frances Wright at 32 in the costume adopted by the New Harmony Community in 1826.

PAGE 6:

Top: George Birkbeck, Courtesy of the Chicago Historical Society.

Bottom left: George Flower, Patricia Flower Martin Collection.

Bottom right: Eliza Julia Flower, 1855 by D. Rooster, courtesy of the Chicago Historical Society.

PAGE 7:

'New Harmony – All Owin' and No Payin'' by George Cruikshank.

PAGE 8:

Top: New Harmony by David Dale Owen, 1830.

Bottom: Robert Owen, University of London Library.

PREFACE

A public meeting of more than ordinary importance took place in London on 14 May 1855, if the handbill that announced it was to be believed. In the chair was the venerable Robert Owen, the former master of New Lanark Mills, philanthropist and – after his own fashion – political theorist. Owen had once been a great voice in the land, his words attended to by princes and statesmen. Now he was a husk of what he had been, a frail but still voluble man of 84, reeling a little from his most recent enthusiasm, a taste for spiritual seances. Miss Marie Hayden of Boston, Massachusetts, had found a way, not of putting him in touch with the dear departed, but of plucking from the Other Side endorsements of his lifelong credo.

On the stage was a three-foot-square board, for the moment suitably shrouded by a cloth. When the time came, Owen had the cloth removed. What was revealed was a graphic sketch of something called the Devastator. It was designed – or at any rate dreamed up – by two mechanics called Sweetlove and Cowen, who, unable to address audiences as confidently as Owen, left him to explain its purpose. Once built, the Devastator would destroy 100,000 lives an hour, spewing shell and shot in irresistible numbers and running the length and breadth of the world upon its six wheels, so ending the will to make war wherever it showed its ugly head. The time for talking was over. If rational argument could not do the job of making the world a better place, then the answer must be force.

Owen had only three more years to live and this was his final commentary on human nature. The meeting at which he unveiled the Devastator was dubbed by him, with characteristic aplomb, The World's Convention Of Delegates From The Human Race. It took place in St Martin's Hall, Long Acre, built in 1850 as a concert venue but leased out from time to time for political gatherings. The World's Convention had other great business to conduct that day – nothing less than the inauguration of the New Millennium. At the end of its proceedings, an age would commence in which the mighty engine of destruction would be set to work. There might be death on an unparalleled scale to begin with – Owen had been warned in spiritualist seances of a 'shattering global event' to take place in 1855–6. But in the end Mr Sweetlove's monster would borrow from its inventor's name and earn its secondary title – the Universal Peacemaker. A velvet glove lay curled inside the iron fist.

There was an immediate use for this terrible weapon of mass destruction, for the Crimean War was not going to plan at all. Once the Devastator had levelled Sebastopol and Kronstadt to the ground, Owen was sure that things would be seen in a very different light. With the Devastator parked on the smoking ruins of the Russian Empire, ready to be recoaled at a moment's notice and sent wherever else terror dared to raise its banner, the world would finally get the message. The new moral order, which bore many resemblances to the old and failed Owenism, would prevail, only this time by main force. Ten hours of the Devastator's operation would deliver up a million souls to their Maker. Ten days would end the war on terror once and for all.

The parallels with our present insanity are easy to draw. We must do Owen the honour of describing him as a good man, though one untroubled by too much common sense. It is not the shadowy impracticality of the Devastator that gives us pause – how can any of us say that who have lived for more than half a century under threat of the Bomb – but the childlike immaturity of Owen's mind. The Board of Admiralty, Horse Guards and the Board of Ordnance had already heard Owen out with varying degrees of impatience and sent him on his way. After their conference, the delegates of the human race disbanded, grew old and died. St Martin's Hall burned down in 1859, was rebuilt, became a theatre, then a warehouse, then was torn down. Offices occupy the site today.

What sends a shudder of recognition through us is something else. For Owen, evil was not a quality but a quantity. This is a view shared in our time (apparently) by the leaders of the one surviving superpower. The war on terror is not a battle of ideas but a matter of straightforward accountancy – hunt the malefactors down, destroy them, rule a line under the profit and loss, move on. The Devastator has changed its nature from a machine to a government. To the dread of anyone living outside the home of the brave and the land of the free, the awesome threat has come perilously close to being embodied in an entire people. That this cannot really be so is in part the argument of this book.

Thirty years before the meeting at St Martin's Hall, Owen landed at New York, his ultimate destination what American historians call the Old Northwest. What he found on his arrival at the frontier and what happened to him there is the truer echo from history. The new moral order had, in those headier and happier days, only one means of delivery – rational argument. In Owen's luggage were multiple copies of his pamphlets which he distributed to those who could not come to hear him in person. Once understood, the arguments they contained would prove irresistible and the way would open painlessly to health, happiness and the enjoyment of mankind's true worth.

In some ways, the aged Owen, who 30 years later convened the human race to a concert room in Long Acre, there to examine the sketch of the Devastator, was being more realistic. Blowing people up to get their compliance has indeed proved to be a better political stratagem and the most recent promulgation of the new moral order is nothing if not wreathed in gunsmoke. The Universal Peacemaker, that smartest of all weapons, will, when it comes – if it comes – fly but a single flag. And that, to those who presently salute that flag, makes perfectly good sense.

The epigraph to what follows in these pages comes from Jean-Jacques Rousseau, who wrote this in his *Discourse on Inequality*:

> 'If I were told that society is so constituted that each man gains by serving others, I should reply that that would be all very well but for the fact that he gains even more by harming them. No profit is so legitimate that it cannot be surpassed by what can be done illegitimately, and a harm done to a neighbour is always more lucrative than any good turn.'
>
> To which our masters reply 'Ah yes, but don't you see? There is no turning back. It is all too late for that.'

PROLOGUE

The Morning opening upon us

There were more than 250 offences for which a man might be hanged in eighteenth-century England. Murder, mutiny at sea or on land, desertion and enlisting in a foreign service were capital offences. These are obvious enough examples but the list included shop-theft, pickpocketing, the maiming of cattle, the sending of threatening letters and some others where it is difficult to see the extreme gravity of the matter – for example, the cutting down of trees in an avenue or garden. Sodomy was a capital crime, as was stealing an heiress or concealing the death of a bastard child. To these statutes could be added scores more for which the offences were punishable by transportation, whipping, the pillory, imprisonment or hard labour in houses of correction. Setting fire to underwood came under these headings, as did pilfering the shroud from a grave, stealing the corpse, robbing orchards, poaching fish from a pond or river or selling fireworks.

The immediate picture is of a society with a very short fuse to its temper. In practice, many fewer people were hanged than the law allowed, but, taken all together, it is hard to resist the conclusion that what was happening in the criminal justice system was the merciless harrowing by those who had of those who had not. Legal violence on this scale brought some consequences beyond the immediate and material. When a man ended up on the gallows for stealing a loaf of bread or a cut of meat, justice could be said to have been done and the law of the land upheld. Looked at in a different light, his fate was like a corrosive stain at the very heart of what makes other people's lives real to us. Taking a life for such unimportant felonies did the society that ordained the punishment no credit.

The London magistrate and novelist Henry Fielding conceded the point. 'No man of common sense can think the Life of a man and a few shillings to be of equal consideration,' he admitted, but went on to give the usual defence of capital punishment. 'The Terror of Example is the thing proposed, and one man is sacrificed for the Preservation of Thousands.'

In London, hanging days at Tyburn were a public holiday. The condemned were taken by cart to the place of execution in stages: at St Sepulchre's, Holborn, they were given a nosegay, at St Giles-in-the-Fields, a last mug of ale. When they reached Tyburn Tree, there was always an intensely appreciative crowd to see them plunge into eternity. The formalities were minimal. Once the nooses had been arranged, the cartman whipped up his horses and left his passengers kicking and dangling at the end of their ropes.

It was a humane act on the part of some to run forward and swing on the bodies of their friends or loved ones to speed the process of death. The mob liked a man who bothered to wear his best clothes to the gallows and their affections were specially aroused by the young or good-looking. When that day's batch was cut down, it was not uncommon for people to take a dead man's hand and apply it to some part of their body in the superstitious belief that it might cure illness. Relatives of the hanged had one more horror to endure. The clothes in which the condemned had gone to their Maker were now the property of the executioner and unless these grubby clouts were repurchased, they were sold on to the old clothes stalls in Monmouth Street. Unclaimed bodies were pitched naked into pits near the gallows.

The last hangings at Tyburn took place in 1783 and then the crowds transferred their enthusiasm to Newgate, where public executions continued to as late as 1868. Once the jeering (and, not infrequently, prolonged applause) was over, it is hard to imagine that many of the crowd walked away with anything of a conscience about the day's events. Little of terror seems to have been inculcated – Tyburn always provided rich pickings for thieves and prostitutes who were there to work the crowd. What pity was engendered was much more like blind sentiment, the treacly stuff that does not flow quickly from person to person and changes nothing. A public hanging, far from being a deterrent, was a spectacle to be bracketed with bear-baiting or fighting with dogs.

In an atmosphere of such swingeing justice, it was as though some people – the numerical majority – grew from a different and lesser branch of humanity altogether. Samuel Taylor Coleridge expressed this perfectly in a letter he wrote to his new friend Robert Southey in 1795.

> It is *wrong*, Southey! for a little girl with a half-famished sickly baby to put her head in at the window of an inn – 'Pray give me a bit of bread and meat!' from a party dining on lamb, green peas and salad. Why? Because it is *impertinent* and *obtrusive*!
>
> 'I am a gentleman! and wherefore the clamorous voice of woe intrude upon mine ear?' My companion is a man of cultivated though not very vigorous understanding; his feelings are all on the side of humanity; yet such are the unfeeling remarks, which the lingering remains of aristocracy occasionally prompt.

Coleridge was young and perhaps too eager to believe the aristocracy already reduced to a rump but he put his finger on a central failure of imagination, one yet to be cured in our own times. His dinner companion, whose lamb had been spoiled by the arrival of the beggar girl, is voicing something to be heard in any epoch, the bewilderment of a rich man being brought face to face with someone he cannot help treating as his enemy.

Our man knows there are poor, for he sees them surging and swarming round him every day. He simply does not wish to meet them while he is eating his meal. This is where the failure of imagination comes in. Coleridge's companion fails to grasp that he and his kind are in the minority – locally, in the teeming streets of London where this incident took place; and globally. The beggar girl with the baby on her hip represents the world's majority. His own feelings might be on the side of humanity in a generalised way – otherwise why would he choose to dine with a young republican firebrand, as Coleridge then was? Yet what is missing in this irritated diner is the sense that he and the girl are brother and sister under the skin. It might be so in books and sermons, but not through the open window of a city inn. Without even knowing it at a conscious level, his responses have been blunted by the age in which he lives. He is a gentleman and across the sill of the window is a nuisance, like a wasp, or the smell of drains.

In early republican America, as its constitution affirmed, issues of common humanity were expressed not as the petulant 'why can't you be more like me?' of Coleridge's dinner companion, but rather 'how are we all alike?' In the old world, simply to ask this last question in the wrong way, or with the wrong emphasis, was enough to imprison people as desperate and king-hating radicals. In America, both by report and in fact, things were done differently. We need a witness to say how differently, some-one who had lived in both worlds. There is no better man suited for the task than Benjamin Franklin.

In 1776, a year after the first shots were fired in the War of Independence, Franklin was appointed American minister to

France by the rebels. He was sent across the Atlantic in the tiny sloop *Reprisal*, knowing full well that were he to be captured by a British ship he would be hanged for treason. He arrived safely and, though surrounded by clouds of British spies, began his true business, which was to procure arms for the rebel armies and act as a diplomatic provocation. Five years later, George III's troops laid down their muskets at Yorktown and British colonial rule was at an end. Franklin now became point man for the new republic and its peace negotiator at the Treaty of Paris.

During this time, he began to receive letters from well-placed Europeans who wanted to know what chance they had of emigrating to the fledgling America on favourable terms. Franklin was approaching 80 years of age yet his deceptively simple writing style had lost nothing of its edge. In 1784, he answered all his correspondents in an essay entitled 'Information to Those Who Would Remove to America'. Despite some tumultuous recent history in which much blood had been spilt in the name of liberty, his advice was completely unpolemical, though touched by sly humour.

Franklin explained that the new republic stood in no need of intellectuals, nor were there great offices of state waiting to be filled by men of an aristocratic background. As he pointed out, his fellow citizens were not in the habit of asking of a stranger 'What *is* he?' but rather 'What can he *do*?' Gently, he steered his readers towards a view of society that was novel to contemplate.

'The Truth is, that tho' there are in that country few People so miserable as the poor of Europe, there are also very few that in Europe would be called rich: it is rather a general, happy Mediocrity that prevails.'

The word mediocrity had yet to acquire its pejorative sense and was used to indicate the mean between two extremes. All the same, there was a flick of wit in Franklin's remark. Taken in context, and coloured by its two adjectives, it was describing a condition of life hardly, if ever, witnessed in modern times. Franklin himself lived in modest luxury at Passy, outside the walls of Paris, and had as his friends men of a philosophical turn of mind who were also members of the political class. Not one of them could claim as much for the benefits of government as he did for the newly born American republic. A general, happy mediocrity was almost the utopian ideal.

The newly created United States of America occupied a land area comparable in size only to China, Russia and the Ottoman Empire. The more startling statistic was that at the time of its creation its white population was smaller than that of Ireland. Nobody had yet found gold in America but the fecundity of its soil and its apparently inexhaustible supply of game were long famous. Clearly, almost any man could succeed there, according to his temperament and ambition; and in the beginning at least, terrain and the climate would make him honest. As to the pursuit of happiness, so famously included in the Declaration of Independence, Franklin had a reflection to make about that, too. In the last paragraph of his essay he says this:

> Industry and constant employment are great preservatives of the morals and virtues of a nation. Hence bad examples to youth are more rare in America, which must be comfortable considerations to parents. To this may be truly added that serious religion under its various denominations is not only tolerated but respected and practised. Atheism is unknown there, infidelity rare and secret, so that persons may live to a great age in that country without having their piety suffer by meeting with either an atheist or an infidel. And the Divine Being seems to have manifested his approbation of the mutual forbearance and kindness with which the different sects treat each other, by the remarkable prosperity with which he has been pleased to favour the whole country.

Full employment, religious toleration and land for all: Franklin had come close to describing heaven on earth. Few Americans could have given their country a more ringing endorsement, nor suggested so subtly its potential for a new moral order. When he looked out of his study windows at Passy, Franklin saw a very different world, one about to come crashing down with the onset of the French Revolution.

Out in the fields, far from Paris and the salons that feted Franklin as a *grande philosophe*, lay the kind of work that does not depend upon ideas for its completion. Good harvests or bad might dictate the ebb and flow of national politics, or (more apparent locally) decide whether a great house was to be raised or stables added to an existing estate. To the sowers and reapers it was all the same. The weather might change but the seasons remained. What the agricultural peasants did last year they would be called upon to do in the same sequence next spring. Stoning unpopular neighbours to death or burning down their miserable hovels out of spite, murdering unwary horsemen, or walking to town to see an execution or the purgatorial regime of the asylum were momentary diversions from an almost animal existence.

For some educated men in the eighteenth century, this was no more than what was ordained by God. The way the poor were kept in ignorance of their situation acted like a benign drug, prescribed in heaven: theirs was the lot of being always at the bottom of the pile, where providence had placed them. To wish anything else for them was to threaten the social fabric but it was also to tamper with the natural order of things. When Coleridge wrote to Southey about the incident with the beggar girl, he addressed his letter like this: 'S. T. Coleridge to R. Southey, Health and Republicanism to be!' But the man with whom he ate dinner that day was of a much more conservative cast of mind and represented the conventional wisdom. The girl with the baby on her hip had been placed in her situation by an all-seeing deity.

So it is that this image of Franklin at his study window, looking out on to landscaped gardens that led away to the shimmering Seine, and thinking of that miracle of politics, a modern republic, becomes an important one. Two years before, his friend Joseph Priestley, the great scientist and Unitarian minister, had written: 'The morning is opening upon us and we cannot doubt but that the light will increase and extend itself more and more unto the perfect day. Happy are they who contribute to diffuse the pure light of this everlasting gospel.'

In these sentences, nominally on the subject of religious enlightenment, are mingled devout wishes and revolutionary zeal, the language of the pulpit and of the barricades. They are an encapsulation of a spirit, a cast of mind that has proved to be irresistible and has changed human consciousness for ever. Something like these words have since been scrawled on the walls of prison cells in every country of the world: they are the charter of the poor and oppressed and an injunction never again to live in despair. Franklin was a very old man when he wrote his advice to would be emigrants to America and the impassioned clarion call was not his style of address. Yet what else was the republic he described if not a great new dawn in the affairs of men?

Once more to Coleridge, briefly. We met him at a time in his life when he had persuaded himself that the old world was not worth saving and the answer lay in finding twelve couples who would agree to go together to the Susquehanna Valley in Pennsylvania, there to farm, to read, to write great works of literature. The republican fury that burnt within him in Bristol would be transmuted into a utopian idyll. He liked the Susquehanna Project for the euphony of its name alone, though there was more to it than that. Coleridge believed – better to say he wanted to believe – that somewhere on earth was a place made just for him and his beloved friends where life could be lived to the utmost of existence.

Just about the last thing Coleridge could be accused of was sybaritism – the Susquehanna was enticing not because it was a desert island but because, as he believed, men of good faith already lived there. Indeed, the great Joseph Priestley had given up on England and was now to be found at Sunbury, where the two arms of the Susquehanna joined. The utopian dream Coleridge held, of taking his friends and their wives and lovers to America, was only that – a dream. He was young, his mind was racing pell-mell, every day that passed seemed to throw up new challenges. Fear of failure did not scotch the great pantisocratic experiment. Love – and poetry – did the job. Coleridge retreated as far as Nether Stowey, where he and his friends turned life in a two-room cottage at the end of the village into a sketch of what the Susquehanna days might have been.

What follows is an account of how two men *did* seek to find the perfect day in America, not in the seaboard cities that Franklin knew so well, nor even in the semi-tamed beauties of Northumberland County, through which the Susquehanna ran, but out along the Ohio River where the frontier beckoned. As we shall see, they were as different as chalk and cheese in personality. The connection between them was not a shared idea or belief, certainly not a friendship or fellow-feeling towards each other, but a town. Such a town had not existed – perhaps could not exist – anywhere else on earth. Had either of them had their way, this place would now be the most famous in history. But the perfect day, the pure light of everlasting gospel, so thrillingly announced, so hungrily sought after, has, as we know, yet to dawn. The sun that rises over the town in Indiana that couples the stories of these two men reveals a heritage site, a visitors' centre and the quiet melancholy of a good idea gone wrong.

ONE

Living Machinery and blind mechanisms

We are in the first decade of the nineteenth century, in the year 1808. England is slower, more densely wooded; the horizons are shorter and news moves from one place to another at the pace of a walking horse, or a pedlar with his pack. The social unit to which most people belong, still, is the country parish – the squire, the parson, the vestry meetings that set the hated tithes; and round about, a few hundred more or less familiar faces.

The content of what people know about the wider world is very uneven: for example, everyone has heard of the great ogre Boney who stalks Europe, his taste for death and destruction never sated, his presence announced in a sudden cloud of smoke, the demon king of the mummers' play. Given a map, not all could point with confidence to France, let alone Paris.

In many villages there was a veteran of foreign wars to be found, or an elderly house servant who had in his youth been carried up to London as part of a great gentleman's annual baggage train. Some current news could be mediated through them, perhaps – His Majesty's foreign policy or the depredations of the London mob, the price of a stone of potatoes in the capital's markets, what a bank note looked like, or a black man. None said this information was accurate, nor even valuable. Left to themselves, villagers had developed a finely tuned sardonic temper, a sly disavowal of what townsfolk and city dwellers thought and said.

In this same year of 1808, boys at Harrow seized the school and flew banners inscribed with the slogan 'Liberty and Rebellion'. Then they set up barriers on the London Road to prevent the besieged headmaster from sending for help. What was any of this to the ploughman with a pint pot in his hand? Sifted with all the rest of the gossip that came his way and bearing in mind the general temper of the times, it might even be true.

In February of 1808, the French occupied Rome and at the other end of the Mediterranean crossed the border into Spain. On the last day of the month they took Barcelona and three days later they were in Madrid. This intelligence was closely studied in London but who is to say when and in what form it reached, let us say, Warminster or Chipping Camden, Beverley or Carnforth? When it did, it was mingled with homelier news, of floods or fires, shocking murders, noble marriages or elopements, market prices for sheep or cattle, shipwrecks, apparitions, hailstones as big as hens' eggs, two-headed lambs, hangings, plagues of starlings, runaway bulls.

But then the countryside, for so long considered the unchanging face of England, the well of tradition and common sense that could never be defiled, had new turmoils of its own to handle. In 1770, the inveterate Irishman and Londoner, Oliver Goldsmith, had written these lines, taken from a work entitled *The Deserted Village*:

> But a bold peasantry, their country's pride,
> When once destroy'd, can never be supplied.
> A time there was, ere England's griefs began,
> When every rood of ground maintain'd its man.

Nearly 40 years later, the politics of England's griefs had become the grumbling bass note of everyday life. The mood of the whole countryside was nervy and anxious; and all that was certain thrown up into the air, like grain at threshing time. There was an ancient tavern joke that appealed to some, the story of the Four-Alls. The king ruled for all, the priest prayed for all, the soldier fought for all – and the peasant paid for all. In times of peace and plenty it was possible to say these things with resigned good humour. But now the staple of country news was increasingly of magistrates, poorhouses, militia and corn prices. The wits in a village pub might not have any clear idea of national news but about their own situation they could be certain, for the evidence was right there in front of them.

A wage labourer with a 20-year-old son could remember that the day his lad was born the average price for wheat was 47 shillings a bushel. By 1808, this had jumped to 80 shillings and in some counties it was said the figure topped 100. Someone was getting rich somewhere, but the shower of coin had not trickled down. War had seen farm prices rise but these – and the curse of land enclosure – had also dislocated village life. On average, four out of ten of the natural population increase in the countryside had migrated to the towns, or been taken up for soldiers, or had otherwise deserted. And still the corn prices were rising.

There was one certain indicator of trouble ahead. A man with a good master might be poor but his bread – however much it cost – was secure. With a willing and uncomplaining wife, half a dozen chickens and a handkerchief of land at the back of his cottage, he could get by the way his forebears had done. Yet at the very bottom of the social heap was a new phenomenon, the landless man who was half day labourer, half vagrant, the sort of desperado who would offer his children to scare birds for a penny or so a day. He had no row of cabbages or beans, the rabbits he took were not his to trap or snare. In a society defined by property, what was to be his future? Who would ever speak for him?

*   *   *

Mr Robert Owen's fine house in Lanarkshire, with gardens running down to the sparkling Falls of Clyde, had formerly been
owned by Lord Braxfield of the Scottish Bench. Though it did
not have an unquiet ghost, it deserved one. Braxfield was a
coarse, arrogant lawyer once described as 'the Judge Jeffreys of
Scotland'. Those who knew his reckless character recalled the
occasion when a defendant appearing before him attempted the
plea that all great men had been reformers, even Christ himself.
Braxfield interrupted with a brutal chuckle. 'Muckle he made o'
that,' he crowed, 'he was hanget.' With contempt for learned
and sophisticated society, he built himself a house worthy of his
title in the tiny village where he was born, a mile or so from the
Royal burgh of Lanark. He died in the last year of the eighteenth
century and it was Braxfield House that was acquired on a long
lease by Robert Owen in 1808.

The new tenant could hardly have been more different in
character. To begin with, he was Welsh, and proud of it. In
appearance, he was neither tall nor handsome, a narrow-
shouldered and unathletic man with pinched features. As a child
he had scalded his mouth and gullet with a dish of flummery
and this made him finicky about diet in an age when it was held
that a gentleman could not eat too heartily. His speaking voice
had only recently been shorn of its strong Welsh accent. He had
no conversation and was indifferent to the manners of the drawing room save for one unexpected and endearing foible. Mr Owen
was inordinately fond of dancing, considered by him a rational
form of exercise. He employed a French dancing-master, a fanatic
who believed a lifetime too short to learn the minuet.

Owen's background was astonishing. Though his life now had
the trappings of a gentleman, he left school – and Wales – when
he was ten and worked as a draper's assistant until he was nearly
twenty years of age. The three employers he had in that time
thought very highly of him and supposed that one day he would

have his own business in a small way, perhaps a modest but well-regarded shop in the high street of some market town. He was unfailingly diligent, sober and attentive – key virtues in the retail trade. He served his apprenticeship in Stamford, Lincoln-shire, with a master who sold to the carriage trade and who liked him enough to hold out the promise of a future partnership. Owen declined the offer and went down the Great North Road to London, where he was engaged by a firm that had premises on the old London Bridge.

When he was still a youth, he came to Manchester for less than a pound a week to stand behind the counter at a draper's called Satterthwaite. This firm did not keep him long. Persuaded by a fellow Welshman to go into machine making for the cotton industry (a proposition that turned out to be a scam engineered by his new partner, whose previous mechanical experience was in making the wire frames for ladies' bonnets), Owen seemed on the way to being a casualty of Manchester capitalism, an over-reacher who was too big for his boots. He leased a floor of an existing mill building, sublet the greater part of it and struggled for his existence in a dark and poky corner. His partner was a crook and he himself had no mechanical ability whatever.

Owen was born in Newtown, Montgomeryshire, in 1771. At the time of his birth, Manchester was a town of weavers and merchants, unrepresented in Parliament, a busy and bustling place but by no means the dominant economic force that it was to become within 30 years. The first cotton mill erected in the town was built in 1783. It was viewed with only mild suspicion because the trade was conducted along time-hallowed lines between outworkers and the merchants who bought their wares. In those days it was not uncommon for a cottage weaver to sit down to dinner with his master when delivering yarn or finished goods. Those who lived in the outlying villages often travelled home in convoy, stopping at favoured pubs along the way to sing and chat and smoke their pipes. Spinning (of flax) had been carried on in Lancashire certainly since mediaeval times and possibly before that, giving rise to occupational surnames such as Webster, Fuller, Walker, Lister and Dyer. The villages surrounding Manchester were no less ancient than those of, say, Dorset, and the town they served as fit for John Bull as any in Britain.

But by 1791 the picture had changed, partly as a consequence of the emerging factory system, partly because the town had become politicised by events in France. The dissenting religions from which the weavers for the most part came were viewed as the likely source of sedition and Jacobinism. Manchester became jumpy – dirtier, much less bucolic, savagely policed, and in some quarters of the town, desperate. Owen left the security of his job at Satterthwaite's when all this was becoming daily more apparent. The move could be seen as an indicator of youthful folly. If Manchester was about anything, it was about capital. The investment flowing into the town was raising no palaces or pleasure gardens: on the contrary, what was building Manchester up was at the same time dragging it down, compared to what it had been only a generation earlier.

The town was riven by political faction. In June 1792, on the occasion of the king's birthday, a meeting of his most loyal subjects assembled in St Anne's Square to see some celebratory fireworks. The newly formed Constitutional Society, which represented the agitation for a wider franchise, advised its members to boycott the event as being likely to engender bad feelings and threaten the harmony and tranquillity of those of the king's subjects who did not happen to be members of the Church of England. This was good advice. The meeting turned into a riot and trees were pulled up, to be used as battering rams against the doors of two dissenting chapels nearby. Not until one in the morning did the mob disperse, leaving behind a scattering of branches, boughs and window glass. No arrests were made.

In December of the same year, with war against the French imminent, a mob attacked the printing premises of the *Manchester Herald* in Market Place, beating in the windows and doors with bricks and staves. The deputy-constable was observed going round encouraging the rioters, who had spent the afternoon in the pubs. The magistrates refused to come out to quell the five-hour riot, which was whipped up by words like these from a special constable: 'I'll give a guinea for every one of the Jacobins' houses you pull down!' Again, no arrests were made, though charges were trumped up against Thomas Walker of the Constitutional Society, who in order to save his house had armed his friends. When the mob attacked, the defenders let off a charge of powder to scare them away. Walker saved his property only to have the magistrates spend a year trying to gather enough perjured witnesses to indict him on a charge of high treason. The hastily improvised firework had become a bomb and – by other accounts – a fusillade of musket fire. Some said they had seen the irreproachably honest Walker exercising files of armed citizens in his back garden.

These events happened at the very time Owen realised his own adventure as a manufacturer of spinning machinery was doomed to failure. A lesser man might have thrown in the towel or looked around for someone – or something – to blame. The mood of the times was an obvious candidate – as well as bitter inequalities of wealth, Manchester teemed with police spies and false witnesses. The only truly safe citizen was a man of property who was also a staunch communicant of the Church of England. Yet the lurid light cast by the 'Church and King' riots utterly fails to illuminate Owen. He had no partisan loyalties and was marching to a quite different drum.

The young Welshman had drive and persistence beyond the ordinary. Without friends, more often than not a mere face in the crowd, he rose through the murk of Manchester to become what we in our time would describe as a player. Only seven years after failing as a manufacturer of cotton machinery, he rode up to Lanarkshire to ask for the hand of Caroline Dale. It was a breathtaking piece of opportunism.

Old David Dale was a rich man and a canny one who had built the cotton mills that were sited a quarter of a mile from Braxfield House and called – not without a certain flourish – New Lanark. Mills got their name originally from the adaptations made to existing buildings with water power – corn mills, for example. New Lanark by contrast was purpose built from the ground up – and it was big. Dale was cautious about letting his daughter go to a man so young and with such a high idea of himself. The former draper's boy astounded him by offering to buy the mills for £60,000, payable over twenty years. He had partners willing to come in with him; these partners were men of the highest reputation. It was a commercial coup that had within it all the elements of a fairy story. As Owen rightly calculated, he had made his prospective father-in-law an offer he could not refuse: he got the girl and what was then the largest cotton mill in Britain. He was two years off his 30th birthday.

Braxfield, Dale and Owen, all linked to such a tiny tract of land, one to be walked end to end in half an hour, make a striking contrast in personality and background. Braxfield had been educated at the grammar school in Lanark and afterwards at Edinburgh University. His neighbour Dale was a grocer's son with a gift for business and a warm heart, a patriarch to his workpeople in the mills and a pillar of the Christian sect to which he belonged. Met with in the street, or walking the banks of the Clyde, these two were eighteenth-century men – square-planted, robust individuals with a beefy confidence about them, not to be lightly challenged or contradicted.

Even a few moments with Owen could leave one with a faint sense of unease. This was a man who neither laughed nor frowned, whose calm seemed preternatural. Over the years, his nervy and unhappy wife gave him eight children and with these he liked to romp; he had an unexpected affinity with all children, even the dirtiest and least-born. Yet in his dealings with adults there was always that perfectly civil but studied distance. It sprang neither from arrogance nor shyness but a much more unusual source, one that gave the clue to the whole man.

From his earliest years, Owen believed he could discover human error in almost every direction he looked. It was his trademark opinion and the secret of his success. The world, that had treated him so well in the material sense, was a sorry place in which to live because what it lacked was rational organisation. There was nothing deep or philosophical about this conclusion – Owen simply looked around him and saw that, according to his own lights, most other people were chasing will-o'-the wisps through a dark marsh. All religion and most politics came under this sombre judgement.

The point is well illustrated by his attitude to books. Though he now possessed a fine library, he seldom dipped into it. As he liked to explain to his bewildered admirers, 'the radical errors shared by all men make books of comparatively little value.' This could be interpreted as a wealthy man's nonchalance. It was actually at the heart of all Owen's thinking. He lived in an age of great sentimentality, when literature was beginning to explore feelings and impulses: in this respect, too, Owen remained staunchly eighteenth-century in attitude. For him, literary romanticism was a dead letter. Poetry fell under the same suspicion as every other source of error.

The new owner of Braxfield House had trained himself never to betray emotion. He did not rant, like the late and unlamented Lord Braxfield, or burst spontaneously into the old Scottish songs, like his father-in-law, David Dale. Not very tall and always younger-looking than his actual age (to compensate for which, he combed his hair forward in a vaguely Napoleonic quiff) Owen had the manner associated with some university dons. Self-doubt seemed to be as foreign to him as the language of the Ashanti, or the history of teaspoons. It was as though what he did not know or had not worked out for himself did not exist – or fell into the general category of error, a gloomy landscape that ran from horizon to horizon in Owen's eyes. If there was a compensatory light illuminating his own circumstances, it was that of reason. To call Owen a rationalist, however, was to label him more generously than he deserved. He was the cat that walked alone.

The three men associated with this out of the way corner of Scotland had deep political differences. First Braxfield. As lord-justice clerk of the Scottish judiciary, he presided over the infamous trial for sedition held in Edinburgh 1793, the bones of which was that the three defendants were members of a society devoted to overthrowing the status quo. Their actual platform was universal suffrage and annual parliaments but Braxfield brushed aside their attempts to turn the case into a political trial and sentenced each of them to fourteen years' transportation. Only one survived the experience.

Seventeen ninety-three was certainly a bad year to call for parliamentary reform. In January, France executed its king and declared war on Britain and Holland. In August, the Committee of Public Safety ordered a levy of the entire male population able to bear arms. In October, it abolished Christianity. These events reinvigorated the counter-revolutionary 'Church and King' movement in Britain, noisily supported by His Majesty's most loyal citizens – the mob. At law, the defendants in the Edinburgh sedition trial were innocent, as Braxfield very well knew: he persecuted them because the mood of the country was with him. As he was fond of bragging, 'bring me the prisoners and I will find you the law' – and in this instance public opinion was only too grateful. The men he sentenced were not wild-eyed incendiaries but mild-mannered and respectable citizens with a constitutional axe to grind. (Two of them returned voluntarily from England to stand trial.) After Braxfield had done with them, constitutional reform became for a while a subject too dangerous to broach for any man of ordinary courage in Scotland.

David Dale was a very different kind of patriot. Starting from little, he made himself a great fortune, yet never as a miserly or unfeeling man. In 1785 he went into partnership with Richard Arkwright to found the New Lanark Mills, the first cotton mill in Scotland. Arkwright gave a great deal of thought to the most efficient layout of the machinery inside the sheds – the mill was to be a model of the most modern applications. Unfortunately, the two men fell out in a ludicrously heated quarrel about where to site the belltower in the new works. Dale's reaction was characteristic of his bluff temperament.

'I don't care to have a man for a partner who would get stirred up about such a trifle,' he rumbled – before adding for good measure – '*and* talk such nonsense about it too.'

Arkwright at once quit the partnership.

Dale was all the better for being left as sole proprietor, for it gave full rein to his fatherly sentiments and deeply held religious convictions. Not many millmasters kept their workers on at full pay during times of slump, nor imported shiploads of food they gave away to the poor. In his time, Dale preached to convicts in the Glasgow gaols, studied both Greek and Hebrew the better to understand the Bible and supported charities that wished to translate the gospel into the languages of India – none of which would have found much support from his one-time partner, Arkwright. Arkwright, too, ended up with a town of his own – Cromford, in Derbyshire – and built himself a castle to go with it. Dale was that rarer thing, a capitalist with interests in practical philanthropy.

There was a tide running here. The American War of Independence, followed so swiftly by the French Revolution, began a
50-year epoch that could truly be described as a sea change in
the way Britain addressed the question of an individual's worth.
Some of that change came about from a higher self-interest among
the rich. In the old days it was common to rattle along in the
mail coach past fieldworkers drenched in rain or with a hoar frost
on their bent backs without giving them so much as a glance.
God, in his all-seeing wisdom, had set them down on earth to
labour for others. But now, to meet the starving poor on the
street corner of what had once been a prosperous quarter of town
was quite another thing. Prayers could not answer their plight,
nor – as had been shown in France – could bullets. A kindlier
attitude to the distressed, as they were generally described, was
only common sense. At the back of the argument about the
unemployed poor was an underlying question, awkward to
answer: if they were to be anything more than the sewage of
society, wherein lay their humanity?

In the same year that David Dale founded New Lanark, a young
Cambridge graduate presented his prize essay for the Senate's
consideration. Its subject was assigned: *Anne liceat in servitutem
dare?* (Is it lawful to make slaves of others against their will?)
Thomas Clarkson, the man who won the prize, entered the competition with nothing more on his mind than to display his skill in
academic argument. As he researched the subject a profound
melancholy overtook him. The evidence pointing to the iniquities
of slaving and slave-keeping undertaken by his own countrymen
was far too stark for him to ignore. He spent the remainder of
his 86 years agitating for the abolition of the slave trade, not just
by Britain but the whole world.

Clarkson's lifelong dedication to the anti-slavery movement
was a striking example of how the conscience of the rich could
be taxed by a single issue. He was not alone in his campaign. His

dogged commitment brought him into contact with the informal grouping of Quakers and Evangelical Christians that became famous as the Clapham Sect and whose chief parliamentary representative was William Wilberforce. Up in Scotland, David Dale was a humbler exponent of brotherly love than any of these men but the same tide ran through him. In his case the object of his compassion was not foreign slavery but the Scottish poor – and it had to be so, by the nature of his business.

Dale employed 2,000 workers at New Lanark. Neither in Lanark itself nor anywhere else in the county could he have found the free labour to work it. Instead, his workforce came from the destitute of Glasgow and Edinburgh – in particular, pauper children. These were dragged from the workhouses and sent to New Lanark, to prosper or not, according to their temperament. Once there, and entered on the books under the fairly meaningless description 'apprentice', they were free beings only in the narrowest sense. They were better off than they would have been under the provision of the Poor Laws but their material prospects were grim. Their apprenticeships generally ended at fifteen. Thereafter, nobody in Lanarkshire wanted them and they had nowhere else to go.

Their situation was softened by Dale's kindliness, though his paternalism also took alarming forms. In 1791 a ship bearing several hundred men, women and children, who had been evicted from their crofts on Skye, was forced into the Clyde. The emigrants were sailing on a free passage to America as indentured labour and their situation was precarious. Moored at Greenock and penniless, with uncertain legal status, there they languished until Dale came down to the docks and cheerfully adopted them, marching them away south to his new mill.

Until very recent times, the condition of the poor had been studied in a rural setting. Their plight was made much more apparent by the sudden deluge of enclosure acts at the end of the eighteenth century. Between 1761 and 1800 two million acres of Britain were enclosed, turning thousands of previously invisible and voiceless men and women into displaced persons, roaming the lanes and trying to find work in the industrial towns. After France declared war against Britain in 1793, many hundreds of men joined the army – 20,000 in Manchester alone, according to one exaggerated report. Their motives were a mixture of patriotism and hunger.

The Christian solution to poverty was to make the rich provide for those who were truly indigent. The question was, how to go about it. The old Tudor system for relieving the poor by making them a charge on the parish began to break down. In the last 25 years of the eighteenth century, the poor rate doubled to four million pounds annually, a burden many considered too high to bear. David Dale, like all his contemporaries, believed in supporting the deserving poor – the old, the sick and those otherwise unable to do a day's work. Yet he also believed there was a significant fraction that was criminal in intent or that could be driven into shiftlessness by circumstance. He could see as much on his visits round Glasgow. There, the alleys and courts were filled with the town poor – drunken bully boys and barefoot whores reduced (or so it seemed) to a subhuman level of existence.

By the time Robert Owen came to ask for the hand of his daughter, David Dale had done as much as any man in Britain to face these matters. He had come to a greenfield site in the leafy valley of the upper Clyde and created both work and housing. In fifteen years he had turned a speculative capitalist enterprise into a community – a rough and ready one, to be sure, but always overlooked by his personal sense of human virtue. If he now chose to live in a fine house on Glasgow Green and visit New Lanark only occasionally, where was the harm in that? New Lanark was not his only business and he was coming to the end of a rich and productive life. His name was associated with philanthropy on the grand scale and his piety was a byword. In business dealings he was a genial and unquestioning supporter of the system.

Then came the wedding of his daughter Caroline to the rationally-minded Mr Owen.

The bridegroom came to New Lanark from what was thought of as the belly of the beast. When he was twenty years old, he had talked his way into managing a Manchester mill for Peter Drinkwater, one that employed 500 hands. What impressed Drinkwater most about his prospective manager was that he demanded a starting salary of £300 without any prior experience in the job. Owen stood his ground. Nobody knew more about finished cloth and the market for it than this calm and confident draper's assistant. The outgoing manager, Mr Lee, was an engineer, a man with oily hands. What Owen had to offer was stunning self-confidence. He simply told Drinkwater that he was the man for the job. In his autobiography, written in old age, he recalls his first day as manager.

> When I arrived at the mill, which was in another part of
> the town from Mr Drinkwater's place of business, I found
> myself at once in the midst of five hundred men, women
> and children, who were busily occupied with machinery,
> much of which I had never seen, and never in regular
> connection to manufacture from the cotton to the finished
> thread.

In six weeks, he mastered the entire operation, not as a mechanical genius (which he never was) but by sitting down and thinking. Owen quickly grasped an essential fact about cotton spinning. The machinery, though it might be improved in minor ways, was already as good as it would get for a generation or more. The way to improve production – and quality – was to concentrate attention on the workforce: or as Owen put it, 'the living machinery.'

The Welshman proved to be a very unusual mill manager. He was the first to arrive in the morning, bringing with him the keys to the premises, and the last to leave, locking up behind him. He lived in modest lodgings, did not drink or womanise, and had no real interests outside the operation of the mill itself. What empathy he had with the hands ended abruptly at the mill gates. Where they lived, what they ate, the kind of sicknesses they endured, all these were of no interest to him. In 1796, for example, there were food riots and a nine o'clock curfew was imposed on the streets of Manchester, patrolled at nightfall by mounted soldiers of the Volunteer regiments bearing spluttering torches. By order of the magistrates all the pubs shut at seven. Owen appears not to have noticed.

He was elected a member of the prestigious Manchester Literary and Philosophical Society but showed little enthusiasm for their debates. The leading lights of the Lit and Phil at that time were doctors with a social conscience, men who founded hospitals, gathered statistics, gave poverty a human face. Owen's view of the same evidence was simpler and more direct. The key thing was to change the man – or child – from whatever he was in the broader social picture to a simpler cartoon of existence. By formalising what was expected of a worker inside his mill, whether or not he had enough bread on the table at home, Owen could and did increase productivity and improve quality.

In his view, it all came down to a matter of character. One of the first questions Drinkwater asked his prospective manager at interview was how many days a week he was drunk. Owen was never drunk. He did not plunge his youngest workers into tubs of icy water to wake them up in the mornings, nor did he take the girls under his care into a dark corner and abuse them, nor swear and rant when things went wrong and the spinning operation broke down. No one who argued the toss with him was beaten or turned off at the gates with a parting kick. It was a simple formulation. To change a man, you had to put him into circumstances where he wanted to work the way you had devised for him. If that did not do the trick, then he must be shamed into it. However it was, he would acquire a 'character' that before he did not have.

Later on in his career, Owen's factory innovations were bathed in a golden light. For many he was the first manufacturer to see that if a man was treated well he would not only work harder but gain an education, at any rate in morals – work would make him a better person. It is doubtful that he saw his time at Drink-water's in the same way. Reason, that guiding beacon in Owen's life, had shown him how to subdivide work and measure it. He was, essentially, a progress chaser. He came to work in the morning not as a kindly man, but as a progressive manager both of men and machines. Personality did not come into it. When Owen talked about character, he meant to imply obedience to the system. The flywheel was obedient to the boiler pressures being stoked – and so it must be with the living machinery.

Drinkwater, though he was by no means an ogre of capitalism, noted with approval that Mr Owen and his odd ideas sprang from a bracingly unsentimental view of the labour force. Reason had long ago told Owen that religion was a principal source of error – he claimed to have acquired his own scepticism at the age of seven, after being badgered by well-meaning Methodist ladies who gave him tracts to study. Accordingly, there was no psalm-singing and hand-wringing in the Drinkwater factory, no prayers in expectation of the glorious life to come. If there was to be a reward in heaven for the labouring poor, that was of no interest to Owen in the here and now. He showed how he could make people more apt for the task, less complaining. Meanwhile, his workers put in the same hours as elsewhere and were paid not a penny more. If at night they slept with rats running over them or nailed down the windows to keep out the stench of open sewers, during the day they span cotton to unheard-of fineness.

At first, it was possible for Owen to ignore the more demanding social problems of Manchester because the markets were strong and there was a manufacturing boom in the town. Exactly where full production might lead in the end, when the machine and the factory system had made the workforce into what amounted to slaves, was left for others to ponder. Owen kept his eye firmly on the situation inside his own mill.

Little by little, however, success led him towards a wider social perspective. The egotist in him was not satisfied merely to return Drinkwater a profit on his investment. His experience had shown how reason could be applied to supply the deficiencies in human character. If it worked in the noise and whirling dust of a cotton mill, why not elsewhere? Why not everywhere?

Friendless by choice and so cut off from the benefits that flow from argument and contradiction; indifferent to luxury; above all perfectly convinced that he was right about most things, Owen now concluded he had something to teach the world in general. If there were wrongs, setting them right was simply a matter of rational reorganisation. This applied as much to society at large as it did to the operation of Mr Drinkwater's mill. In Owen's eyes, Manchester went to bed each night in a state of intellectual squalor. For that, he had a prophet's answer. What he had done for Drinkwater he could do for everybody. He could change human nature.

The New Lanark Mills made the ideal test-bed for this seductive idea. The location was remote, the workforce not very different in character or temperament to the hands he had employed at Drinkwater's. The housing associated with the mills made the foundations of a community. Of course, New Lanark was hardly a town in the traditional sense but there were many more ancient places in Britain that called themselves towns and supported smaller populations. As a child, Owen had run about Newtown in Montgomeryshire, where his father was postmaster. The population of New Lanark was twice as large. In every way, here was the clean slate his ideas demanded. He arrived intending to live among his workforce and teach them the benefits of reason. What he found proved very shocking. In Manchester, the workforce had clattered away to their unknowable hovels. Here, they lived right under his nose.

> 'They were a very wretched society: every man did what was right in his own eyes, and vice and immorality prevailed to a monstrous extent. The population lived in idleness, in poverty, in almost every kind of crime; consequently, in debt, out of health, and in misery.'

The workers, when they bothered to turn up, put in a thirteen-hour day, starting at six in the morning. A child would be lucky to take home six shillings a week, earned at the rate of a penny an hour. A grown man might pocket twice that. It is not surprising that absenteeism was common. The workers drank, they fought, they fornicated. The existing management in the mills included much-hated toadies who had been given their positions because they aped the Christianity the former proprietor had observed with such gusto. As to the housing that was provided, it was no more than banks of single storey, one room hovels, each with its pile of cinders and kitchen waste at the door. In short, New Lanark, for all the surrounding sylvan beauties, was as vile a place to live and work as anywhere in Britain.

Another man – especially a newly married one – might have put in a manager, taken the profits and moved away to a place where he did not have to think too often about where his money came from. This was not Owen's way. He set about the task of turning these suspicious and recalcitrant millhands into useful living machinery. He added a second storey to the dwellings and chivvied people into cleaning up their own filth. A committee was formed to inspect and report on the conditions inside each household – 'The Committee of Bughunters', as it was swiftly labelled. Owen was genuinely baffled by accusations of interference and snooping from the hapless women he put under investigation. He persevered; and as happens in army barracks, the worst were brought up to the standards of the best, though not by rational enlightenment. Fear and shame did the trick. Under David Dale, the troops had been left to their own devices. With the arrival of Owen, some of what he saw as moral re-education was in practice barrack-room bullying under a different name. Reason was as rare as soap among his workers and not much less of a luxury. They changed their behaviour because they had no choice in the matter.

The new proprietor formed a band and inaugurated healthy exercise in the form of dancing and military drill: the ungrateful hands complained they found it more tiring than being at work. David Dale had long ago founded a school for the factory children in his employ. Owen increased its scope and paid for the improvements by taxing the sale of alcohol in the village shop. He set up a savings bank; withheld a sixtieth of every worker's pay to create a sick fund, and generally busied himself in telling the man in the street what great good would follow from changing the street. The large building he erected for the education of his workers' children was called, ominously, the Institute for the Formation of Character.

While things certainly improved, there were no indications that the lessons had been taken to heart in a longlasting way. Twenty years after he arrived among them, the workers he had set out to re-educate had this to say, in language he had taught them: 'We view it as a grievance of considerable magnitude to be compelled by Mr Owen to adopt what measures soever he may be pleased to suggest on matters that belong entirely to us. Such a course of procedure is most repugnant to our minds as men, and degrading to our characters as free-born sons of highly favoured Britain.'

There had always been a smattering of millmasters – men in the mould of Owen's father-in-law – who tried to temper the effects of the Industrial Revolution by kindliness and what could be called a higher self-interest. In the early years of the nineteenth century, such simple philanthropy began to reshape itself. A variety of experimental communities came into existence, designed to soften the blow of the new. Most of them were of an agricultural kind – Owen had a neighbour who charged with the Royal Scots Greys at Waterloo, came home to resign his commission in disgust and then set about a more communitarian way of working his estates with a view to improving the plight of the poor. For such men as these, the answer to all the dislocations and miseries of the machine age was to return people to the land. Quixotically, for a millmaster, Owen had some sympathy with the idea. He supported a crank idea current at the time to abandon the plough and replace it with the spade. As well as creating employment, he considered the change would give back dignity to manual work.

Meanwhile, the sheer novelty of the industrial landscape acted like a magnet on the curious. There was a vogue for visiting the new mill towns to wonder and exclaim at their rawness. Louis Simond, a French-born American, visited New Lanark in 1810, gathering materials for a travel journal he published five years later. The site was only moderately interesting to him because it was a mill run upon water-power and these he had seen before. Simond was much more excited by his visit to Glasgow and a tour of its steam-driven mills and factories.

> The eye of a child or of a woman watches over the blind mechanism, directing the motions of her whirling bat-talion, rallying disordered and broken threads, and repairing unforeseen accidents. The shuttle, likewise

untouched, shoots to and fro by an invisible force; and the weaver, no longer cramped upon his uneasy seat, but merely overlooking his self moving looms, produces forty-eight yards of cloth in a day, instead of four or five yards.

Simond was lucky in his visit: he did not see an accident, such as maimed or occasionally killed a child crawling about under the loom beds. The heat in the spinning sheds was, as he admitted, 'quite insupportable', even for a Virginian, for the temperature was kept at 100 degrees winter and summer. There were windows, but none of them opened, and the turbulent air was filled with the overpowering stench of vaporising engine oil and unwashed bodies. Simond asked no questions about the hours worked or the rates of pay, nor did he raise the issue of child-labour with his hosts. He had not come for that. The hero of the story was the machinery.

'It is impossible to see without astonishment these endless flakes of cotton, as light as snow and as white, ever pouring from the carding machine, then seized by the teeth of innumerable wheels and cylinders, and stretched into threads, flowing like a rapid stream, and lost in the *tourbillon* of spindles.'

Simond, like many of his contemporaries, was entranced by the expressionistic energy of the machine age. There was a thrill in seeing coal burnt in such huge quantities, the steam it generated turning machines that gave out the clattering and hammering of a thousand village blacksmiths. There was nothing like it in America, nor could a traveller find anywhere like Manchester, Leeds or Glasgow in the whole of Europe. Smoke, fire and the incessant drumming noise of the shuttles produced a visceral excitement that formerly belonged to battle and the clash of great armies. At the end of a factory tour, a visitor like Simond could retreat to his hotel or lodgings and listen to the window glass thrum, absolutely convinced that he had seen the future. He might turn his head on the pillow, reflecting that an industrial economy was a beast difficult to tame and one with an insatiable appetite, but only a fool would argue that it could be stopped in its tracks.

Yet for anyone with eyes to see, machines – 'the blind mechanisms' – were creating disease, despair and death as well as cheap cloth. Streams and rivers quickly turned as black as ink, whole quarters, sometimes entire towns became no-go areas for those with money to move elsewhere. In 1801, the Court Leet of Manchester summonsed eleven manufacturers whose mills were run by steam engines, imposing fines on them for a failure to consume their own smoke. Within another decade or two, words like the following would acquire a pantomime comicality:

> The furnaces of factories worked by steam are of a magnitude that want some prompt and effective remedy. The town is in every direction surrounded by them, and numbers are daily erecting in the midst of it. It is the subject of universal complaint, for the houses, the furniture, the persons and the clothing of the inhabitants are all contaminated and the health of thousands impaired by this offensive and unsalutary nuisance, which if suffered to continue will in a short time render the town unfit for the habitation of man.

New Lanark was by comparison an idyll. Curlews flew overhead and the mill-wheel churned up water that was pure and full of fish. What struck many of his workforce as Owen's incomprehensible innovations seemed to those gentry that came to see them admirable. For example, each man in the mill had a colour-coded plaque hung by his machine which did not record his productivity (for the machine itself decided that) but his attitude, his moral character. As for his children, within the Institute for the Formation of Character there existed what many considered the high-point of their visit – Britain's first nursery school.

Corporal punishment was abolished in the mills as well as the schoolroom; the usual petty crimes of theft and dishonesty when at work were ended by a rigorous system of stocktaking. Public drunkenness fell – it became so rare that once, when one of Owen's children ran to his father to describe a man with a terrible disease staggering about in the street, it turned out to be a drunk on his way home. All these changes in the way people behaved came directly from Owen's interventions. He never fell into the trap of making friends with his employees – the whole point of his system was to leave sentiment out of it. He merely made it more difficult for the denizens of New Lanark to be 'bad'. As to what was good, he was the sole judge.

After 1815, when his methods began to attract national attention, Owen claimed that New Lanark received 2,000 visitors a year. Some of these – like William Wilberforce – saw what they thought of as practical philanthropy on a grand scale. Although Owen had no Christian affiliations and turned his back on all religions, nevertheless what he was doing could be said to be saving souls. Other enthusiasts interpreted things more prosaically. If there were going to be factories, this was surely the most cost-efficient way to organise them. That was the opinion of Grand Duke Nicholas of Russia, later Tsar, who was so taken with New Lanark that he offered to move two million of Britain's 'surplus population' (his ideas on the density of population in the British Isles were, to put it mildly, sketchy) and found his own factory system in St Petersburg with the great Welshman at the helm.

When the royal brothers, the Dukes of York and Sussex, came to New Lanark, Owen laid on something of an elementary school lesson. They were shown a heap of cubes, which their host began to assemble as a pyramid, representing the relative numerical strengths of each part of the social order. Perched on the very top was the the smallest cube, representing the Royal Family and the peerage. This, Owen tells us, 'appeared so strikingly insignificant, compared with all below, and especially when compared with the cubes representing the working and pauper classes, that the Duke of Sussex impulsively pushed the elbow of his royal brother, saying – "Edward, do you see that?" And the whole party for the moment seemed confused.'

It happened that the Duke of Sussex was a man of great liberal and intellectual tendencies (he later became President of the Royal Society) and though his brother was not even halfway as acute, the confusion Owen felt he had sown was hardly likely to have been more than polite condescension. It was typical of him that he thought he had done something useful and instructive, without realising that the Royal Family had been born to this view of society. The Duke of York, whom Owen saw as consternated, had been elected Bishop of Osnaburg in Westphalia when he was a year old, made a Knight of the Bath when he was four, and Knight of the Garter when he was eight. By the time he was seventeen, he was a colonel in the army. For him, Owen's cubes were a statement of the obvious.

In truth, the master of New Lanark was at heart as deeply conservative as the royal dukes. He had no wish to topple the social order and went out of his way to explain to his manufacturing colleagues that in fifteen years he had more than doubled the value of his capital investment. In the period between 1809 and 1813, New Lanark made the partners £160,000 in profits. Owen was not an egalitarian by instinct and certainly not a democrat. What obsessed him was method: the application of his principles would lead not to revolution but what Owen called 'harmony'. The pile of cubes would remain as they were but without 'distrust, disorder and disunion' between the classes.

No one who had seen the new mill towns could deny that in

terms of human dignity Owen's workers at New Lanark were better off. They earned less than hands in Glasgow but worked fewer hours. Their children, many of them, were literate after the fashion of the age and distinguished visitors, who included the prime minister Lord Liverpool, treated them with an awe-struck respect. They wore kilts (the girls' very slightly longer than the boys') not because they were Scottish patriots but because the trouser-wearing Owen considered the kilt a most rational form of dress. Only the elderly now remembered David Dale's happy-go-lucky regime where good intentions went along with the cheapest whisky.

Owen had done what he set out to do by methods he had invented and others derided. He had, by the application of reason, driven out error. The company's books showed how successful this had been in commercial terms but there was an even wider social benefit. He had made an entire community happy in the utilitarian sense of the word. He had changed the face of humanity.

'Any general character, from the best to the worst, from the most ignorant to the most enlightened, may be given to any community, even to the world at large, by the application of proper means; which means are to a great extent at the command and under the control of those who have influence in the affairs of men.'

This assertion is taken from essays gathered together under the title of *A New View of Society*. A copy of this work was dispatched by Lord Sidmouth, home secretary, to all the universities and courts of Europe, not forgetting Napoleon on Elba. Owen gave Napoleon his due. The dictator had been blinded by ambition but 'has contributed to this happy result, by shaking to its foundation that mass of superstition and bigotry, which on the continent has been accumulating for ages, until it had so overpowered and depressed the human intellect, that to attempt improvement without its removal would have been most unavailing'.

In other words, the late Emperor of France and master of Europe had done Owen a favour by clearing the ground for more rational arrangements.

Owen was 44 when he published *A New View of Society*. To do him justice, he was far more concerned with being right than being famous. His writing style was repetitious, his grasp of social ideas blithely independent of other people's experience and opinions. The man who built the house he lived in, Lord Braxfield, would have kicked him downstairs without a second thought for being an interfering radical with jumped-up ideas of his own importance. His father-in-law might have reprehended a want of religious sentiment in the new New Lanark. Owen's response to both men would have to been to invite them to look at the evidence. When last had the prime minister, the future Tsar of Russia, royal dukes, the Archbishop of Canterbury and other assorted clerics made their way to that part of Scotland?

Owen subscribed to a journal called *The Philanthropist*. One day in 1816 he browsed through an article in it by John Melish, a Glaswegian merchant, which on closer inspection turned out to be a chapter from a book he had written on America, where he now lived. The piece was an out and out eulogy of a town in western Pennsylvania run along communitarian lines. A particular detail caught Owen's eye. The town was called Harmony.

TWO

Wie den Zaun haelt, haelt er auch das Gut

When John Melish first saw Harmony, the town was less than ten years old. It was located on indifferent land at a right-angle bend of the Connoquenessing Creek in Butler County, western Pennsylvania. Melish did not stumble on the place by accident but rode out north and east from Pittsburgh especially to inspect it. He was gathering materials for a book, *Travels in the United States in the Years 1806–11*, first published in Philadelphia.

Travels was intended by Melish to be his calling card and a bid to make himself a name. His character was that of a steady and sobersided Scot in his forties – he was born in the same year as Robert Owen – who was also a canny judge of the pride Americans took in their own achievements. He knew that among the new towns now springing up all over the republic, Harmony was something of a celebrated case and he went there to boost what he found.

John Melish first came to America as an agent for Georgia cotton. He had a taste for topography and statistical information and we can see something of the set of his mind by his later works. In 1815, he published a map of the United States 'compiled from the latest and best authorities'. He followed this a year later with a *Geographical Description of the United States*, a gazetteer intended to supplement his map. He was careful to send a copy of this work to Jefferson with the dedication 'Presented to Thomas Jefferson, Esq, By his friend, John Melish'.

According to the 1810 census, the population of Butler County, where Harmony was sited, was 7,346. Of the thirteen 'townships' in the county (that is, designated tracts of land, six miles square, purchased in the first instance from the government) only some were actual and active communities, or towns at all in the European sense of the word. Butler, the county township, had been founded in 1803 and after seven years of sweat and struggle boasted only 34 houses, sheltering 250 people. Young as it was, Harmony greatly exceeded this, both in population and real estate. Straggle-bearded backwoodsmen who rode in to get their corn milled or buy another puncheon of whisky stayed to gawp. The place had landed among them like an enormous cuckoo.

What gave Harmony its reputation was its citizens' capacity for unrelenting hard work. The community was founded by a Württemberger called George Rapp, and Melish was shown over what had been achieved by this man's adopted son, Frederick. This was interesting in itself, for Rapp had two children of his own and Frederick was no foundling when he came into the family. Had Melish asked the right questions, he would have discovered that Frederick was 21 before ever he clapped eyes on his new family. His 'adoption' was a sign of spiritual favour from the prophet. Melish correctly supposed that what was said by this lanky young man was spoken on behalf of George Rapp himself. He took the same name as his adoptive family but was a son only in the most metaphorical sense – his real name was Reichert and both parents were living.

Some startling figures emerged from Melish's conversations. From an initial investment of under $11,000 the value of the land alone had risen by a factor of seven. Frederick Rapp, with his quaintly fractured English, estimated that the total book value of what had been accomplished in five years stood at $220,000. Melish could see by looking around him activities like milling, weaving, chandlery, the manufacture of hats and shoes, a brewery and a whisky distillery. There was a hotel already famous for its cleanliness (the competition was not great) and on Sundays possibly the first town band in America played hymns and patriotic marches. The place, young as it was, buzzed.

This was all the more remarkable because western Pennsylvania beyond the Allegheny mountains had long been a thorn in the government's side. Huge tracts of land had been taken up for settlement by speculators, who had been badly burned, unable to sell on the divided lots to the public, or not in sufficient numbers. The soil was not as fertile as elsewhere and until the end of the first decade of the nineteenth century there was always the threat of marauding Shawnee Indians. The white settlers that came to this frontier country were the poorest kind of immigrants, many of them Irish, without the capital or the expertise to do well. There were many empty cabins out in the backwoods.

We have a description of travelling in western Pennyslvania at this time. The English emigrant George Flower was once on his way to Pittsburgh as a solitary horseman and found himself lost in the forests. He was a resourceful man and hit on the expedient of climbing the tallest trees he could find to look for smoke, the tell-tale sign of human occupancy. All he could see was 'an endless ocean of treetops, without sign of human life'. Towards nightfall and just when he was beginning to despair he heard a distant tinkling bell and by following the sound came across a stray black mare. He mounted her and she led him, not along any recognisable track, to a cabin. It was deserted. Next day at noon and completely by chance he came across a scarecrow Irishman who put him on to a path that led to what passed for the man's 'town'. Flower was dismayed enough to ride straight through it, exclaiming 'a more forlorn place could never be seen'.

Harmony had been purchased in 1804 at rock bottom price, the vendor passing on his unimproved land at a profit to himself of not much more than $2,000, or fifty cents on the acre. From his point of view, he had scrambled free of a bad investment by the skin of his teeth. It did not take long for Melish to grasp that the town's present wealth had come about by forming the citizens into a society, one in which all goods were held in common and all labour freely contributed. Harmony was in effect a closed town, sealed from the outside by articles of association. No stranger could take up land there; instead, it was peopled by peasants from seven Württemberg villages, newly brought to America by George Rapp.

There were other examples of faith-based communities in Pennsylvania and for Melish that was not the point of interest. What engaged him more was the rapid economic success these Rappites had made of their migration. Many of his own compatriots had fled their native country to settle in Canada and America, often to end up as little more than subsistence farmers or indentured labourers. In the cant phrases of the day, they had escaped the fell hand of tyranny to come to the land of liberty – and paid a heavy price. Some of them in the not too distant past had probably found their way to western Pennsylvania on the promise of land at two dollars an acre, only to be beaten back by the enormity of the challenge the backwoods presented. It would have been noteworthy for Melish to have found a single family of settlers living in even moderate comfort off the indifferent soil of the new frontier: to find a whole town – and such a new one – in boom was remarkable.

America wanted settlers. The federal government held millions of acres in trust for 'the people', that political abstraction enshrined in the preamble to the Declaration of Independence. In practical terms, the identity of 'the people' had altered dramatically in 30 years, from the ideal of liberty-loving revolutionaries prepared to take up arms for their freedom, to a more complex but much more modest character. In 1775, the faintly preposterous Patrick Henry had addressed his fellow Virginians in these inflammatory terms: 'We have petitioned, we have remonstrated, we have supplicated, we have prostrated ourselves before the throne . . . Why stand we here idle? What is it that gentlemen wish? Is life so dear or peace so sweet as to be purchased at the price of chains of slavery? Forbid it, Almighty God! I know not what course others may take, but as for me, give me Liberty or give me death!'

Henry died in 1799 and although he and other revolutionaries had ensured that no political speech in America would ever be complete without the word liberty in it, what was actually wanted in the new century was something rather more mundane – men who were prepared to go out into the vast wildernesses and build. This was a country almost without roads, densely covered in forests, and with western lands beyond the Mississippi that hardly anyone other than trappers and government expeditions had ever seen. Such a huge country stood the risk of partition and foreign intervention. The way to combat these threats was to encourage the hardy and courageous to fill up the empty spaces of the map, take their axes to the tall timbers – and stay put.

There was no shortage of immigrants ready to make the gamble. After Britain introduced the Passenger Ship Act of 1803, which regulated the numbers permitted to take passage on a ship on a scale determined by the tonnage of the vessel, unscrupulous captains left port in compliance with the Act, sailed to a remote beach in Scotland or Ireland and filled their holds to bursting with unregistered emigrants. Then, before entering the St Lawrence or the Hudson, these unfortunates were rowed ashore more or less anywhere the tide and winds dictated. There they were left, with a few pitiful possessions in sacks at their feet, and a continent at their back. They quickly found there was no such thing as occasional labour: they must settle, squat, or perish.

A pioneer settler needed three things to make a start on his

new life – an axe, a rifle and a woman to breed up free labour
for the days ahead when he had cleared enough forest to plant
and reap. But if he was to succeed he needed to hit the ground
running, growing (or killing) enough in the first year to keep
him alive but going on as swiftly as possible to creating a surplus.
Settling was in the end trading. A man could dress himself and
his family in deerskin, go without shoes, eat from hollowed-out
gourds, dose himself with Indian medicines; but sooner or later
he would need shot and powder for his gun, nails, horseshoes,
bar iron, a place to mill his grain, rope and harness for his ox.
To survive, in a country virtually without circulating money, he
needed to find others willing to help him and trade with them
what little he had – skins, honeycombs, whisky, even feathers.

The ideal American citizen was the yeoman farmer, a way of
life Jefferson held out to the Indians, too, as a means of pacifying
them and offering them a stake in the country. But the Indians,
as every backwoodsman knew, had adapted to the environment
as restless but highly sophisticated hunter-gatherers, moving in
large family groups. Centuries of experience had brought them
into a relationship with the land that had nothing to do with
title. Famously, the land belonged to no one and was viewed by
Indians much as a European might think of the sea. It was a
good, to be respected (and sometimes feared), but not a piece of
real estate. As white traders and missonaries discovered, out there
in the primeval forests there were Indian summer camps that
passed for villages and in one or two places permanent defensive
positions that could at a stretch be described as towns. What
there were not were lone Indians living in log cabins. In their
whole history, up to the time of the white man, the Shawnee,
Wyandot, Miami and Delaware, the tribes that lay along the line
of encroachment from the east, had found no need of the ultimate
sign of domination and desecration, the boundary fence.

White settlement, possibly the one constant of conversation

and debate, was easy to promote but much more difficult to achieve. George Flower discovered this in his meeting with the lost mare and the deserted and gardenless cabin. One further example can be adduced. Potter County, on the northern borders of Pennsylvania, was created by a stroke of the pen in 1804. The 1810 census discovered just one township there, a forested area six miles square in the geometrical centre of the county. The *total* population of Potter County was 29, of whom only six were women. Two families, the Lymans and the Ayers, slugged it out in the lone town called, after the name of the man's wife who had sold them the land, Eulalia. There, surrounded by dense forests that stood until logging companies began their operations in the 1880s, the tiny settlement ambled along with its hogs and oxen and a few scratty fields of Indian corn.

It was against this background that Melish came to Harmony. In a staggeringly short space of time (if Frederick Rapp's figures were to be believed) he could report what seemed to him a paradise of moneymaking. It was true that English-speakers were in the minority but that was not so unusual in Pennsylvania, which had long been a magnet for German immigration. There were some odd rules to this particular community – men and women lived apart in separate dormitories and marriage was strongly discouraged – but Melish's eye was fixed more on the economic detail. He was taken to see a newly erected spinning and weaving shed. Inside were sixteen girls operating handlooms, unable to converse with him in English but – wonderfully – singing hymns. Everywhere he went, accompanied by Frederick Rapp and an amiable but light-headed young man who turned out to be George Rapp's natural son, John, there was a similar story of unpaid hard work undertaken in a cheerful spirit. Melish was enraptured.

> It is impossible to convey an adequate idea of the diligent
> industry and perseverance of this extraordinary people.
> Wherever we went we found them all activity and con-

tentment. Here, at a situation where they carry the clay
for bedding the dam in wheelbarrows, they were carrying
it in baskets upon their backs; but they have every
inducement to perseverance – they are all on an equal
footing – every member is equally interested in the good
of the Society.

Melish had discovered Christian communism and found that
it worked. Because he spoke no German (his interview with
'Father' Rapp was little more than a feast of handshaking and
grinning), he was seeing things through a refracted light. Nevertheless, he was an experienced traveller and Harmony was in his
judgement as sober and tidy a place as any in America. The
houses were well built, each with its fenced garden of fruit and
vegetables. The German passion for flowers grown in window
boxes and tubs was very apparent. While the Society distilled
excellent whisky, its consumption was forbidden to members.
Sullen and suspicious neighbours riding in from the back country
to hitch their horses at the hotel found all round them hymn-
singing Rappites, identically dressed in drab brown smocks, not
lounging but marching to some fresh task.

Walking back from the fields one morning with the community's doctor, an intelligent man named Muller, Melish was
told an interesting story. Recently, a child in school had burst
into uncontrollable tears. On being questioned, he explained that
he felt wicked. Soon the whole school was sobbing and the hysteria spread to the adult community. Muller himself had been
afflicted. So what was the outcome? The doctor had gone to
'Father' Rapp, who 'pressed him to his bosom and told him that
he now knew his whole soul'. Then he sent him back to work.

Melish found this inspiring. Though he stayed only two or
three days, his account of his visit to Harmony is the largest
single notice he gave to any town in America. Before publishing
the *Travels*, he sent Frederick Rapp a draft of the pages concerning

Harmony to be sure he had correctly interpreted the figures. Here, west of the Alleghenies, on the far side of the mountain range that had for so long marked a boundary for settlers, was something approaching a utopian dream – a rich and prosperous community that was also a model of Christian endeavour.

It was, moreover, exactly the direction the federal government wished to take. When Melish published his *Geographical Description*, he calculated from the 1810 census returns that about 810,000 citizens inhabited Pennsylvania. By a little arithmetic he showed that the average population per square mile was 16. In his native Scotland, the figure was 63; in England, 181, and in Ireland, 156. Harmony, with its aggressive management and communitarian ideals, had room and more to grow and prosper. It was the future. Melish was careful to echo his friend Jefferson's views on expansionism.

'The right which man has to appropriate any portion of the earth to his exclusive use, arises entirely from his having expended labour in its improvement,' he declared. 'As population and power overspread the land, the Indians must of necessity betake themselves to agriculture and virtuous industry. It is the interest of both the white and the red children that it should be so, and this doctrine cannot be too frequently or too strongly enforced.'

The last verb gives the clue to how he thought in general and by how much a town like Harmony fitted his views. Unfortunately, by the time Melish published his *Description* all his Rappite friends had disappeared from Pennsylvania. Had he stayed longer among them and asked some sharper questions, he might have discovered that Harmony was built from more crooked timbers than he imagined.

The prophet Rapp – the bearded and beetle-browed German peasant Melish had met along the Connoquenessing Creek and talked to in such cheery dumbshow — was born in Iptingen in the Duchy of Württemberg in 1757. His childhood was relatively calm and peaceful. Iptingen was in the heart of wine country, where generations of labour had been expended in the same vineyards. The better houses of the village were tall and half-timbered, dating from a century or more earlier; there was a market place and a church. Rapp's father died young, leaving him, his mother and three siblings a fairly substantial dwelling built in the old style and enough of a smallholding to eke out the winters. From March until the grape-harvest in October, the whole countryside worked in the fields.

Iptingen, like everywhere else in the duchy, subscribed to a characteristically German piece of folk wisdom: *Wie den Zaun haelt, haelt er auch das Gut* (As a man tends the fence, so he tends the farm). Rapp was raised in the spirit of this dictum to be resourceful, methodical and — about anything other than field work — blithely incurious. The family was not rich but neither was it poor. In physical terms, the young Rapp was something of a giant; temperamentally he was slow in thought and earnest to a fault.

The capital city that governed over Iptingen and little towns like it was Stuttgart, located on the Neckar River. It was generally bypassed by travellers on the road to Italy or Austria. For those making the Grand Tour, there were no great savants to be met with there, no fine galleries or opera houses to visit. The duchy's university was not even located in the capital, but twenty miles away, in Tübingen. Stuttgart (the word means 'stud farm') was not much more than a princely sleepy hollow.

In the days of the cheerfully wicked duke Charles, who died in 1737, recruiting officers sometimes made lightning raids from the capital to conscript the most able-bodied peasants and sell them into foreign armies. These unwilling soldiers repaid the attention shown to them by deserting as soon as they were able and making their way home again. There *was* a regiment of Württembergers serving in the French army, cuirassiers easily distinguished by their white coats and tall fur hats. No man of rank from their own duchy ever followed them into service.

Württemberg slumbered peacefully throughout the greater part of the eighteenth century. However, it had an achilles heel. All the German dukedoms and principalities had a religious history that was very much darker than what passed in present times. The Protestant reformation of the sixteenth century had not been won without blood, nor without stirring dark fantasies about the world turned upside down, when beggars would ride on horses in a landscape denuded of priests altogether. Martin Luther's attack on the Catholic Church unleashed much more than he bargained for – those that he saved from Rome set about saving themselves from him as well. Thousands of Anabaptists who felt confident enough to interpret their faith in their own way, without the help either of the pope or Martin Luther, were slaughtered. First in the upper Rhine and then in the north-west of Germany, there was a frenzy of killings, burnings, the sacking of cities and suicidal peasant uprisings.

One such example was Münster in Westphalia. In 1533, this episcopal city-state of 10,000 inhabitants suddenly became Lutheran. The bishop fled and his clergy were forced by circumstance to preach the new theology. But to some of the more inflammatory elements in the town the year also marked the fifteenth centenary of Christ's death. For them, the extirpation of the bishop was interpreted as a sign of the so-called Third Age, the time of vengeance and triumph for Christ and his Saints. In a world grown wicked beyond repair, the time was coming when all must be put to the sword and the present world extinguished. In February 1534, Anabaptists ran through the streets of Münster in a state of ecstasy, announcing that this cataclysmic event would occur at Easter.

The entire city fell under the spell of prophecy. Those with money fled, or were seized from their homes and counting houses and beheaded. Their goods and effects were taken to central depots and redistributed to the poor. All property rights were abolished and polygamy introduced, with men taking as many as fifteen wives, down to barely pubescent girls – measures attracting both the poor and the lecherous from as far away as Holland. The New Jerusalem was declared: Münster was to be the chosen citadel from which a vengeful Christ would lay waste the world. The hour of Armageddon had arrived. Messengers who were promised the invulnerability given only to the righteous were sent out to raise the surrounding countryside. They barely cleared the city gates. Hunted down by the bishop's mercenaries, they were hacked to death with axes.

The New Jerusalem lasted until June 1535, when Münster was finally starved into submission. Before the end, the leaders dreamed up more and more fantastical punishments for those who exhibited doubts. Backsliders were beheaded and their quartered bodies exhibited in the streets, a trunk here, an arm or a leg nailed up elsewhere. Jan Bockelson, the self-styled king, liked to employ the Sword of Justice on this work himself. The poor of the town dressed themselves in the velvets and fur clothes of the rich and there were parades and grotesque beggars' banquets at which the only thing missing was food.

Outside the walls, the bishop's policy had nothing about it of Christian charity. Those emaciated believers with second thoughts who escaped Münster or surrendered were either put to death by the axe or the sword, or in the case of women and children, kept in no man's land to crawl about eating grass, like cattle. When the siege finally ended, the ringleaders were tortured to death with red hot irons and their mutilated corpses hoisted in cages to the gables of the church. These cages were still there in Rapp's time and indeed lasted into the twentieth century.

Münster was the last major battle of the militant Anabaptists. The most violent sectarianism burned itself out, leaving more peaceful forms of dissidence to stutter along in forgotten villages or on the estates of rich men. As for Württemberg, it had become Lutheran in that same year, 1534, in consequence of a rather desperate political expedient, expressed in the Latin tag *cuius regio, eius religio* – that the religion of the people should be that of the ruler. In the subsequent two centuries this imposed (and unopposed) settlement proved to be beneficial to the duchy. It prospered economically and maintained a large and for the most part docile population.

However, the echoes from the past continued to swirl. There was always an instinct among the peasants towards a greater pietism than that to be found in church. The youthful George Rapp shared in this to the full. In his early manhood he left his village to travel the region as a journeyman vine-dresser. It was now that fate dealt him a high card. On his travels he came across a self-styled 'prophet' called Michael Hahn, who held meetings in the houses and barns of those who had fallen out of love with Lutheran doctrine.

Hahn was and remains an obscure figure but his teaching was a harking-back to sixteenth-century days when the very word prophet spelt trouble and men like him had risen from nowhere and soon enough commanded armies. His text was the incandescent last book of the Bible, Revelation, and the sermon he drew from it was an ancient one. Sooner or later – perhaps much sooner than anyone else realised – the world would be judged. Christ would come to Jerusalem to cast out sinners and inaugurate a thousand years of perfection, after which humankind would be extinguished, along with night and day and the waters of the earth. These times, Hahn taught, were just around the corner. Armageddon was no poetic metaphor but an imminent event. Only 144,000 of the earth's population would survive the first cataclysmic harrowing. For many, these apocalyptic warnings came as an injunction to look into their souls and declare their sins. George Rapp, the vine-dresser from Iptingen, had found the focus of his life.

Rapp returned to Iptingen in 1783. He married a woman from a neighbouring village and two years later he and his wife Christine fell foul of the local pastor, a man called Genter, by refusing to attend church services. Without knowing of Rapp's contact with Hahn, to the pastor of Iptingen this would have seemed an inexplicable defection. After consultation with the consistory, Genter demanded that Rapp explain himself in writing. The last few sentences of an unexpectedly prompt and stark reply explained the effect Hahn's teachings had made on Rapp.

> For this only pleasure I still find in the world, to meet with the righteous, true and upright souls, the more seriously the better. This briefly is the cause. If I should now withdraw from this I would have to withdraw from Jesus, his spirit, path and truth, and consider it a spirit of temptation, and this would be a mortal sin for me: in fact I could not do it because Jesus has already shown me so much loyalty and still does. If any man should like to ascribe this to reason, let him do so at his own responsibility. The pawn and seal of the Holy Spirit is too dear to me, for I would rather suffer the enmity of all men than knowingly deny a bit of it. Right must remain right, and all pious hearts will be attracted to it.

Pastor Genter must have read these words with a sinking heart. The remark about reason was directed at him personally: what his parishioner was experiencing had nothing to do with rational objections to doctrine. Rapp had been born again. His disobedience in the matter of churchgoing was compounded by other dramatic gestures. He grew his beard long and left it untrimmed and uncombed in the manner of mediaeval prophets.

Soon enough, others in Iptingen did the same, changing their appearance from obedient citizens to defiant outsiders.

Whether or not a man wore a beard was a small point but what started as an individual protest soon gathered strength. Many others joined Rapp, abandoning the church and going so far as to drive their pigs past the church doors on Sundays. These devotees were enjoined to forgo sexual congress with their wives on the basis of an interpretation of Genesis, which appeared to indicate that in the beginning God intended Man to be of both sexes and so replicate himself. Like Hahn, Rapp began to hold his own meetings out in the vines, or in the houses of friends. The long hair, the wild beards, the hedgerow services emphasised separateness. In time, the movement spread to surrounding villages and over the next ten years police spies estimated as many as 20,000 had become followers or fellow-travellers. This figure was an exaggeration but points to the nervousness of the times. After 1789, events in France were casting their long shadow.

Rapp was twice interrogated by the civil authorities (and briefly imprisoned, though not for more than few days). No evidence of political agitation could be found against him. He did not have a quarrel with the duchy especially: his argument was with all mankind. His exasperation was also Christ's: the time was fast approaching when sinners would suffer everywhere. However, Stuttgart was not Paris and the police authorities and magistrates could afford to discount the more lurid statements their spies reported. Napoleon's name certainly came into the files mounting up at Maulbronn, the regional seat of government. For some of Rapp's followers the Corsican was the great liberator, the messenger of the Second Coming; and yet for others the ravening Antichrist, the Beast. What was needed in assessing Rapp's activities was a cool head. The balance of evidence was that here was a charismatic preacher with a blistering command of biblical exegesis. In other matters he was more hesitant and, having roused the countryside, he did not know quite what to do next. It was not unnoticed that he advised his followers to continue to pay taxes.

In 1798 the movement was given a sudden impetus by the arrival in Iptingen of the young stonemason, Frederick Reichert. Looking for somewhere to stay, he was invited to lodge with the Rapps. It was a fateful meeting. Reichert, who was barely 21, proved to have a genius for organisation and from the moment of his arrival things took on a new complexion. The stonemason saw at once that nobody had it in mind to march on Stuttgart with sickles in their hands: the movement had no politics. The key to Rapp's popularity was the millennial hunger he stirred in his flock. These were not angry men who wished to change the world, but rather to depart from it and all its vanities.

The Book of Revelation was quite clear about what must be done to prepare for the coming apocalypse: those who wished to be saved must go out into the wilderness and search for the Woman Clothed in the Sun. It was Reichert who moved this from a poetical figure to a straightforward injunction. Father Rapp must put his sermons and whirling words to the test and set off to find a real and actual geographical wilderness. West of the Rhine was out of the question; Poland and Russia were possibilities; but the most obvious choice was America.

There were precedents. In 1694, a man named Johannes Kelpius had gone from Württemberg to found a utopian community which he named the Woman in the Wilderness, sited not far from Philadelphia. More recently (1774) a semi-literate Manchester woman, Ann Lee, had fled with her followers to the woods and swamps of upstate New York, styling herself as the living embodiment of the Woman Clothed in the Sun. The ecstatic dancing and twitching of her adherents gave them a local name which stuck and became common currency: they were the first Shakers.

In 1803, egged on by Reichert, George Rapp sailed down the

Rhine and took ship from Amsterdam to Baltimore. He travelled with his son John and two admirers, the doctors Haller and Mueller. They intended to spend a year reconnoitring a suitable site for about a thousand families, one where preparations could be made for greeting Christ on his return to earth. They went with the blessings of the entire community, for they travelled, not as economic migrants, but in the fulfilment of prophecy.

The little party landed at Baltimore in July 1803. It was the most dangerous season of the year, when all milk and meat was suspect, the month when ship-borne diseases were most likely to erupt. Rapp moved north and west into Pennsylvania, riding from community to community, always seeking out places where the welcome was likely to be spoken in German. He must have made an interesting traveller to those he met along the road – he had no English and, perhaps even more strikingly, no particular business to transact. He was a (relatively) rich man with an ample purse yet having the manner and appearance of a clumsy peasant. The money he carried comprised subscriptions from his followers.

In 1766, Benjamin Franklin gave evidence to the House of Commons on the number of Germans then resident in Pennsylvania. He estimated that about a third of the colony was German in origin, a figure which he calculated to be 53,000. There were, according to him, as many Germans as there were Quakers. The term 'German' demanded a very loose interpretation – it included citizens of Switzerland, Luxembourg, Alsace and Lorraine and the Low Countries. Many had fled religious persecution; all but a very few had prospered. By the time of Rapp's arrival, the Germans were an indispensable part of the economy. German ironmasters cast the cannon for the revolutionary wars and in Codorus Creek, York County, locals drank to the revolution with a German toast: 'Ohne Schweffel und Salzpeter gibt's keine Freiheit!' – without sulphur and saltpetre there can be no freedom.

A complete retreat from the vanities of the world was impossible in most of eastern Pennsylvania, as Rapp soon discovered.
Kelpius's Woman in the Wilderness utopia had vanished but
nearby Rapp could ponder the rise of Germantown (now a suburb
of Philadelphia). Founded a century earlier by only thirteen men
and women, this minuscule community had grown into a solid
manufacturing base, a religious centre and a standing advertise-
ment for good citizenship. Rapp saw how within one generation
families like the Rittenhouses had grown rich and influential. A
Rittenhouse had founded the state's first paper mill but perhaps
more significantly a member of the family had also risen to become
the country's leading astronomer.

In other words, Rapp was witnessing something he had not
bargained for – not the inviting empty spaces of the new world
but the rise of American capitalism. What was most valued in
this nation was weak government, low taxes, good credit arrangements and a chance to exercise those prime American virtues,
self-reliance and a capacity for hard work. From these bricks
more modest Pennsylvanian Germans were creating the origins
of the moral majority. Their idea of a Christian life was far less
radical than Rapp's – full barns and healthy stock, dutiful wives,
obedient sons and daughters, neighbourliness: these were the
threads of their faith. Rectitude was of more concern to them
than revelation. The itinerant prophet who joined them at meals
and was never shy about delivering a fiery sermon was interesting
but, in the wider scheme of things, irrelevant.

There were places in Pennsylvania that had something of what
Rapp envisaged as his own way forward. In 1741, the Unitas
Fratrum, more commonly known as the Moravians, based at
Bethelsdorf in Saxony, bought land in Northumberland County
and established not one but two closed communities, at Bethlehem
and Nazareth. In Lancaster County there was Ephrata, founded
by a Palatinate German called Beissel. This particularly ascetic

group spawned another in Franklin County, called the Snow Hill Nunnery. All these communities had two things in common – they had come into existence originally to lead a life apart from the mundanities of the material world; and they had managed to survive by adopting a communitarian way of life, the chief part of which was the pooling of all wealth and labour. If these sites were considered utopias by some, they were also ruthless adaptations to an unforgiving economic climate. Nobody prospered in America by praying on their knees.

That autumn of 1803, Rapp wrote a startling letter from Philadelphia to his flock in Württemberg. 'I am not returning to Germany; if my citizenship still exists, I will give it away. I am a citizen here already. In this country, all people are very courteous to each other, all people are good to each other, one must admire the friendliness. Whoever wants to work here can obtain enough wealth. There is no pauper here, unless a person refuses to work.'

These few sentences would have given an intelligent Rappite something to think about. Father Rapp would hardly have written to say how difficult, how unpromising the new start was going to be, how delicate the balance that held all their futures, but here in this letter was the language of the share prospectus. While he had been quick to see the Whore of Babylon rampaging over the old world, in America the lady was proving remarkable by her silence. In Württemberg there was economic depression. Those Rappites who were making the decision to follow him across 3,000 miles of salt water, however exalted their mood, were struggling with weak property prices and falling land values. Meanwhile, Rapp was leaning on farm gates watching peaches fed to hogs, so reckless was American bounty. He seemed in no hurry to search out the wilderness that Revelation demanded.

The truth was that Father could be indecisive and petulant without his adopted son Frederick to keep him focused. His sense of politics, of what it was possible to demand from Babylon, was always naive. In his old age, he revealed that he had written to Napoleon in 1802 suggesting that his flock be given lands in Louisiana. The First Consul replied suavely that he was in negotiations at that very moment to sell Louisiana to the Americans and so could not accommodate him. In 1804, Rapp petitioned the president to make him a personal gift of lands – he had in mind 40,000 acres – in the Ohio Territory. Jefferson pointed out that it was not in his power to do any such thing and that his petitioner, who had written in German and was not yet technically a citizen of the USA, should study the laws of the country more closely.

It was a Moravian, John Heckwelder, who first tried to get Rapp to see that his future lay far beyond the settled and prosperous counties he had so far been touring. Heckwelder was a seasoned traveller along the Ohio River, which in the absence of roads was the gateway to the west. The further down it one went, by flat-bottomed barge or keel boat, the more sparsely populated the country became. As the river approached the Mississippi, there were empty lands as fertile as any Heckwelder had seen. When he mentioned the Wabash River, for example, he had in his mind's eye a place 1,000 miles from the sea, at the very edge of white settlement. Heckwelder was a missionary as well as an adventurer, and his life was devoted to the Christianising of the Indian. No obstacle was too great, no rebuff too daunting when it came to that purpose. He supposed that Rapp saw God's intentions in the same light.

Unfortunately, the Württemberger did not. Rapp was not a lazy or insincere man but neither was he the flaming sword of prophecy. His instinct was always to move slowly, with peasant caution. He vacillated. What brought things to a head was the arrival in 1804 of the first of three shiploads of his disciples. Frederick Rapp had not been able to hold back the tide of 'America Fever'. In all 1,400 Württembergers made a final and irrevocable break with the old country and now found themselves penniless in a strange land, with no home to go to. Rapp's adopted son arrived on the third boat and found that so piteous was the plight of his fellow-countrymen that Philadelphia citizens raised $600 for their relief. It was the time for action.

At the end of 1804, Rapp contracted for 4,500 acres on Connoquenessing Creek. The vendor was a former German aristocrat called Basse-Mueller, a bankrupted diplomat in his early forties, trying to extricate himself from yet more debt. It was the winter season when the sale went through and what there was at Connoquenessing Creek was blanketed in snow. Neither Rapp nor anyone else in his flock had ever seen what lay beneath it.

THREE

*Neither said any of them that aught of what they possessed
was their own*

The first 40 Rappites to arrive at Connoquenessing Creek in the
winter of 1804 made their most urgent task the fashioning of log
huts and A-frame shelters in what was a trackless and unbroken
field of snow. These pioneers (they included both men and
women) were in the worst possible situation: they could get no
credit and until they produced their first crop they had nothing
to sell and everything to buy. The charity shown to them by
German-speaking Philadelphians was already a distant memory
– to the more ribald of their neighbours watching from the tree-
line they were figures of fun. Gathered round huge bonfires, their
cloaks trailing in the slush, they made a disconsolate picture.
Detailed surveying had to wait until the snows melted but the
bitter cold told these pioneers one thing: their first idea of growing vines on a commercial scale was an impossibility. The frosts
were too severe.

A log hut was made by forming the shape of a hollow box.
Only when all four walls had reached to the height of the eaves
was a doorway sawn out on the lee side of the structure. The
floor was bare earth with the larger and looser boulders removed.
When it came to roofing, winter was a specially bad time to do
the work, for what normally sealed the purlins and rafters were
sods cut from a meadow, a job much easier done when the earth
was not stiff with frozen water. The final task was to collect up

boulders and lay them in courses roughly sealed with mud to form an external chimney. The crude dwelling that resulted was draughty and filled with woodsmoke. Soon enough hair and clothes acquired an acrid stench, hands blackened and the skin split; the pioneer homesteader commonly looked out on the world with a prickle-eyed defensiveness as if searching for one more thing that might go wrong.

Nothing illustrates the temperament of the newcomers better than their first communal labour, the excavation of a mill-race. This project was a clear statement of commercial ambitions. The trench ran for three-quarters of a mile and the brigades that dug it worked regardless of frost and snow. It was a demonstration of the extraordinary tenacity of purpose that was to raise Harmony to its eminence. Women worked alongside men all the hours of daylight and their sheer stubbornness shamed their critics. Out on the ice and snow of Connoquenessing Creek were wives whose only pride, before Rapp came along to claim them for God, had been their man, their children and their kitchen. If they, even more than the men, could survive such cruel conditions, anything was possible.

The bill of sale for the land had been signed by 'Georg Rapp mit Gesellschaft'. Legally, no such society existed and this the prophet hastened to put right. In February 1805 he drew up articles of association in what was called the Harmony Society, a quasi-legal entity which survived in ever dwindling form until 1916. The relevant biblical text for this document can be found in Acts, 4:32. 'And the multitude of them that believed were of one heart and of one soul: neither said any of them that aught of what they possessed was their own; and they had all things in common.'

In the Bible, this revolutionary event takes place after the Apostle Peter has convinced the elders of Israel of the power that lies in the word of God. The story favourably mentions Barnabas, the citizen of Cyprus who sold all his lands and gave them to the common good – and contrasts him with Ananias, who with-held some of his land and was struck dead. The fate of Ananias was not lost on those who signed the articles of association, for the movement was already split, or at any rate splintered. Dis-gusted at Rapp's vacillations about where to buy, Dr Gloss had taken a party down the Ohio River and Doctor Haller led another band towards Lycoming County, up on the northern borders of the state. Two of the best educated lieutenants to the project had quit. Father Rapp was clear about their fate: divine retribution would follow after them into the woods and strike them dead.

The number of men and women who actually signed the Society's articles fell well short of the 1,400 who had crossed the Atlantic and may have been as low as 450 – ten pages of the record of signatures have been torn out of the document at some point. They put their names to six brief paragraphs, three of them identifying what the individual must contribute and the remainder outlining what he would receive in return. Legally, it was a sketchy and naive document – even a moderately competent Pittsburgh laywer could have overturned the whole thing.

Under the terms signed on 15 February, subscribers transferred all their real and personal property to the Society, not just for themselves but for all their heirs and descendants. They pledged obedience to 'the laws and regulations of the congregation' and held their children accountable to the same. They undertook that if they chose to leave, they would not sue for services rendered – 'whatever we jointly or severally have done or shall do, we will have done as a voluntary service for our brethren'.

On the other side of the contract, Rapp permitted the signa-tories to attend all religious meetings and enjoy the benefits of whatever instruction, religious or secular, the Society might offer. He undertook to look after the membership and supply them with 'all the necessaries of life' both in sickness and in health.

If they could not stomach the regime and wished to leave, Rapp and the Society promised to refund – without interest – the value of all the property they had subscribed. Those who had entered poor would receive a cash donation of an unspecified sum.

Though at heart a money contract, there is the possibility that for the signatories what Rapp created was not so much a secular society as a church – and since his creation outlived his own death by nearly 80 years there must be some truth to this. Faith was certainly as important as common sense in reading over the articles. Suppose for example a Harmonist died and his family – not in America but in the old country – sued for the return of his investment? Again, could a child be bound by articles signed by his parents? Was there nothing that might constitute an unreasonable demand by the community on the time and labour of the individual? The Society had no officers other than Rapp himself – who then was to keep account of whatever profits might accrue and decide how they were to be reinvested? These questions could only be ignored by those who were truly blithe in spirit.

The immediate benefits of incorporation were astounding. In 1805, when the main body arrived from Philadelphia, the original temporary shelters were augmented by the construction of 46 substantial log houses, a large barn and a gristmill. Within six months of its foundation, Harmony had overtaken in population and buildings the turnpike town of Butler. That summer, the community began construction of a hotel. While only 200 acres had been cleared for the planting of Indian corn and potatoes, the garden plots round each house were filled with beans and cucumbers.

Uncomplaining, fanatically sober and industrious, the Harmonists rose early and went to bed not long after sunset. They prayed, they sang, they worked, they slept. The town was open to strangers for trade; it was swiftly noticed by those who came that all the talking was done by Rapp's adopted son. The mass of the inhabitants had no English and attempts to josh an old man passing by with his barrow or flirt with any of the younger women failed. The Harmonists were polite, but completely incurious about the world outside. Their eyes – and their minds – were turned inward.

Within a year the fledgling community was attracting both admiration and resentment. There was the pleasing picture of Father Rapp summoning the entire population to Bible-reading in the town's first orchard, peach blossom falling on their heads. Backwoodsmen riding in to get their corn ground would be startled to hear the sweetest singing out in the woods and just make out, up on the ridge, a slender stooping figure working by the side of a garlanded horse. Music was important to these strangers. At the time of haymaking, the town band would assemble out on the fields and play the slow and stately hymns they had carried over from Germany, while their comrades reaped and tied.

Set beside these idyllic moments was the incoherent rage Father had shown during the construction of a bridge across the creek. Stamping out to show how it was to be done, he fell through the ice and was in danger of being swept away. The reaction of outsiders was significant. 'Let the tyrant drown!' they yelled to the distraught Harmonists.

The town's hotel was followed by a store. Though they were not permitted to drink whisky, the community distilled it to a high standard and promoted it as a brand – Golden Rose. They brewed excellent beer, made shoes and hats and sold on their surplus food. They gave up the raising of cattle (on which Rapp had made a rash investment of $2,000) and bought sheep instead. Soon they began weaving cloth – not of the best quality, but strong and serviceable. For a price, this could be tailored into a jacket, or a suit. The commercial genius of the town was Frederick

Rapp, struggling to teach himself English. 'Sir, I send you hereby the watch of Smith Tavernkeeper again back, as soon as I brought her home she would not go. If you can repair 'er before the bearer goeth out of town, do so to send me back, if not, send me the other one Smith gave you to repair.'

The gristmill was followed by workshops, a library was added to the central meeting house. It was all relative: the point of comparison was not with, for example, Pittsburgh, 26 miles and eight hours distant, but the lives of Harmony's more immediate neighbours, slugging it out in smoky clearings and forced to come into this cuckoo town to get their corn ground or guns mended, teeth pulled, shoes replaced. Hymns and the profusion of flowers set before every homestead did nothing to soften the mood of these backwoodsmen when they made their visits. The Harmonists would not give up an acre of land to them, and charged the full cent on any services rendered. Their womenfolk, who had the attraction always attaching to foreigners, were as unavailable as nuns in a nunnery. No Harmonist woman ever married outside the community – indeed, even inside, none shared the same bed as a man. Husbands and wives slept in separate dormitories.

There were dark currents beneath the surface. In September 1805, the three skilled carpenters who were working on the construction of the mill downed tools at the very time that the community was running out of both flour and the money to buy more. Their reasons for abandoning the project sent shockwaves through the new town – they had been approached by the despised defector Dr Gloss. God had not struck down this Ananias after all: instead, Gloss invited the carpenters to join him in Columbiana County, Ohio. One of them, Lang, left town the next day, but the other two changed their minds at the last moment and begged to stay, amid scenes of great emotion. As Father Rapp put it with grim satisfaction, 'God's righteousness set the fires of

hell burning among them.' Two days later, a contrite Lang came
back to plead forgiveness. He was turned away.

This was the sort of incident certain to raise doubts among
liberty-loving Americans. Lang had gone no further than a few
miles before experiencing his agony of repentance. No amount
of tears and prayers could save him now. Father Rapp had a word
for him and anyone like him – he was filth. This was ugly and
– for a frontier community – impractical. What other place would
so lightly dismiss and humiliate a skilled carpenter? The following
year, there was a second mini-revolt, this time led by the teacher.
On Whit Sunday, the feast in the Christian calendar that cele-
brates the descent of the Holy Ghost, the Harmonists gathered
in terror to hear Father preach.

'On Pentecost day I suffered greatly within, likewise several
other brethren, so that I could barely get myself together to give
an address, but I cried out to Jesus and was strengthened so that
I gave an address that brought about a separation. Thus the evil
spirits were discovered and all five men came forward who were
against us.'

Their fault was in pressing for a restructuring of the Society
along more equitable lines. All five were expelled. In 1807, an
unwary critic of the system called Joseph Kister was set upon in
his home and beaten with sticks by Frederick Rapp and six others.
A charge of riot resulted. In 1808 two more families could take
no more and were cast out, completely penniless.

These incidents point up the authoritarian side of Rapp's
character, as well as a wilfulness amounting on occasion to hysteria. Unlike Robert Owen, Rapp ran his town by playing directly
on the emotional susceptibilities of its citizens. A passionate and
short-tempered man himself, he kept the Harmonists in a state
of dread, consistent with the great purpose that had brought
them to America. They were sinners and Christ's judgment was
at hand. Even after the great sacrifices they had already made,

they could not be sure of salvation, so steep was the path, so narrow the gate. Rapp's judgements might seem to be cruel and tyrannical to outsiders but his disciples understood why he was like that. His one duty of care to his flock was to save them from the world. The Day of Judgment was at hand and then all that had been achieved by them would go for nothing, along with the rest of Creation.

It is difficult to accept that Rapp believed this as whole-heartedly as did many of his followers. If Harmony was such an urgent religious retreat, then it was surprising – to put it no higher than that – that the Society had a commercial agent in Philadelphia. Later on, it appointed shipping agents in Pittsburgh for its trade down the Ohio River, for which it had opened a general store and warehouse at Beaver Point. (An instance of its fine-tuned competency in commercial matters is that it managed to sell whisky to Kentucky.)

On the surface, the unpaid labour that made all this possible was content with its lot. The man who delivered the milk at dawn also had with him, written on the side of his cart, that day's tasks, devised by Frederick. So many to the fields, so many to cut timber. Ten people here to quarry stone, in another place ten to shear sheep. There were no backsliders. Whatever the day brought was accepted with a grateful heart. Men separated from their wives by the demands of the work details met them on Sundays when the man they called Father preached. What was tyrannical about Rapp to outsiders seemed not to strike the majority of his congregation that way. Or if it did, they were not talking.

In 1832, however, the *Pittsburgh Gazette* published a list of 215 former Harmonists who wished to denounce Father Rapp and his son Frederick. Forty-three of the names were those of men and women who had been children at the time of the early purges. They had harboured their resentment for nearly 30 years.

It may have been a single horrifying incident that turned their minds.

Father had two children of his own. The most favoured was Rosine, born in Iptingen in 1786. She was a founder member of the Connoquenessing Creek community and, obedient to her father's wishes, she never married. Her brother John (Johannes) was three years her senior. As we have seen, he came to America on the exploratory expedition of 1803 when he was twenty years old. John Rapp was never a serious adornment to his father's activities and what might have been his proper role in the family had in any case been usurped by the adopted son, Frederick. John's dilemma was an obvious one, which he expressed in a way bound to set him against his father.

There were only ten marriages permitted during the whole of the time the community stayed on Connoquenessing Creek and John Rapp's was one of them. In the end his libido or perhaps only his uxoriousness got the better of him. One day the Harmonists were shocked to learn that he had fallen from an apple tree and jagged his stomach, some whispered his groin. The darker rumour was that his father had tried to cure his promiscuity by taking a knife and emasculating him. Whatever the truth, the wound he suffered cut into an artery and he bled to death.

There was no jail or courthouse in Harmony, any more than there was a town hall. No sheriff patrolled the streets. If this was manslaughter, it passed in silence, the day of its happening melding with all the other days; sunrise, and the tramp to work; nightfall, and the brief lighting of lamps before prayer and sleep.

Though Harmony's sole proprietor – for in practical terms that is what he was – had no more than a few words in English and took next to no interest in state or federal affairs, the town he founded had *Made in America* stamped all through it. The labour that created its little economic dominance was freely given and though even the most devoted follower could see there was spite and irrationality in Father Rapp from time to time, the project could not be faulted. Harmony did things better and on a grander scale than its neighbours.

It was the American way: presented with the opportunity to make real money, Rapp had seized it in both hands. Each day that passed was a step in the same direction. Every penny earned a penny. Though they never saw any of the accumulating wealth, the Rappites were better off materially than those that came to scoff. In a small way, they were the epitome of American citizenship – hard-working, uncomplaining, sober and resourceful. Money – say as much as would fill even a housewife's purse – was unknown among them but then so it was on many a neighbouring farm. That they were free to worship as they chose was more important to them and this freedom they delivered into one man's hands without public commentary.

There is a contemporary point of comparison. The Shakers were no less devout and no less exercised in spirit than Rapp's Harmonists but the gifts they made to American history were essentially different. They were evangelists. Though they had a permanent base in New York, their real place, as they saw it, was on the road. Three Shaker preachers had recently bypassed Rapp's community to go down the Ohio River to spread the word of God, a journey of some 1,200 miles. They spoke at camp meetings and lodged with sympathisers where they found them, always putting their faith in the faith of others.

These first Shaker missionaries found a permanent welcome on the farm of Malcolm Worley at Turtle Creek, Ohio, which later became known as Union Village. After seven years of unremitting hard work they sent home a report.

> The present situation stands thus – in the new house
> there is 56 young Believers – in the house we built 32.
> Chiefly the most aged & Some young people – where

> Richard formerly lived half a mile east is 22 – also in
> about a quarter of a mile is thirteen brethren and Sisters
> that have the care of 80 children – these have all come
> into a joint Interest – besides the hatter Robert Baxter
> that lives in the Saw Mill with a family of six in number
> – the rest of the Society without [that is, outside the
> village] there is four large families and 12 small ones.

Altogether a little under 200 people made up the numbers in
Union Village. You were always more likely to meet a Shaker on
the trail, or riding in half starved to a revivalist meeting in
the dripping woods. The reception he received was not always
friendly, nor was his purpose to conciliate the opinions of others.
He was there to utter the gospel as he saw it, with whatever the
consequence. For this very reason, his profile was a high one.

To many European eyes, backwoods America was an uncouth
and uncultured society. One thing it was not was godless. Perhaps
nothing surpassed the great Cane Ridge revival meeting of 1801,
when between 10,000 and 20,000 Kentuckians gave themselves
up to the word of God, as preached by scores of ministers. The
Gospel acted on them like grapeshot, felling them where they
stood. Men and women sinners lay writhing on the ground in
ecstasies of self-recrimination, howling and tearing their clothes.
The meeting only ended when the preachers were exhausted. By
that time, even the most hardened reprobates were stretched
out under the trees, talking in tongues, or listening to sermons
delivered by four-year-old children.

The Harmonists on the other hand had not the slightest interest
in 'the outside' and none in converting others to their way of
thought. Far from wishing to proselytise their neighbours, they
wanted nothing from them but their trade. When it was asked
how a celibate community could replenish itself (a question the
dazzled Melish did not consider) the answer Rapp gave was a
brusque one. When death or infirmity took a hand, he would

send to Württemberg for younger replacements. Meanwhile, the membership worked, it sang, it slept. Only the most trusted members of the community travelled more than a mile or two outside Butler County, Pennsylvania.

In January 1806, Father Rapp himself went to Washington. He spent seven weeks in the new federal capital – then not much more than a muddy village out in the woods – lobbying for the passage of a bill that would allow him to buy government land in the Indiana Territory, about as far west as anyone had ventured. Helpless without his interpreter and having only two shirts to his name (he was dismayed to find an insistence on clean linen among the country's legislators), his visit was an unhappy one. The delays he encountered left him in a truculent mood.

'As far as I am concerned,' he wrote to Frederick, 'it makes no difference who owns the world. I certainly would have run off long ago, if that would not offend Hoffman too much.'

Hoffman was the Philadelphia merchant who served as his interpreter. One bitterly snowy afternoon it did seem as if Rapp had acted on his feelings and fled the capital. But the truth was rather less heroic. To vent his irritation, the prophet had gone for a walk in the woods, lost himself, and spent the night in an icy and fireless forest hut, where he passed the time in composing a 24-verse hymn, 'Kinder seyd nun alle munter' (Now children all be joyful). On 19 February, the worst of all news came. His bill was thrown out, defeated on the casting vote of the speaker, the Virginian Nathaniel Macon.

It may have weighed with Congress that its petitioners had yet to qualify for citizenship, granted only after five years' residency in the country. It was also widely assumed that in a time of European war, all immigrants brought with them dangerous political baggage. The Harmonists were clearly successful businessmen but who was to say that out on the frontier they might not turn to something more inflammatory? Macon cast his

deciding vote on grounds of 'nativism' – the people he wanted
to see develop the west were, ideally, Virginians.

In Indiana, there was just such a man. The territorial governor
was a young Virginian named William Henry Harrison. He was
a renowned Indian fighter and treaty-maker who relieved the
frontier tribes of millions of acres of land, endearing himself to
the hungriest and most energetic of settlers by persuading Congress to sell on the land in penny packets, rather than ceding it
in bulk to land companies (that was, after his own commerical
connections had wetted their beaks). When he took office there
were only 4,875 white inhabitants in Indiana, from the Ohio River
to Lake Michigan. By the time he left in 1813, Harrison had
increased this number tenfold and made the territory eligible for
statehood. This energetic man was not done with politics. In 1840
he ran for the presidency of the United States, dubbed by an
eastern newspaper critic as the Log Cabin and Hard Cider candidate: he won, but by then he was 67, and caught cold while
delivering an inordinately prolix inaugural address. The cold led
to pneumonia and Harrison became the shortest-serving president
in American history.

The Log Cabin and Hard Cider campaign – a sneer cheerfully
adopted by Harrison as a title of honour – illustrates the desire
some Americans had to romanticise the immediate past, when
settlement out along the frontier, as it then was, favoured the
brave. What started as a jibe had enough resonance to get
Harrison to the White House. Although he was rich and well
connected, Harrison knew Indiana best from the back of a horse,
or being led by guides to an Indian camp. His parleys (and
subsequent battles) with the great Shawnee chief Tecumseh were
the stuff of frontier legend.

With this context to hand, it is easier to see how Congress
turned down George Rapp's petition in 1806. What Indiana
wanted was settlers whose stake in the land was large enough to

give them hope of a good life yet not so large as to encourage market speculation. The greatest civic virtue they could display was to stay put. As one pioneer put it, with brutal honesty, this was the country 'of log cabins, tall timbers and ugly women'. The biggest town in the Indiana Territory was the long-established Vincennes, where Harrison had his house and headquarters. Built by the French in the 1740s, occupied by the British and for many years the most famous place-name in Indiana, Vincennes had less than a thousand citizens in it.

Rapp's claim that it made no difference to him who owned the world reads not so much like a stern renunciation of Babylon as straightforward petulance. He had very little political sense and was more than once made to look foolish when the situation called for shrewd judgement. Melish, who had every reason to show him in the best possible light when he visited Harmony, was cheerfully patronising in his description. 'The old man's face beamed with intelligence, and he appeared conscious of having performed a good work, but he could not speak English and as we could only communicate our sentiments by an interpreter, we had but little conversation with him.'

Casting his host as a benign and elderly patriarch was a careless piece of reporting, for in the event Rapp easily outlived him, making nonsense of a twenty-year age difference. Melish might have asked the question (if Father had not allowed himself to be addressed as some genial and bearded old cove in a Dürer hat) how it was that such an apparently modest man had persuaded so many others to follow him? Then, having got them to America, how he kept them under his control?

Whatever there was that was charismatic about Father is lost to us today, with our generally more cynical mentality. In the Christian world, we do not embrace millennial fantasies with the same intensity and when we find rare examples of those who do

– like Jim Jones of Jonestown or David Koresh of Waco – we expect the story to end in tragedy, seeing the followers of men like these as dupes. Getting a clear view of how Harmony cohered is difficult. Very few of Rapp's followers stand out as individuals and most of these were in the inner circle that controlled the fortunes of the rest. Knowing something of half a dozen people cannot explain the undoubted devotion of many hundreds.

The sociologist Max Weber was the first to point out that charisma is as much a gift freely proferred by the majority as it is the quality of any individual. The Harmonists *wanted* to idealise their leader and in some senses gave him the power he exercised over them. The work they did was hard but that was not a novel experience – it was how they had lived in Württemberg, generation upon generation. What Rapp gave them was an endlessly reiterated admonition and the justification for a communitarian way of life: that unless they conducted themselves in an uncomplaining and sinless fashion, the Day of Judgment would find them out.

Christopher Mueller, the Society's doctor, probably spoke for the majority when he commented ruefully that 'Father Rapp is a despot, but his heart is good.' It was not in their leader's nature to be amiable, nor even approachable – and this suited the psychological needs of his flock. They were not fighting *him*, after all, but the life of impulse that would, if it were given free rein, shut them out from heaven. A stern and aloof leader was a very necessary thing. The Sunday sermons he gave were often several hours long and rose to heights of invective and vituperation that were wonderful to witness; for the rest of the week he kept apart, it was supposed to mediate or pray. His habits were exactly those of the severe and distant father.

One indication of the hold he had over his flock was the number of times he threatened to abandon them. His exasperation with his people rolled like thunder. 'I would rather bear the greatest disgrace with my family and be apart than live in strife and quarrels among a people that claims to be the Lord's and is not; or, on the contrary, to them we are not the Lord's.'

Though the Society had severed connection with the old country, 'America Fever' still ran very high in Württemberg. There, spiritual hunger for the life of a Harmonist vied with straightforward envy. A local wit put it about that when the first Rappites arrived in America in 1804 they had been greeted by a 100-gun salute and driven round Baltimore and Philadelphia in post-chaises. Within six months, this piece of mockery was reported back to him as fact. For the people left at home, Harmony was the city on the hill spoken of in the Bible – but it also doubled as a material heaven on earth.

It even had its own ambassador, a thumping crook (as it turned out) called Peter Ulrich, hired by Father Rapp to go back to Europe and settle money matters between those that had left and those who stayed behind. Ulrich was exactly the kind of man you would not wish to handle your financial affairs: he converted the money he collected into goods (watches and clocks) and was duly arrested by the US Collector of Customs. A better clue to his activities was given in 1817 when he arrived at Philadelphia on the vessel *Francis* with a group of 430 Germans, enticed to America by his blandishments. Only a very few had any intention of joining George Rapp. Ulrich sold them the dream of plenty, booked them on an assisted passage and once he had them ashore, dumped them to work in the quarries until some other employer might come along and take them up as indentured labour.

His reports back to Harmony about the fortunes of anxious family members searching for news made dismal reading.

> About Wagner in Eberdingen they are saying that he has disinherited his son, but he did not say a word about it to me . . . Christoph Friedrich Weeber from Pforzheim also has little to expect because his grandmother has made

a will, according to which his father Weeber may draw from the income of her estate until his death . . .

Kohler from Schwieberdingen has been disinherited by his deceased aunt in Seresheim. She had willed him fl 150 in case he should appear or send some word to her during her lifetime. Since neither happened he is entirely disinherited.

Sometimes the heartbreak flowed from those left behind. Little Christina Margherita Muhlhauserin wrote from Hochdorf to her grandparents in Harmony in 1814. What she said was a postscript to a letter written by her father and her words were probably dictated by him, but the pain and bewilderment strikes home: 'I beg you, dear grandparents, that you would leave me what you promised me 9 years ago. You can still give your lawyer in Benzwagen 800 gulden, so I beg that you may not cast me, your grandchild, further out than your dear lawyer, who has never yet dealt rightly with you.'

Sometimes the grief of separation was perfectly expressed in a single sentence, as here, words flying across an ocean: 'Dear Mother, if you are still living, I would be happy if I could spend but an hour with you with my three children, but of course that cannot be.'

Aged parents were reported in their graves, or grandchildren born: news that, when it was received in America, was already a year old. The Rappites adopted from the start the unsentimental practice of burying their own dead without markers (John Rapp was one of the very few to have a headstone); but who could not be touched by news from overseas that spoke of a child or a parent never to be seen again? Those who followed Rapp to America had given up the world to become the Lord's but they would have been inhuman not to suffer the pangs of isolation and homesickness.

Few individual accounts have come down to us, but one such

is the story of Jacob Schick. He was a founder member of the Society, joining with his wife and children as a penniless labourer. He hoped to be taught the art of tannery but was taken from that work and sent to tend sheep. In 1812, the year of John Rapp's emasculation, he left Harmony, unable to budge his wife but taking the two children with him by force. Schick fled to Pittsburgh and there set up a small farm of his own, living as man and wife with his sister-in-law. In 1816, he wrote to relatives back home. He starts by acknowledging he will never see his mother again – even assuming she is still living – and then wastes no time in denouncing Rapp.

> The so-called Harmonie Society I left four years ago. Error, superstition and religious mania combined have among this handful of ignorant men reached the highest degree. Rapp, this concentrated monk, allows himself to be honoured as divine; he speaks of himself as divine by setting himself up as immortal and by professing to have the keys of Peter as the ruler of the Universe. Woe to the man who must buy his indulgence from this scoundrel; there one must pay dearly for one's sins.

This is the language of a bitterly disappointed man. His contempt for Rapp's secular activities has the ring of righteous indignation about it. 'Money controls the world and especially here in America, where the court is all English and goes through the hands of lawyers, where a common man understands nothing. Thus Rapp has built a silver wall around his slave colony and a person must be happy to get away with empty hands.'

The articles of association that gave rise to Harmony were never tested in court nor was a cash dividend ever paid by the Society to its members. Schick found his former neighbours gullible about both religion and money. Father was made all-powerful by their wish to see in him elements of the divine: that wish in turn enslaved them. Since they never left the community, they had no measure of what was usual elsewhere. If like Schick they absconded, the consequences were irreversible. Frederick Rapp made this clear in a letter written to a Philadelphia sympathiser in 1808, just after two errant families had been expelled from the community.

> And so the Harmonie will quickly cast out all filth in order that the body may be cleansed and purified of all foreign substance, and this is a good sign, although it gives offence to many. Whoever has been in Harmonie and has left it again, be it for whatever cause it may, is not worthy of the Kingdom of God and is a despiser of the sufferings of Jesus, therefore also of His salvation which He has won through suffering, and therefore such are persecutors and scorners of His name; therefore hate such and have no sympathy with them.

The seasons and the years passed. Harmony began to export goods to the eastern seaboard, as far as New York; some of this trade continued across the Atlantic and found its way to Bristol. More locally, 'outsiders' were married in Harmony suits and warmed their new brides with Harmony stoves. They walked to the town to buy their shoes, or bonnets for their children. The more discerning palates bought a puncheon of Golden Rose whisky or jars of peaches. And then, in the edition of *Niles Weekly Register* of 25 June 1814, published far away in Baltimore, came news that hit like a bombshell.

> The extensive settlement of *George Rap* and his associates at *Harmony Pennsylvania*, with all the buildings, improvements, etc, etc is offered for sale. It consists of three villages – many mills, workshops, factories etc and 9,000 acres of land; 3,000 of which are highly improved, with orchards, vineyards, meadows, etc. They have on the premises 3,000 sheep and 600 horned cattle. The stock is

not offered for sale. The concern is about to remove to
the *Indiana* territory, and settle on the *Wabash*.

In the early months of 1814, without consulation with the Society,
Father and two companions set off on horseback along the
Kentucky Trail. One of them was an English-speaking Rappite
called John L. Baker who in Württemberg had been Johannes
Langenbach – without him Rapp would have been as silent as a
stone. It was still the snowing season as the party made its way
towards Louisville. Pleasingly, at every inn they stayed the locals
had heard something of them. For their part, they were scandalised by the indolence of the Kentuckians, who assured them a
man need work no more than three days a week, so rich was the
soil. The only problem was, as these tavern wits went on to point
out, both banks of the Ohio were already settled and the best
land taken up. There were fewer people in Louisville than there
were in Harmony, not all of them as sober and industrious as
Father might wish: on the other hand there were 57 counties
state-wide, supporting something like half a million people.

Rapp and his companions crossed to the north bank of the
river below Louisville, intending to enter Indiana about halfway
along its southern boundary. They rode west and north for a
hundred miles along the Buffalo Trace, finding their way at last
to the government land office at Vincennes. Money talked in
Indiana: without the slightest difficulty the three newcomers
bought 6,000 acres of bottom land on the Wabash, twelve miles
as the crow flies from its confluence with the Ohio.

Back in Pennsylvania, Frederick Rapp was busy taking an
inventory. Nearly ten years of backbreaking effort was about to
go under the hammer and whatever comforts the community
had fashioned from their stay on Connoquenessing Creek were
transformed suddenly to empty vanities. There was no discussion
about the move and nothing so redundant as a vote. Rumour had

it that the journey would be made down the Ohio River, which none of the Harmonists had ever seen, to a place none of them had ever heard of. It was said to be far away; and virgin land. The 6,000 acres Father had purchased had not one stone standing upon another. No axe had ever rung out in its woods.

If there was to be a revolt among the Harmonists, now was its time. Instead, the men gathered and sharpened their tools, the women turned away from the little gardens that had been their pride. In the fields, whatever had been sown in the spring would be reaped by someone else.

FOUR

Easy to say somewhere; not so easy to say where!

In Scotland, Robert Owen had grown a little tired of having always to open his company's books to defend his principles. In 1806, his original partners, with whom he had completed the purchase of New Lanark, were scandalised when he insisted on paying full wages during a catastrophic hike in raw cotton prices that brought production in the mills to a standstill. The proximate cause was a trade embargo imposed by the United States but it took place in a generally inflationary year. The crisis lasted four months, at the end of which Owen's gesture of goodwill towards his workforce had cost the company £7,000 – a piece of philanthropy not well received by the other partners in the enterprise. Their dismay touched at the heart of the New Lanark project.

Paying wages for men to stand idle when, after the embargo was lifted and trade resumed, Owen could have had his pick of thousands of starving spinners, was going against the grain of business. The price of labour floated or sank according to the 'natural' laws of supply and demand. To the argument that here at New Lanark Owen had secured an element of trust between master and hand that could only bode well for the future, his colleagues had a simple and brutal reply. In the cotton trade, as everywhere else, it was necessity that drove men to work, not co-operative loyalty.

The partners had other issues on their mind. Over in America, it made no difference to Rapp's sleep that in October of 1806, the Holy Roman Empire came to an end, nor that nine days after that Prussia very incautiously declared war on France. (Frederick William III gave a dramatic twist to a very bad decision by visiting Frederick the Great's tomb at Potsdam and bestowing a kiss on the marble effigy of his illustrious great-uncle.) Five days later, Napoleon smashed the Prussians at Jena and Auerstädt. Within a fortnight he was in Berlin, where he too paused at Potsdam in order to pay his brief respects to Frederick the Great before, as an afterthought, looting his sword and the Order of the Black Eagle for shipment back to Paris. Once at Berlin, he issued a series of decrees outlining the new 'Continental System' he envisaged as dictating the fortunes of Europe.

All this news was at least three months in the future for Rapp, and while when it finally arrived it might have cast (from his point of view) a welcomingly lurid light on the coming end of the world, it did not curdle the milk in his cow parlours or stop by a single day the grindstones turning in his gristmill. Harmony might not be located in the sort of biblical wilderness envisaged by St John of Revelation but it was all the same as remote from the fallout of world politics as anywhere could be.

The prosperity of New Lanark, on the other hand, could never be wholly insulated from great events taking place far away. Owen might ignore them, with his characteristic loftiness, but his partners were more sanguine. Nor were all the problems of the trade to do with foreign wars and blockaded ports. In the period 1801–11, the home population increased by over two million. Coming to terms with this and its consequences for social and economic life depended on where you stood. Out in the lanes of Lanark it might seem an almost unbelievable increase: in Manchester, Leeds or Glasgow and their satellites, it was only too apparent. What did this huge percentage jump in population mean for the trade – bigger home markets, or imminent social breakdown?

In London, where the politics was made, the population now topped a million. Artisans' wages, which were set by an Act of 1563, began to buckle. Combination – unionism – became a political force for the first time. In Spitalfields, once the capital's prosperous silk weaving district, unemployment was almost 100 per cent. Now not every beggar met with in the street was born to poverty – there were men who once had honourable trades who had lost them, possibly for ever. Radical agitation was being led by men who had been weavers, shipwrights, cabinetmakers, printers and the like.

Owen was in many ways the last person with whom to discuss such issues. His two principal partners were more attuned to the fragility of the markets – and the political volatility of the masses – than he was. Though they presented him with a testimonial silver plate in 1806, three years later they were staggered at the scale of a proposed school building, for which the ground had already been cleared and levelled. For them it was an innovation too far. Some form of education among the workforce was no doubt valuable and even prudent; nor had they forgotten what the genial David Dale had attempted by way of schooling in his days. But what Owen had in mind seemed to them excessive. They made an inspection of his plans and listened patiently to his lengthy arguments on the subject. But they would not be budged. 'Each of your conclusions is true individually; but as they lead to conclusions contrary to our education, habits, and practices, they must in the aggregate be erroneous, and we cannot proceed on such new principles for governing and extending this already very large establishment.'

Temperamentally, they were reacting like Tories of the old school. A little private philanthropy might be all very well in its place but they were, or thought they were, investing in an industry and not in social experiment. All his life, Owen displayed a genius for the sudden and dramatic gesture and to contradict him in this way could only have one outcome. He forced their hand. The partners could have his share in the mills, or he would buy them out, whichever they preferred. They chose to sell, inviting him to name his price. He proposed £84,000, a figure they accepted with gratitude. The return on their capital had risen by more than a third in a mere nine years.

Though Owen was a much richer man than when he first came to New Lanark, he was in no position to find this kind of money from his own pocket and he formed a second partnership, this time comprised of Scots, two of them his wife's relatives. It was a short-lived and unhappy arrangement. The new men were even less disposed to indulge the visionary in Robert Owen. In 1812, they outvoted him on the board of the company and forced New Lanark into sale at public auction. Their motives seem to have been vindictive: they disparaged Owen's ideas, disliked him personally – and intended to show it. Hatred of the company they owned was so irrational that they valued it at only £40,000. It was a calculated piece of spite, wrapped in a not very dangerous financial gamble, for they could be fairly certain that the knock-down price at auction would far exceed this figure. The thing that would suffer was Owen's reputation, as locally it did.

The complexion of Owen's third partnership, which re-purchased the company at £114,000, is an indication of how far he had moved meanwhile towards a more openly radical view of his communitarian activities, as well as demonstrating the breadth and quality of his social contacts outside Scotland. Six people joined him in finding the new purchase price, three of them extremely rich men, all of them with strong philanthropic interests. Joseph Foster was a Quaker from Wearmouth, who inherited a fortune from his father's bottle-making business in London. William Allen, a fellow Quaker, was the son a silk manufacturer who became a distinguished chemist and whose second wife was Elizabeth, daughter of his neighbour and partner, another chemist called Hanbury.

Allen was an indefagitable servant of good causes. He met Thomas Clarkson in 1794 and through him was introduced to William Wilberforce and other members of the Clapham Sect. He had a house in the City at Plough Court and a manufacturing laboratory at Plaistow, then a muddy village. In 1811, Allen used some of his money to found the journal *The Philanthropist*, appointing James Mill as editor. Owen found Allen a 'very busy bustling meddling character', possibly because he took the most direct interest in New Lanark.

Of the remaining partners Michael Gibbs was a City merchant who afterwards became Lord Mayor of London; Joseph Fox was a dentist. John Walker was a member of the Taylor and Walker brewing dynasty, a highly cultivated man who lived in studied indolence at Arnos Grove and was quite rich enough to have purchased New Lanark out of his own pocket. The last member of the consortium was the philosopher Jeremy Bentham.

This partnership shifts the view we had of Owen when he first arrived at New Lanark. Then he had been an unknown venture capitalist with a bee in his bonnet about how society should be managed; now, if he chose, he could join such eminent phil-anthropists on his own terms. He had broken through the under-growth, as it were, and was standing now on something of a sunlit upland, peopled by men whose minds were habituated to thinking on social issues. William Allen, through his friendship with Wilberforce, gave him access to Parliament; John Walker stood ready to lead him towards scholars, writers and artists. In Bentham's writings he could find a compendium of good causes lengthily argued, from the inadequacies of the poor law to prison reform.

True, the sunlit upland had its geographical location in London and the people who occupied it were for the most part far better educated men than he; nevertheless, the third partnership gave him his chance to present himself to a wider audience. As a cotton mill, New Lanark had never been out of profit. Now, people who had no interest in it commercially – who had never even seen it – began to speak of it as a philanthropic experiment of the highest public interest.

John Stuart Mill wrote of Bentham after his death: 'There is hardly anything in Bentham's philosophy that is not true. The bad part of his writings is his resolute denial of all that he does not see, of all truths but those which he recognises.' Unfortunately, this judgement might have been applied just as aptly to Owen himself. Characteristically, he described his most intellectually distinguished partner as having 'little knowledge of the world except through books and a few deemed liberal-minded men and women who were admitted to his friendship'. This is narrow; and unpleasant. For someone famous in history for his later co-operative ventures, it is always alarming to come across instances of how little Owen seemed to trust and respect other people.

The problem of the age was not that there was too much bookreading, but far too little. What the early nineteenth century lacked in its fevered discussions on social issues was hard evidence, in the form of statistics. It was clear that something irreversible was happening to the old society, for which the old laws had been been framed, but nobody could say for sure what it was. So, for example, when it was first proposed that no child under ten should be allowed to work in factories, opponents of the measure (many of them employers of such children) asked what mischief they would get up to, what awful moral danger they might fall into, if they were not kept busy at work. Only a man who had never seen a mill in operation could have asked this question sincerely.

For many people, what still worked best was the custom of their fathers and grandfathers. This was true in almost every sphere. In the Peninsular campaign, for example, the languid but generally good-natured Captain Gronow of the Guards (another Welshman) had witnessed a soldier given 800 lashes, having been found guilty of making counterfeit coins from the pewter spoons of his mates. The man died of his punishment long before his backbone appeared through the pulp of his flesh and Gronow did wonder idly whether it might not have been simpler to have shot him at the outset and have done with it; but it never crossed his mind to ask whether such ferocious punishment was of itself wrong. (Gronow composed his reminiscences, from which this anecdote is taken, as late as 1861, which sharpens the point.)

In the end, flogging was not abolished in the peacetime army until 1867. Shoving a child up a chimney like a human brush only became illegal in 1842, the same year that girls under the age of twelve were prevented from working underground in mines. The agitation to reduce the labour of children in factories to no more than ten hours a day lasted more than 50 years. These are illustrations of a difficulty all reformers faced in the early part of the nineteenth century. It was useless to urge a principle upon an even moderately well-disposed public when they had no direct experience of the wrongs the principle was supposed to set right. Very few of the well-off had ever stepped inside a factory or a military barracks, sent their young sons up chimneys or watched their naked daughters drag coal tubs along underground tramways on their hands and knees.

Culpable ignorance – which Owen lumped into the general category of error – was cruelly pilloried 50 years later in *Our Mutual Friend* in the character of the testy Mr Podsnap (said to have been modelled on Dickens's friend and biographer, John Forster). Dickens had explored the fragile and dangerous world of the workhouse child in *Oliver Twist* – Gamfield, the hideously cruel sweep, nearly indentured Oliver, who was saved only by the intervention of the magistrates. What Podsnap was made to say in 1865 had an echo reaching all the way back to the beginning of the century – indeed to the circumstances of Dickens's own childhood.

> 'There is not,' said Mr Podsnap, flushing angrily, 'there is not a country in the world, Sir, where so noble a provision is made for the poor as in this country.'
> The meek man was quite willing to concede that, but perhaps it rendered the matter even worse as showing there must be something appallingly wrong somewhere.
> 'Where?' said Mr Podsnap.
> The meek man hinted, wouldn't it be well to try, very seriously, to find out where?
> 'Ah,' said Mr Podsnap. 'Easy to say somewhere; not so easy to say where! But I see what you are driving at. I knew it from the first. Centralisation. No. Never with my consent. Not English.'

If Owen was about anything, he was about centralisation. Everything could and must be reduced to a single central tenet. He was not an ameliorist like the Allens or the Hanburys, for whom improvements were made incrementally – a school here, a seizing interest in some new social ill there; friends and supporters gathered patiently, the whole going forward slowly. Men like these looked for the local social evil and applied their wealth and their sentiment – and the lives of their children – to putting things right. If they could not change the whole world, they could at least right wrongs where they found them – in prisons, or slums, among homeless children or those who were starving in the streets.

Five minutes of conversation with William Allen would have disclosed another thing foreign to Owen. One of the engines of change among philanthropic Quakers was marriage between like-minded families. Elizabeth Paterson, who interested herself in prison reform, became the second wife of Cornelius Hanbury, whose first marriage had been to William Allen's only child, Mary. There were also Allen family connections to the rich Norwich banker, John Gurney. Two of Gurney's daughters were the prison reformer Elizabeth Fry and Hannah Fowell Buxton, whose husband, the son of a baronet, was introduced to philan-thropic causes – particularly the abolition of slavery – by William Allen. (Sir Thomas Fowell Buxton has his statue in Westminster Abbey close to Wilberforce's.)

None of this useful cousinage suited Owen temperamentally, any more than the theoretical discussions on, for example, the relationship between poverty and population undertaken by Malthus. He had no talent for association or social interaction and in any case his lack of religious sentiment cut him off from the London Quakers and evangelical Christians just described. Most damaging of all, he suffered from the disability shared by all autodidacts: no power on earth could ever change his mind.

In 1813, he published the first of four essays with the overall title *A New View of Society*. The strap gave the important clue to their content: *Essays on the Principle of the Formation of the Human Character and the Application of the Principle to Practice.* Nothing here about soup kitchens or ragged schools, prison reform or the plight of the poor: Owen went straight to the heart of the matter, as he perceived it. What was wrong with society was the lamentable warping of human character that had be-devilled history since its beginnings. In every past age, right down to the present time, man had been raised to inherit insti-tutions and ideas that were founded on intellectual error. We can see at once where this is coming from: Owen was codifying thoughts that had first occurred to him in his Manchester lodg-ings, after a hard day's work at Drinkwater's Mill in Manchester.

What would put things right, therefore? Only the realisation that any child could be formed into any character the world over 'by the application of the proper means; which means are to a great extent at the command and under the control of those who have influence in the affairs of men'. As to what these 'proper means' might be, the undiscovered key to right behaviour, the author of *A New View* has a pleasant surprise for his readers. He has already employed them himself 'over a twenty years period', with nothing but success!

This provides a reassuring note to an otherwise bleak analysis, though there remains a worrying problem of scale. Owen insists: history can only be brought to a shuddering halt by employing worldwide what he has accomplished in little at New Lanark. Unabashed, he hammers home the point. 'Some of the best intentioned among the various classes in society may still say: All this is *very delightful and very beautiful in theory* but *visionaries* alone can expect to see it *realised*. To this remark only one reply *can* or *ought* to be made: that *these principles have been carried most successfully into practice.'*

When italics failed him, Owen had his text set in capitals. Thus these stark assertions:

> THAT THE CHARACTER OF MAN IS, WITHOUT A
> SINGLE EXCEPTION, ALWAYS FORMED FOR HIM;
> THAT IT MAY BE, AND IS CHIEFLY, CREATED FOR
> HIM BY HIS PREDECESSORS; THAT THEY GIVE
> HIM, OR MAY GIVE HIM, HIS IDEAS AND HABITS,
> WHICH ARE THE POWERS THAT GOVERN AND
> DIRECT HIS CONDUCT. MAN NEVER DID, NOR IS
> IT POSSIBLE HE EVER CAN, FORM HIS OWN
> CHARACTER.

Quite apart from whether all this is true, it has several consequences that Owen does not explore. Mankind can only be made better by direction, and then only by someone much like Owen himself. Love and affection do not change circumstances. Nor can churches do the job – they are a part of the problem. So, too, Parliament, universities, the law, even the advice a doting father might offer to his son. The situation is stark. Man has had his character decided for him in all preceding ages and the net consequence has been nothing but harm. What has been inculcated, with whatever good intention, has been error piled on error.

Setting things straight might have suggested to some nervous readers the need for a nihilistic rendering of everything in the world to rubble, before it could be rebuilt on new foundations. But this is not Owen's point at all. He is at pains to make clear that such a cataclysm will not be necessary: simply to acknowledge the existence of universal error is the first step towards correcting its consequences. In some way that Owen does not yet specify in any detail, the renewal of society will follow. History will change direction.

We know that one of the authors Owen did trust was the London police magistrate, Patrick Colquhoun, a Dumbarton man with a taste for statistical enquiry. Like John Melish in Georgia, Colquhoun spent part of his early life as a commercial agent in the Virginia cotton plantations. When he came home he settled in Glasgow and was appointed lord provost at the age of 37. The following year (1783) he was re-elected, and during this tenure he founded the Glasgow Chamber of Commerce. In 1789, Colquhoun moved to London and three years later was appointed one of the new stipendary magistrates.

What made him interesting to Owen was his gift for examining society in a statistical light – one of his first pamphlets was *Observations and Facts Relative to Public Houses*. Colquhoun had a practical turn of mind and his enquiries always led to sensible recommendations. He invented the idea of soup kitchens, promoted schemes to enable skilled workers to redeem their tools from pledge or to provide fish to the poor when the price of bread rose beyond a certain level. The West India merchants asked him to investigate theft from their shipping in the Thames – the outcome was the establishment of the River Police. From Colquhoun first we get the idea of a board of education, national savings banks, police commissions and a uniformly calculated poor relief (or national unemployment benefit).

His statistical enquiries were not complex, nor were they slanted to demonstrate any particular theory: he simply went out and counted heads. As his interests broadened (and his fame increased) he began to calculate how to divide the population according to rank. Accordingly, he found that 2,880 individuals formed what he called the Highest Orders – that is, 'the Royal Family, Lords Spiritual and Temporal, the Great Officers of State, and all above the degree of a Baronet, with their families'. The word he chose to distinguish the rest was class, and he found, by his tabulation, that there were six such classes, of which the lowest was described as containing 'Paupers and their families, Vagrants, Gipsies, Rogues, Vagabonds, and idle and disorderly persons, supported by criminal delinquency'. These numbered 1,828,170.

The biggest single class was those 'who subsist by labour in various employments'. Over thirteen million such people were engaged in productive labour and created what Colquhoun described as 'new property' every year. Sitting on their heads were less than half a million persons 'whose exertions do not create any new property'. They were the Royal Family, the nobility and gentry.

Owen had no sense that these figures might suggest class conflict as a more probable agent of change than the country waking up one morning to adopt Owenism. The very idea of conflict dismayed him. As he had demonstrated to the royal dukes with his pile of bricks, the trick was not to topple the whole social edifice but rather to rearrange it so that the working man was more content with his lot and his masters more benevolent towards him. The keyword was harmony.

The only way things would ever change was by engineering human character so that it led to a better and more harmonious society. Like the effects of a neutron bomb, while the change to the individual might be drastic, property would be left standing. The principal dedication in *A New View of Society* was to the very unlikely figure of the Prince Regent, who could be reassured that Owen's big idea was not going to leave him swinging from a cupola in Brighton, hanged in the guts of a bishop. If the prince bothered to read these essays at all, he could easily persuade himself that their overall thrust came close to saying not much more than if everybody were nicer, the world would be a nicer place in which to live (which proposition has, of course, its adherents to this very day). If you took Owen's word for it, there were already straws in the wind. 'Happily for man, this reign of ignorance rapidly approaches to dissolution: its terrors are already on the wing and soon they will be compelled to take their flight, never more to return. For now the knowledge of existing errors is not only possessed by the learned and reflecting, but is spreading far and wide throughout society; and ere long it will be fully comprehended by even the most ignorant.'

Unable to help himself, the role of man in this new dawning is to wait with joy for someone else to come along and form his new character for him. By the logic of Owen's argument, man has no choice in the matter, for all other systems have proved quite inadequate for the task and have simply added to the aboriginal mountain of error. Even the great work of educationists like Andrew Bell and Joseph Lancaster is mistaken and fruitless: the true saviour of mankind is made clear to the sympathetic reader of these essays – it will be Robert Owen.

A New View of Society was the first time Owen had put his ideas down on paper and though they are intended as an irrefutable critique of society, there is much in them that is foolish, not because he was a bad or foolish man but rather that he was deaf and blind to many aspects of life about which he knew little. He could point to huge changes in behaviour successfully accomplished at New Lanark, without seeming to realise that if had he suddenly demanded of his workforce that they wear lincoln green hats with a feather sticking out, or that on alternate Thursdays they hopped on one leg for eight hours, they were hardly in a position to refuse him – not if they wanted to eat.

New Lanark was in the end a story about coercion. As Owen insisted, people could be made into any shape at all. He did not realise that human nature could not be beaten into shape as if it were wrought iron. 'Thou needest to be very right,' his good-natured father-in-law had muttered before he died, 'for thou art very positive.'

The Institute for the Formation of Character in New Lanark was officially opened on 1 January 1816 before an audience of 1,200 people. The principal speaker was, of course, Owen, who delivered an address so long that it was (by intention) interrupted by a musical interlude played in another room. He was easily persuaded that his listeners believed this to be some mysterious reinforcement of what he had to say, musical harmonies delivered as if from heaven. Though he himself had no view on heaven, the effect was carefully calculated. It was almost impossible to speak of great changes and the advent of a new age without recourse to the language of religious enthusiasm. Whatever his address intended by way of rational exposition, it was delivered – and received – much as a sermon might be.

'What ideas individuals may attach to the term Millennium I do not know, but I know that society may be formed so as to exist without crime, without poverty, with health greatly improved, with little, if any, of misery, and with intelligence and happiness increased a hundredfold; and no obstacle whatever intervenes at this moment, except ignorance, to prevent such a state of society from becoming universal.'

This is encouraging the devout wish that exists in many to see the world cleansed and scoured before being made over in a new form. Owen affects not to know what millennianism is but all the same aligns his thought carefully with it. What he says – and especially the tone in which it is said – reflects the sermons and homilies heard in many a kirk or chapel of that time of millennial enthusiasm. These are not the irrational rantings of Joanna Southcott or the unfortunate Richard Brothers, who styled himself 'the Almighty's nephew': all the same the world is hungry for a Redeemer. Owen, he lets it be known by indirection, may be that man.

> Hitherto, I have not been disappointed in any of the expectations which I have formed. The events which have yet occurred far exceed my most sanguine expectations, and my future course now appears evident and straight-forward. It is no longer necessary that I should silently and alone exert myself for your benefit and the happiness of mankind. The period is arrived when I may call numbers to my aid, and the call will not be in vain.

This is a claim that goes far further than demonstrating to the prime minister or the Archbishop of Canterbury how to run a cotton mill along philanthropic lines. It is the first sign in Owen that the balloon was about to slip its moorings and fly off over new and unfamiliar terrain.

He had written some of the essays comprising *A New View of Society* in London while enjoying the hospitality of William Godwin; and we know, too, he showed the manuscript to the radicals Francis Place and James Mill. These debts were never acknowledged. Yet Godwin's *Enquiry Concerning the Principles of Political Justice*, which first appeared in 1793, contained this sentiment, fuel to much of what Owen had come to believe: 'Ten pages that should contain an absolute demonstration of the true interests of mankind in society could not otherwise be prevented from changing the face of the globe than by the literal destruction of the paper on which they were written.'

Parsed: the gospel, when it is revealed, cannot be contradicted or suppressed. These are progressive sentiments, derived from a genuine pyschological shift that can be characterised as impatience with the old ways and an absolute conviction in the existence of something better. In Godwin's case, the overarching authority was reason, which he believed in with a passion equal to Owen's. So we can read in Godwin this: 'Legislation, as it has been generally understood, is not an affair of human competence. Reason is the only legislator and her decrees are irrevocable and uniform.'

The feminine pronoun suggests how easily language slips from rational exposition to an enthusiasm that is at heart semi-ecstatic. Not every reader of *Political Justice* would have followed its author in declaring that the monarchy was 'founded in imposture', nor that having two Houses of Parliament was 'the direct method to divide a nation against itself'. On the other hand, Godwin's characterisation of reason stirred a fundamental yearning that was at heart religious.

The year after the publication of *Political Justice*, Christianity was abolished in France and at Paris the cathedral of Notre Dame became for a while a Temple of Reason, presided over by a buxom 'Goddess', a young dancer from the Opéra called Thérèse-Angelique Aubry. In place of the Mass was a 'rational' form of worship that was hardly less ritualistic. Owen was likewise tugged in two directions. Reason had led him to a simple, if misguided proposition, that the whole world was marching out of step. This placed him in the political camp of men like Godwin, though he lacked any sense they had of a democratic solution.

At the same time, there was a messianic strain in what he had to say, which greatly offended the faith of men like his partner William Allen. The real point of difference between Owen's democratic friends on the one hand and his philanthropic millionaires on the other was Owen himself. Greatly to their disgust, in the *Address to the Inhabitants of New Lanark* he announced himself much as would a prophet. By the logic of his argument only transfiguration could follow.

He made a start on his ministry by drafting a Bill to limit the labour of children in factories, putting it forward in the Commons by the hand of Sir Robert Peel, MP for Tamworth, first baronet and father of the statesman. The Bill was introduced in June 1815. Unfortunately for Owen, he had next to no understanding of how Parliament actually worked and the proposals were not considered again until April of the next year, when Peel, who was a mill owner himself, moved for a committee to be appointed to take evidence. Owen thrust himself forward as a principal witness without realising that he was taking on the whole of the textile industry. He fared badly. To the argument that the Bill as drafted would be the ruination of the industry, he replied that he thought it would not, if his experience of New Lanark was anything to go by – and then added, much more recklessly, that if it was, it was.

The textile lobby in the House of Commons was well aware that cotton manufacture was indispensable to the economy. The committee gave Owen a roasting, producing some highly dubious evidence of their own to show that the Bill was unnecessary because most of its provisions were already active. Medical witnesses affirmed that mills and factories were healthy places, beneficial to growing children. The general tone of the evidence is given here by an extract from the examination of James Pattison, a silk manufacturer who also happened to be a director of the East India Company.

– Could any system of inspection of the mills be established without inconvenience?

– I conceive certainly not: some years ago it was very
much the practice for persons to visit mills of this description from curiosity, but it was found so inconvenient that
these visits have been declined as much as possible, as
the attention of the children was always drawn from their
duty by the appearance of any new faces; and inspectors,
for the purpose of seeing all is right, it is conceived by
those who are the best judges of the question, would
very much weaken the authority of the masters over the
children . . .

There is a strong suspicion that the witness was stonewalling
in a reply like this; even that he was inviting the committee to
see him at it. For a man like Owen too much of this sort of thing
was galling. The art of the possible was utterly foreign to him.
He came to the House with the truth, stamped as it were with
his own personal seal. His fellow manufacturers should act on it
without demur. What happened in fact was the committee report
was shelved and the Bill failed.

In the early summer of 1816, a large public meeting was held
at the City of London Tavern at which the benevolent Duke of
York took the chair, its business to discuss the severe distress
that had followed the end of the war against France. The Archbishop of Canterbury was invited to form a committee to enquire
into 'Relief of the Manufacturing Poor' (namely, how to combat
unemployment) and Owen was invited on to it as a member. A
fellow member was the statistically minded Patrick Colquhoun. In
this way, Owen had a second bite at the cherry: at the committee's
request he submitted a lengthy report, which included in it such
strong recommendations that it became known as 'Mr Owen's
Plan'.

He had at hand the evidence supplied by cotton manufacturers to the House of Commons committee. Statistical information had been given to show the number of looms and spindles now in operation, with the intention of showing how powerful and irresistible an industrial undertaking cotton had become. Owen accepted these figures but drew a different conclusion from them. Twenty-five years of machine spinning had broken the cottage industry and, as factories turned increasingly to steam power, diminished the value of labour generally. He gave ground to the cotton interest: there was no way back from the situation as it now was. 'Under the existing commercial system, mechanical power could not in one country be discontinued and in others remain in action, without ruination to that country in which it should be discontinued. No one nation, therefore, will discontinue it; and although such an act were possible, it would be a sure sign of barbarism in those who should make the attempt.'

The machines were here to stay and it was in their nature to create unemployment among manual workers. There was no logic in attempting to reintegrate men with machines. Trade margins in the cotton industry would never permit full employment of unskilled manual labour for the mere sake of it, nor could manufacturers be expected to give bread to the poor from humanitarian considerations. Meanwhile, the parish system of relief was buckling at the knees. There had to be another way out of the crisis.

Owen's solution was as alarming as it was original. What was wanted was an entirely new form of village, for which he provided detailed drawings and costings. The poor should be redistributed in communities not smaller than 500 and not much larger than 1,500, each village to work by spade cultivation 1,200 acres of land. The drawings of an individual village indicated a vast square, redivided into parallelograms, with areas designated as communal kitchens and dining rooms, schools, an infirmary and the like. Each of these villages would have its superintendent, schoolmaster, surgeon and clergyman. Owen calculated that the cost of building such a village would be cheaper than paying the individuals in it poor relief and would give back dignity, labour and a properly responsible moral attitude to its inhabitants. Once in operation, every village would be self-sustaining.

It was the rational solution and it terrified the committee. Charles Manners-Sutton, the archbishop who had commissioned the report, was especially dismayed. He had begun his ministry at Averham-with-Kelham in Nottinghamshire; thence to Whitwell in Derbyshire; after that as Dean of Peterborough and Bishop of Norwich. He must have had special difficulty in rendering Owen's plans into the likeness of the country parishes he knew from the days before his elevation to the Deanery of Windsor and his present eminence; his consternation must have been shared by others on the committee. Where would these villages be sited? How would they co-exist with more ancient communities? Were weavers, the proudest and most independent examples of village life in the old and unregenerate days, to pick up a spade and work beside some spavined ditchdigger or redundant potboy? And in this context, who would be the voice of the new communities – the parson, the superintendent, or simply the man with the biggest fists?

The archbishop admired Owen in a general way but could not overcome the objections that sprang from common sense. He took the coward's way out and suggested the master of New Lanark take his drawings and his charts to another House of Commons committee then sitting to discuss the poor law. Its chairman was a lawyer least calculated to see the good in Owen's plan, William Sturges Bourne, of Winchester and Christ Church. He kept Owen waiting in the ante-room to the committee for two whole days before languidly sending out to say that his evidence would not be called. It was a personal and political snub of the greatest magnitude. Owen, his drawings and cost sheets under his arm, was sent packing.

It was now 1817. Two parliamentary committees had turned him down: Owen's most obvious strategy was to beat a dignified retreat to New Lanark where some at least of what he was advocating already existed. This was not the way of a Redeemer. He had conceived a plan on a national scale and he intended to see it through. He published what he had to say in *The Times* and *Morning Post*, both of which papers gave him a supportive leader. Copies of his plan were posted to every parish in the kingdom, all magistrates and provincial bankers, all MPs. The Secretary of the Post Office complained that the volume of such correspondence was holding up the London mail coaches by twenty minutes.

At two meetings in August he attempted to reintroduce his ideas, now rewritten as the fifteen 'Resolutions' it would be necessary to adopt before the regeneration of society along Owenite lines could commence. Both gatherings were rowdy ill-tempered affairs unlit by the noble torch of reason. Liberal gentlemen could not easily let go of the experience of their fathers and grandfathers; radical working men, who attended in great numbers, were not about to approve what Cobbett had called 'parallelograms for paupers'. But what wrecked the meetings was Owen's extraordinary insensitivity to people he presumed to be less rational than himself. Shouting to be heard in an overcrowded and smoky meeting room, he faced down his restless audience with this: 'My friends! A more important question has never yet been put to the sons of man! Who *can* answer it? Who dare answer it – but with his life in his hand: a ready and willing victim to truth, and to the emancipation of the world from its long bondage of disunion, error, crime and misery?'

Never give a heckler a rhetorical question to answer and never pose as a rich man whose life is threatened by a statement of principle. Over the din, Owen persevered with what he considered the meat of his address.

Behold that victim! On this day – in this hour – even
now – shall those bonds be burst asunder, never more to
reunite while the world shall last. What the consequence
of this daring deed shall be to myself, I am as indifferent
about as whether it shall rain or be fair tomorrow. Whatever may be the consequences, I will now perform my
duty to you and to the world: and should it be the last
act of my life, I shall be well content, and know that I
have lived for an important purpose.

There were clergy present at this meeting and he was hissed by
them; but the greater part of his audience were radicals. They
were there to abuse him for failing to see that what mattered was
the political representation of the poor and not their incarceration
in what appeared to be some new form of barracks, or augmented
workhouses. In his old age, Owen described this meeting as 'the
day on which bigotry, superstition and all false religions received
their death-blow.' But when the meeting ended and the doors
were opened, releasing clouds of tobacco into the street outside,
the greater part of the audience streamed away thinking they
had been wasting their time with a madman.

It was the year of the suspension of the Habeas Corpus Act,
when men less well-heeled than Owen, who did not have the
Archbishop of Canterbury as their patron, were taken up on the
evidence of police spies for imprudent remarks made in a tavern
or even in the street and chucked into prison without trial. One
of those awaiting the pleasure of the home secretary that night
was the weaver-poet Samuel Bamford, who had been brought to
London from Manchester in chains on a charge of high treason.
After a brief initial appearance before the Privy Council, he and
five companions were banged up in Coldbath Fields. They drank
tea, talked about their families and, before turning in, sang the
Union Hymn, part of which went:

> Oh! Worthy is the glorious cause,
> Ye patriots of the Union;
> Our father's rights, our father's laws,
> Await a faithful union.
> A crouching dastard sure is he
> Who would not strike for liberty,
> And die to make Old England free
> From all her load of tyranny;
> Up! Brave men of the Union.

Bamford was not yet 30. A silk-weaver, he had a clear and affectionate view of 'Old England' founded on his memories of Middleton, near Manchester, where his father had been a weaver before him. The sort of liberty he had in mind was of the sentimental backward-looking kind, a return to the quiet decencies of a rural life with long traditions, lit by fond reminiscence. Bamford was discharged by the Privy Council on this occasion but was not so lucky two years later. In 1819, the Middleton boys went up on the moors to practise their marching and wheeling and then set off for Peterloo. The weaver-poet was an easy target for arrest and subsequently served a year in Lincoln goal for his part in the demonstration; but although he liked to call himself a radical, he was too soft by far for many of his contemporaries. We can say this at least about Owen and the radical detractors who gave him such a bad time: they each understood that Old England in the Bamfordian sense was as dead as Falstaff and his buttered eggs.

FIVE

Accustomed despotic habits

We are seldom out of sight, as we travel on this grand track towards the Ohio, of family groups behind and before us. The New Englanders, they say, may be known by the cheerful air of their women advancing in front of the vehicle; the Jersey people by their being fixed steadily within it; whilst the Pennsylvanians creep lingeringly behind, as though regretting the homes they have left. Often the back of the poor pilgrim bears all his effects, and his wife follows barefooted, bending under the hopes of the family.

This was written in 1817 to describe travellers on the turnpike road from Philadelphia to Pittsburgh. The witness was a recently arrived tenant farmer from Surrey named Morris Birkbeck, travelling in a party of nine other English men and women, one of whom, George, was the son of his radical friend Richard Flower, a brewer and banker from Hertford.

Very few English immigrants to America were rich but those that were had the reputation of bringing everything with them but the kitchen sink, toting carpets and paintings as well as silver services and their finest plate. Some even brought their carriages, with the intention of bowling about the backwoods much as they had been used to doing in London or Bath. In this case, Birkbeck and his party were moving along the turnpike on horseback but he had the edge on his fellow-pilgrims all the same, for he was carrying with him enough credit to buy up to 20,000 acres in the far west, wherever he chose to lay his head.

Birkbeck was a widower in his fifties with four children; a short man, highly opinionated, exasperated with the England he had left behind and (once safely away from his native shores) republican in sentiment. The Quaker in him had all but disappeared and he had begun to affect a high-minded agnosticism he considered – wrongly – to be appropriate to his new circumstances. It was already in his mind to publish the journal he was keeping, partly from motives of vanity but more importantly to encourage others to follow where he led. The plan was that when he found them, his 20,000 acres would draw the better sort of British artisan and small farmer after him like a magnet. Meanwhile, he shrugged off the difficulties of the journey with a fine disdain.

He and his companions were unusual in that they chose to ride west all the way, electing not to travel down the Ohio by boat, with the greater ease and economy that route promised. They landed at Norfolk in Virginia and were taken to Richmond by steamer. From there they struck north for 200 miles, crossed the Potomac and joined the Philadephia–Pittsburgh trunk road. Travelling west from Pittsburgh, they crossed the Ohio at Wheeling and rode right across the state to Cincinnati. The more agreeable features of the journey began to dwindle the further west they travelled. Once mounted, the party resigned themselves to as much as twelve hours a day in the saddle, which in Indiana was spent blundering about in the half dark of the forest floor. Even for Americans, who as Birkbeck pointed out, were by their restless travels more knowledgeable about their own country than the English were about theirs, this was a major expedition.

Birkbeck carried letters of introduction furnished by Lafayette and that other old friend to America, William Cobbett. In his saddle bag there was also a copy of John Melish's book, which undoubtedly led him to search out Harmony before he crossed the Wabash into Illinois. He made little of his visit to Father Rapp. With the sort of stubbornness that afflicts rich Englishmen in a foreign land, he was looking for the greatest prize of all, a pristine landscape where no foot had ever set. Once arrived, he would build a town to be reckoned with, consistent with the view he had of himself as an enlightened proprietor from the old country who was also a friend to America. It was a high ambition and also something of a mistaken one. The journey to the hinterlands had uncovered a quality in Birkbeck that had lain dormant in the tamed beauties of Surrey. He was a natural explorer, the sort of man who might easily forget the original object of the expedition and end up as a pile of bones under a bluff or in some forsaken river bed.

His partner in this scheme was still in England. Richard Flower was a more querulous man and yet at the same time more finely drawn, more distinguished by his years. It was the bald and heavy browed Birkbeck who looked like a pugnacious bank clerk: Flower fitted his station in life like a rose in a stem glass. Though they were of the same age and considered themselves intellectual equals, Flower had one important advantage over his friend. In England, he was a freeholder, which Birkbeck never was, and he exercised this independence in a thoroughly modern way. At his home in Marden, near Hertford, he kept open house for men of a radical disposition who took their politics at a slant. His brother Benjamin had edited the *Cambridge Intelligencer*, one of the very few journals to support the progress of the French Revolution and oppose the war with France. His sister Mary, though rich, was married to John Clayton, a Unitarian minister who preached to convicts in the hulks.

These ill-matched partners, Flower and Birkbeck, had come together out of disaffection with the government and a hatred of recent legal repressions. They shared vaguely utopian ideals of freedom and perfectibility. It is interesting that they expressed these not so much in connection with people as with land. Birkbeck was a passionate agriculturist who farmed 1,500 acres on a long lease from the Earl of Onslow; his colleague Flower devoted much of his time away from the counting house to the breeding of merino sheep that dotted the parkland in front of his handsome property on Marden Hill.

There was nothing of Coleridge and Southey about their plans, no dream of poetical musings along the banks of the Susquehanna with their bosom friends – the idea was they would go to America and turn back the clock to a better time, with themselves cast as lords of the manor. For Birkbeck, the incentive was to own his own land and be his own master. His grudge against England was very particular. Flower, who already had the experience of being a rich and settled man, would transfer his political and aesthetic loyalties to a country where the tree of liberty had been watered by the blood of patriots and the battles now raging in Britain had long been decided in favour of the brave.

Birkbeck finally purchased 20,000 acres on behalf of the partnership in the prairie country of Illinois, twenty miles from the second Harmony. The transit through Indiana depressed him. He found the forests sombre and overwhelming; but then, little by little, the trees gave way until, on the far side of the Bon Pas Creek, there was grassland. And such grassland it was, too. No sod had ever been turned here and the horseman could ride through a landscape that had not changed for thousands of years. Horse and rider disappeared into grass so tall that it overtopped them: cattle would wander for five or six miles from homesteads, lost without horizons to orientate them. The very emptiness was intoxicating to someone of Birkbeck's character. Yet, as was to prove, he had many flaws. He was a fine man for a journey and a stoic when it came to the frustrations and irritations of the trail.

Only when he got down from his horse did his faults become apparent.

The new arrival immediately set about writing two works that had an enormous vogue in Europe and went through several editions and translations – *Notes on a Journey in America* and *Letters from Illinois*, both published in 1818. In some ways these books were like prospectuses. But the scheme dreamed up in the drawing room of Flower's home at Marden Hall was to founder on the conflicting personalities of the partners. The falling out between Birkbeck and Flower was accelerated by the alluringly young and beautiful Eliza Julia Andrews, a Flower kinswoman who travelled out to Illinois in Birkbeck's party. She was eighteen years old. The elderly widower was so smitten that before they reached journey's end he proposed to her – and was refused.

To his chagrin, she soon after married his partner's son, George. This was a double blow because Birkbeck knew George Flower – or thought he did – even more intimately than he did his father. Nor did it help matters that George was already married and had left behind in England a woman he did not love and who did not love him, though she had borne him two children. To Birkbeck's disgust, Eliza Julia gave herself up to bigamy with the enthusiasm he hoped she might have reserved for his own suit. The wedding was solemnised at Vincennes, Indiana. The disappointed lover insisted on acting the gentleman's part and standing as best man. It was a gesture he was to regret.

Eliza Julia was not the only fly in the ointment. Birkbeck's one time friend, William Cobbett, also a Surrey man, had a second and more practical objection to what became known as the English Prairie. In his view, it was a case of overreaching. The sort of farming Birkbeck and Flower had in mind would have been better begun in the eastern seaboard states, where the land had already been cleared and sweetened. Cobbett knew that his radical friends were not pioneers: they were improving farmers who lacked the fund of common sense he felt he had himself and that he liked to assert at length to others.

At the time of Birkbeck's expedition, Cobbett was holed up on Long Island, a refugee from the suspension of Habeas Corpus in England. He found it irritating that what good advice he might have to give about farming prospects in the republic was going unheeded. He was, after all, the expert, the muscular giant known to thousands. There was also a question of pedigree here. Birkbeck's father had been a mere Quaker minister, though a distinguished one: Cobbett was born in a pub called 'The Jolly Farmer' which *his* father ran alongside a successful smallholding. Birkbeck farmed for the eccentric and even fatuous Onslows, father and son. Cobbett would not have opened a gate for any earl in England.

George Flower and Morris Birkbeck had already travelled together in France in 1814, looking for property. They found the influence of the Church in *la France profonde* more than they could stomach, even though their steps were guided by Lafayette. In Illinois, all religious and legal objections were removed – this was as close to virgin soil and the utopian idyll as could be pictured. It had the thrill of the new in other ways, too. Birkbeck's land was sold to him under its original title as Bolting-house Prairie. It was so named after the first man to build a cabin out in the tall grasses. One night the unfortunate Boltinghouse fell into a quarrel with a marauding Shawnee and was killed. The Indian – or an Indian answering to the general description – was captured, had a slab of stone tied to his chest and was flung into the Little Wabash River. To some temperaments, this was an energising example of how the west was to be won. Birkbeck always had a strong element of the colonial adventurer in him, in which both the Shawnee and their American usurpers were seen as disagreeable and sometimes fractious natives. About abroad, he was incurably English.

However, when Richard Flower finally arrived from England in 1818 with bags of money and noble aspirations, his partner met him with some alarming words: 'I am sorry to see you, I had rather not see you . . . I cannot, will not see you.' The marriage of the delectable Eliza Julia to George (and maybe his own unhappy part in it as best man) had turned his mind against the whole family. So it was that the English Prairie set about building not one but two towns – Wanborough, where Birkbeck smouldered, drinking cheap whisky and smoking cigars; and, less than three miles away, the high-sounding Albion, over which Richard Flower fussed and worried.

It was an absurd solution to a quarrel over a woman. The two settlements were soon 'the abodes of contention, party spirit, speculation and feuds' according to a book published in 1823 by William Faux, a work that bore the enticing but finally misleading title *Memorable Days in America, Being a Journal of a Tour to the United States Principally Undertaken to Ascertain, by Positive Evidence, the Condition and Probable Prospects of British Emigrants; Including Accounts of Mr Birkbeck's Settlement in the Illinois*. Faux had a great capacity for sneering. He liked Birkbeck slightly better than the Flower family, but not by much. On one gloomy visit to Wanborough he posed the proprietor a direct question and got back this defeated answer: 'Birkbeck tells me the reason why he does not cultivate his land is because he can buy produce cheaper at Harmony, much cheaper than he can raise it.'

It seemed a poor outcome to a 4,000 mile journey, especially one designed to show the world how true-born Englishmen could turn the prairie into a goldmine. The farmer in Birkbeck had gone the way of the Quaker. He was lost. It was a further gall to his soul that Richard Flower had not only turned up with examples of his prize merino sheep but also the many choicely engraved silver plates they had won at agricultural shows in England.

*   *   *

In October 1819, a traveller visited both Harmony and Wanborough on the same day. He wrote of what he saw in a letter to a
friend in Kentucky. It happened to be a Sunday when he rode
into Harmony and the whole community was gathered to hear
Father Rapp preach.

> [W]e had an opportunity of seeing them all together in
> their going and returning from meeting, attendance *at*
> meeting being denied strangers. About 1 o'clock pm a
> fine band of musick struck up in the street and headed
> a procession which marched about ¾ of a mile to the
> Wabash. We followed at a short distance & on our arrival
> at the dry and Gravelly bed of this beautiful river the
> irregular procession paused, the Band again played a tune,
> 'mournful, yet soothing' to the heart of the stranger. The
> motley group now seated themselves round their vener-
> able leader who addressed them in German in a most
> animated & pathetick manner, this was followed by read-
> ing for some time.

The author of this letter – probably an Englishman – had no
prior knowledge of Harmony but had sharp eyes. Father, he
observed, lived in a fine brick house and the rest of the Rappites
in log cabins. Like many another casual visitor, he was fascinated
and yet faintly repelled by the community. Young though it was,
the town was clearly the outcome of unremitting hard work,
derived from the strange hold Rapp had over his congregation.
'How so numerous a population are kept quietly and tamely in
absolute servitude it is hard to conceive – the women I believe
do more labour in the field than the men, as large numbers of
the latter are engaged in different branches of manufactures.'
This made the fact that 3,000 acres of Harmony land – half the
total estate – had been put under cultivation in only four years
all the more remarkable. Three thousand acres of felled trees and

cleared scrub bespoke a huge communal effort not to be bettered in any township for hundreds of miles.

Late that same day, towards dusk, he rode into the English Prairie, found Morris Birkbeck sulking in his cabin and spent the evening there. He had the advantage of being able to speak English to his host but otherwise the comparison with Harmony was stark. Birkbeck had yet to put into practice the big idea that had brought him to America. His visitor was quite amazed at his indolence. 'He did plant six acres of corn but unfortunately not having taken the usual precaution to protect it from the inroads of cattle by a fence, they ate it up before it was fully grown – how he came to expect that his corn would be more sacred in their eyes than that of American settlers it is difficult to imagine.'

Birkbeck, it seemed, had given up on rolling acres. In preparation for the arrival of emigrants to this wilderness he built a sort of barracks, squalid in the extreme, and his advice to dispirited newcomers expecting a bit of Surrey set down in America was to buy land from him and push out even further into the prairie. There was certainly little for them at Wanborough. His own first task had been to dig a well and in this he had beginner's luck, finding good water not much more than twenty feet down. Once found, he refused to share his well with another living soul.

This was not the way things were done in Harmony. In 1814, when Rapp arrived on *his* virgin site and hardly before a tree had been felled, he astounded his neighbours by ordering 3,000 bushels of Indian corn. Despite the malarial fever that prostrated the advance party, two men (just two) were set to begin planning and constructing a watermill, in order to be independent of the horsemill nine miles away. Writing to Frederick about the sick, Father was his usual brutal self.

The following will still probaby die: tailor Durr, Josua
Vayringer's wife and two boys have been buried, Launer
is dead, Leibbrand, the Steinhauer woman, the Fester
woman are dead. Old Reif and Kreil will scarcely make it;
Waldman is still living but will scarcely make it; Ludwig
Schreiber is in a bad condition; Jacob Laupple will die
as well as the Schmeid woman, the Waldman woman
also is in a bad condition. The rest I hope will recover
gradually.

The Rappites had suffered their first encounter with the mosquitoes, held by locals to be able to bite through the sole of a
boot. In every other respect Rapp had chosen his property
extremely well. At the back of the area marked out for the new
town was a hill that hid the only quarriable stone for many
miles around. Four substantial creeks gave opportunity for water
power, exploration revealed both clay and surface coal. There
were huge banks of freshwater mussel shells along the Wabash
from which to make lime; and opposite the beach on which Rapp
had harangued his congregation there was an island. Admittedly,
they had first to evict an enraged squatter discovered among the
reeds, but once removed they set fish traps in his place and built
a landing stage.

One of the signs of how things were intended to turn out took
place as early as Christmas Eve of 1814. Staggering up from the
river came Frederick Rapp, his clothes stiff with frost. He had
made the descent of the Ohio from Pittsburgh in the worst season
of the year, when ice floes clattered against the rocks and the
swollen waters boiled. More than that, he travelled the whole way
without stopping, careering along under the stars – an unheard of
feat of daring and endurance. It set the tone. By the early months
of 1815, the entire community arrived from Connoquenessing
Creek and hurled themselves into a frenzy of building.

The second Harmony was even more impressive than the first.

Rapp got his gristmill, his sawyers their prime spot on one of the four creeks. The tanners and the blacksmiths set up extensive workshops and the weaving shed began to turn out cloth of such quality that soon the territorial governor himself sported a Harmony suit. Feeling in need of a bell for Sunday services, Father sent to a foundry in Liverpool and had one cast. It was shipped across the Atlantic and dispatched by wagon and keel boat more than a thousand miles inland to its destination. To the further astonishment of the locals, the community ordered a steam engine from a works in Pittsburgh, the first of its kind ever delivered to Indiana. It came with a long-suffering mechanic called Hamilton, whose job it was to assemble the parts and prevent the new owners from blowing themselves up.

In those early days, before Frederick brought down the main party, Father claimed to have suffered a sort of Birkbeckian cafard.

> I am rather spoiled by solitude and have lost even my taste for reading. I seem to myself to be a real idler, a man who is waiting for something and he does not know what, but I am as if resting thereby but do not know, is it indifference or sluggishness? I cannot make much out of anything because according to my innermost being, I am aware that a wish is expressing itself to become nothing. May it happen now by whatever means it will.

This was a mood that quickly passed. US Congressman William Hendricks and Senator Waller Taylor hastened to send Rapp their compliments from Washington and Governor Jennings made 'a pleasant visit' to Harmony a year after his inauguration, staying two nights. Thus, while it pleased Rapp from time to time to play the part of an anguished prophet in his solitary wilderness, the truth was very different.

An English visitor named Courtney looked over Harmony in 1819 and counted 175 dwellings, including a three storey church.

His eye was taken by the poplars lining every street, planted for their shade. (Father Rapp was also persuaded they would deter mosquitoes.) The town was set out in formal blocks created from two principal streets running at right angles to each other and at regular intervals there were public wells and – a novelty – communal bread ovens. Courtney found the lack of family life around an individual hearth as intriguing as anyone who had come before him but the hotel was the most comfortable he had stayed in during his American travels. This was partly due to the efforts of Christopher Hobson, a rare outsider admitted to the Harmony site and a refugee from Birkbeck's Wanborough. All in all, Courtney was in no doubt he was visiting a commercial and manufacturing centre much like a thriving English market town. The only bugbear was that it remained a closed and German-speaking community.

'During the short time I remained in the settlement, I should suppose that from 30 to 50 saddle horses and a few wagons arrived daily from within a circle of about 100 miles in circumference, with customers of both sexes, to purchase European, East and West Indian goods, or to buy and sell country produce.'

All these customers were free to raise a glass in the tavern but they never met a Harmonist there. The town was famous for its cleanliness and the absence of crime – no drunken brawling, no shots fired off at random or screams in the night. And nothing either of the three-day week so famously boasted of in other backwoods communities. These people worked from sunup to sundown. *Arbeit ist der Burgers Zierde* said Schiller: what adorned the Harmonist and crowned his brow with laurels was work. As visitors sat in the tavern they could look out of the window at any time of the day and see Schiller's dictum in action. Among the otherwise placid and unquestioning folk who lived in Harmony, work was raised to an almost philosophic principle. It was as hard to find a loafer as it was to discover a kissing couple.

Left Robert Owen, mill-master, from a society miniature by Mary Ann Knight.

Below New Lanark Mills as they were in 1825. The Royal Burgh of Lanark is in the background.

Georg Rapp, idealised by a primitive portraitist as the white-bearded patriarch of unblemished conscience.

Above right Rapp's Iptingen home, which matches with the idea of him found in his portrait – and (*below*) the house he had built for him in Harmony, as large as any in Indiana.

Wabash country, after a painting by Karl Bodmer. The awesome and romantic forest – and in the distance, Harmony and its three thousand acres.

Robert Dale Owen and his brother, William, sketched at Hofwyl in 1821.

Left William Maclure, as memorialised by the Philadelphia Academy of Natural Sciences, of which he was the honoured president.

Below One of many pencil sketches by the naturalist and scientific illustrator, Charles Lesueur, associated with Harmony. This one shows the Philanthropist, or 'Boatload of Knowledge' trapped by ice along the Ohio River, January 1826.

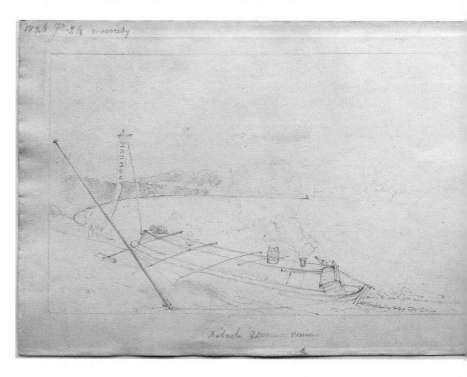

Above Frances Wright, drawn
after her fling with George
Flower and flirtation with
Robert Dale Owen.

Above right Guillaume Sylvan
Casimir Phiquepal d'Arusmont,
provincial dentist, Pestalozzian
teacher, and protégé of William
Maclure.

Right Frances Wright in the
costume adopted by the Literati.
It was designed to indicate
unisex politics and a high tone
but was widely reported as
being provocative and indecent.
From the *Illinois Gazette*,
published in Shawnee-Town:

In beauty there's something to
    hide and reveal
There's a thing that we decency
    call;
The old system ladies display
    a great deal,
But the new system ladies –
    show all.

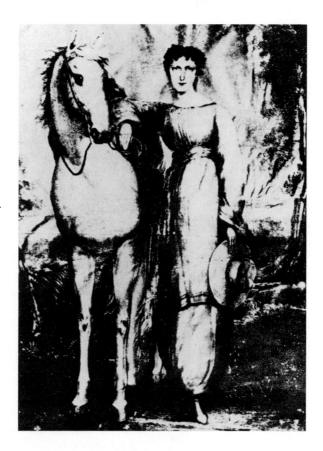

The only known likeness of George Birkbeck, founder of the
ill-fated township of Wanborough, out on the English Prairie.

George Cruickshank's lampoon of New Harmony, entitled 'All Owin' and No Payin'', an inspired reading of the actual situation.

OPPOSITE *Left* George Flower in his later years. Though already married with two children, he snatched the eighteen year old Eliza Julia Andrews from under the nose of George Birkbeck and married her at Vincennes in 1823. He survived – but only just – a liaison with Fanny Wright.
Right Eliza Julia Flower, the object of so much passion, painted in the primitive style towards the end of her life. She and her husband died on the same day in January 1862 – she in the morning, he in the afternoon.

Above A sketch by David Dale Owen of Harmony (with Rapp's old house in the background) done in 1830, when the gale had blown over the town and those that were left rediscovered the virtues of fences – and private property.

Right Robert Owen, sketched at the door of a newsagent's in Manchester, when he was approaching sixty.

Duty was too important a matter and if George Rapp, studying the balance sheets of the community with secret satisfaction, might by now be taking a longer view of the coming Armageddon, his followers were not. They were working to save their souls.

There were cultural assets not visible from a bench in the tavern. Father had a $300 piano fetched down the Ohio; many hundredweights of books came up the Mississippi from New Orleans. (The Harmony library of German texts was famous all the way to the coast.) The town boasted its own Stansbury printing press. It produced religious pamphlets and in time a single sheet newspaper. The congregation met regularly and discussed religious matters to a depth not common even in other closed communities. There was a homogeneity of purpose and interest here that contrasted strongly with other religious townships, where the young were often disaffected. In Shaker communities, for example, it was not unknown for recalcitrant girls to be rolled in barrels or boys to be harangued for hours by their exasperated elders. Strikingly, it seems the Indians understood the spiritual aspects of Harmony in a way the locals did not, with the consequence that they left the town alone. At Vincennes, on the other hand, they ringed the place with encampments, riding in to buy whisky and acting up to terrified strangers.

The underlying reason for Harmony's economic dominance was also hidden from common view. In letters passing between the old world and the new, it was very apparent the Society had huge reserves of manpower at home in Germany, enough that if the entire population of the town in Indiana had been seized by mortal illness all on the same day, their numbers could have been replaced within a few months. In 1817, the royal duchy of Württemberg issued 25 paragraphs of new regulations in an attempt to overcome 'America Fever', most of it occasioned by news – and wild rumours – about life out west. The religious hysteria that triggered the first exodus had gone and what was left behind was its residue, stoked by straightforward envy. Harmony's fame and wealth, even so misreported as it was, remained a magnet. The United States were attractive in their own right but by how much more when one of the principal adornments was a Württemberger from Iptingen.

His Royal Highness Duke Wilhelm's warnings about overhasty emigration came too late. Only a month before his proclamation, 600 Württembergers, including Father's elderly sisters Barbara and Dorothea, took ship from Holland. Many of those who set sail were unable to pay passage but were assured by agents that Harmony, from a love of God, would redeem their debts on arrival in Philadelphia. Rapp took a very much more sanguine position. He had not asked them to join him and, since he did not need them, he let the new arrivals stew. Their only way off the ship was to accept indentured labour, principally as house servants. Until then, the captain of the vessel held them hostage as his unearned fee.

A year later, another uninvited emigration took place, with even more awful consequences. A shipload of Germans was sailed up and down the North Sea in raging gales until the vessel was dismasted. They were finally dumped ashore at Bergen (Norway was then in union with Sweden), penniless. Two hundred of them died even before they were landed, since the captain of the ship refused to feed them. Funds got up to relieve their misery – including one from the port of Hamburg, which contributed £200 sterling – were misappropriated or went astray. Only a year later did 107 of the original party land at Philadelphia. They, too, faced indentured labour and were for the time being imprisoned on the ship.

When John Melish first came across the Harmonists in Pennsylvania he was not quite sharp enough to realise that the town was the outcome of a huge pool of unpaid labour, wedded to central

planning. The move to Indiana made this all the more apparent
– Harmony prospered because it had aspects to it that could in
some ways be described as socialistic. The good of one led to the
good of all; conversely what benefited the community led to the
happiness of the individual. Only a little investigation showed
that the system worked as well as it did because in practice too
much individualism was cried down – for example, though the
town was renowned for its love of music, no one was allowed to
shine as a soloist. Nor was it ever possible for a dissident to stand
up at one of the interminable meetings and criticise how things
were run, any more than would have happened in the Politburo
150 years later. Harmonists met to listen – and concur. One
instance of the rightness of their cause was the degree of downright hatred they occasioned among their neighbours. It was the
fulfilment of prophecy.

Meanwhile, central command worked. Labour was divided into
brigades, led by men who had some prior knowledge of the task,
or who had shown a willingness to take orders and carry them
out to the utmost. Frederick and George Rapp judged others
generally by their capacity for obedience – individuals who were
attracted to the community out of emotional need were not
encouraged and seldom admitted. Nor did Father have any com-
punction about leaving prospective but untried Harmonists on
the dock in Philadelphia. Writing on his behalf to their Württemberg agent Ulrich (a letter which also calmly removed from him
any powers of attorney and closed all accounts), Frederick Rapp
made the situation brutally clear. The Society had freed about
150 emigrants at a cost of $8,000. For the rest, he had no great
interest in their future.

'The people are so impaired in their manners and morals that
we will have a great deal of trouble in forming them into good
people . . . It is better for such people to be bound for their
passage. The Americans can break them better than we, and

when once they are free, they can move wherever they wish.'

Among those that were freed, there were stories of children and women left by the side of the road not because they were sick but rather that they did not know how to ride a horse. Even in the comparative orderliness of Pennsylvania, parties found themselves hopelessly lost: those lucky enough to find the turn-pike road shed their baggage and in time their weaker brethren. Tavernkeepers broke open jealously guarded trunks hefted down the Rhine and across the Atlantic and took what they wanted by way of payment for a few nights' lodgings or a plate of food.

All this, Rapp considered, came about because his fellow countrymen were too weak, too lacking in character to merit a place in the Society. Some sent letters to the old Harmony, which had reverted to a drunken Alleghenian nightmare; some, with pitiful ignorance, wrote to George Rapp 'at Pittsburgh'. It made no difference that many of these lost and hapless souls had rela-tives in the Society. Rapp's unsentimental view extended even to his own sisters: one of them, Dorothea, walked all the way from New York to the Wabash without a penny to her name. She was 57 years old.

This ruthless streak was perfectly apparent locally. In January 1818, 21 influential citizens of Posey County petitioned the State Legislature and House of Representatives, asking for redress for grievances lodged against the Society. All the signatories had fought in the war of 1812 and some of them were Revolutionary soldiers: it particularly irked them that what they freely admitted was a better town than any other in that part of western Indiana should evade taxes on new buildings and refuse military service. Furthermore, the entire town voted en bloc at elections 'by the advise of their Head, Mr Rapp'. The neighbours did not like it: it was all profoundly un-American.

Their feelings were put into almost these exact words in 1820. Early in the New Year a quarrel began in the Harmony tavern between locals and the German tapster; blows were exchanged and a riot ensued. Karl Arndt, the most scrupulous of Harmony's historians, cannot discover a single overarching reason for this particular bout of violence: it seems merely that the locals did not like the Germans and the feeling was strongly reciprocated. The case led to a jury trial in which the lawyer General Washington Johnson was retained for the American defendants. The general had a robust courtroom presence.

Gentlemen of the Jury, you must always remember that the Harmonites are not of the same free blood as you are, but emigrants out of a foreign country; consequently not entitled to the same degree of freedom as the real sons of Columbia, who either themselves in person or their fathers before them fought for the American liberty. And if you do not stand your guard well, the Harmonists will by and by subject you to their accustomed despotic habits and make it necessary for a second Washington to come and re-establish the original liberty.

This was unjust by any standards. It took five years to establish citizenship and the Harmonists were by now as American as the general. The 'accustomed despotic habits' he alluded to would not bear much examination either, although it is interesting to see the imputation of tyranny attached to Rapp, harking back to the derisive shout when Rapp fell under the ice at Connoquenessing Creek: 'Let the tyrant drown!' The judge who presided over the case made no comment on General Johnson's defence and the jury found for the real sons of Columbia. Perhaps they were predisposed to see it Johnson's way but they were also probably bribed.

At a greater distance than the Vincennes courtroom, Birkbeck's fondness for the pen, Flower's own books, the works of William Faux and more than a dozen other published sources built up an enticing picture of that part of America. The first advantage that struck the stranger was the cheap price of land (although near

Harmony itself the value had been driven up to $32 an acre). Being one's own master was a seductive proposition and for the poorest immigrant the realisation of an impossible dream. It may have been a divine imperative that had sent Rapp and his followers to America but for dispossessed Highlanders or starving Irishmen crouched in misery over a peat fire the pull was different. Such men had nothing to lose and everything to gain by migrating. Once ashore, necessity drove them west.

They were battened on by shrewder and richer men who saw an opportunity for speculation. Land was land wherever it was and yet the hapless and feckless would always be attracted to the impossible adventure: a cabin cut from the forest, with water drawn from the nearby creek and the hollow echo of children's voices by day and the howling of wolves by night. On the other hand, Ohio and Indiana had already joined the Union and Illinois was about to follow. People who sat in offices in New York with not much more than Melish's map for guidance could grasp that the next big wave west would carry along with it men of substance, politically ambitious men. The days when only Virginians and Revolutionary War veterans occupied the empty spaces were coming to an end.

'I was born by a saw-mill, was early left an orphan, was cradled in a sugar trough, christened in a millpond, graduated at a log school house and at fourteen fancied I could do anything I turned my hand to, and that nothing was impossible . . .'

This is William B. Odgen speaking, who started dealing in property the year after this realisation hit him. He went on to become the true father of Chicago, which in General Johnson's time was an abandoned fort with a population of hardly more than a hundred. Ogden lived from 1805 to 1870, by which time he had raised the population of his adopted city (he was actually born in the Catskills) to 300,000. His trick had been to get there first, buy land cheap and sell it dear.

Harmony was an example of this trend. It had a second importance, one that had begun to interest men of a philosophic turn
of mind. Money might drive the relentless settling of the interior
of America ('settle and sell' was the watchword of the wise)
but what kind of a country would result? The Declaration of
Independence was not yet 50 years old and men like Jefferson
never wavered in their view that what America had to offer was
a standing reproach to Europe. The question arose: what had he
and his countrymen to put in its place that was better? Liberty,
to be sure, but then liberty was like quicksilver. While it might
be the greatest of individual rights it was not the most obvious
or even most useful component of civic and national cohesion.
Here in Harmony was surely a model for the future – for some
an exemplar of Christian communism, for others the utilitarian
ideal at work.

In August 1820, Robert Owen sat down in his study at Braxfield
and addressed a letter to someone he called 'The Reverend Mr
Rapp'. After a polite introductory paragraph, he came to the meat
of the matter.

> My first attention was called to [Harmony] by some travels
> published by a Mr Melish who in 1811 visited the original
> settlement near Pittsburgh – and who gave many details
> which to me appeared to promise many future advantages.
> You have since had an opportunity of creating a second
> settlement under the full benefit of the experience derived
> from the first & the particulars of the result of these two
> experiments would be of real value to me in order to
> ascertain the practical inconveniences which arise from
> changes from a state of private to public property under
> the peculiar circumstances by which your colonies have
> been surrounded.

Owen mentioned his own successes at New Lanark and
enclosed copies of his pamphlets. He arranged to have the letter

and its enclosures delivered by the hand of his neighbour, William Newham Blane, who was planning a tour of Canada and the United States. A gap of nearly two years resulted before Blane finally pitched up in Harmony and Frederick Rapp opened the package. He did not reply, perhaps because he knew that his guest was yet another author writing a book about his travels and Owen could find out what he wanted to know from that source. There were, however, other reasons to ignore this letter. Over the years, the Harmony Society had received many such enquiries and Owen was in Frederick Rapp's eyes just another ignorant stranger from what was considered 'the outside'. And talk of what Owen called 'practical inconveniences' denoted a man who had not read his Bible and did not understand the divine injunctions that governed Harmony.

It was a little lofty of the master of New Lanark to dispatch a letter in such a laconic fashion and Blane, who wrote quite a detailed report, was obviously given short shrift during the week that he stayed in what Owen had called the 'colony'. He described the physical appearance of Harmony very sympatheti-cally, noting that (in 1822) there were now more than a hundred brick buildings. But as an English gentleman and a former cavalry officer, the organisation of the Society distressed him. As he explained: 'it presents the extraordinary spectacle of a most com-plete despotism in the midst of a great republic, for with the exception of being perhaps a little better clothed and fed, the lower orders of the Harmonites are as much vassals, or more so, than they were in Germany'.

Blane put up at the hotel during his visit, an experience he found, as had everybody who stayed there, very enjoyable. But there was, he concluded, something fishy about Harmony. 'What struck me as very singular was, that no one would answer any questions. Even my host Eckensperger [the landlord], when I asked if they were permitted to marry, what became of all the money they collected &c, invariably replied "We never answer those questions."'

It was rum: Blane was much more used to having Americans bend his ear about their triumphs and achievements and this reticence struck him as sinister. As for Owen, whose polite enquiry had been ignored by the Rapps, the summing-up of Blane's report showed what we have already learned of the town. It was big, it was wealthy, and it had a stranglehold on the local economy. Birkbeck bought his groceries there and the Flowers' little town of Albion had already spent $60,000 in the stores and workshops.

Without meaning to, Blane completely misjudged Harmony and sent Owen a report that could only have misled him. Like many before him, he failed to see that what held Harmony together was not fear of Rapp, but fear of God. Unconsciously, he – and, of course, many native-born Americans – would have preferred more humility from the Harmonists, more of a sense of debt to their American hosts as being in some way parents to their success. That Harmony's economic dominance was – or ever could be – the outcome of a consensual religious conviction was quite beyond Blane. He saw foreign devils who would not give a straight answer to a straight question.

In 1822, the Society received reports from two emissaries sent to Württemberg to clear up the mess the commercial agent Ulrich had left behind. What they had to say throws a clearer light on the self-confidence that existed in Harmony. The two men were hardly recruiters: on the contrary, they actively discouraged further emigration to Harmony, for they discovered that among the people of the old country:

> the decline in morals is too great. In some cities it is reported that up to ⅓ of the children are now born illegitimate, besides other frequent immoralities. On the other hand, persons who want to search a little further, for the

greater part are much too badly educated and taken in
by themselves; consequently as angry with the communal
living of the brethren [that is, the Harmonists] as with
the devil, especially because tremendous lies are still
being spread out about us, which are accepted and
believed here and there.

The emissaries found a way to express their sense of moral
superiority to those already in America. 'Pray that for us the
bearing of the disgrace of Christ and his members may never at
any time and at any opportunity become heavy for us, but that
we may learn to prefer this with all our heart to Egypt's joyous
gain.'

Better to suffer under Christ than give way to the life of
impulse. Frederick Rapp's natural brother, John, was a co-
signatory of these reports. Some of what he discovered came close
to home. Their father, Gottlieb Reichert, had died disinheriting
his children. Their mother had soon after remarried their uncle,
a man in his sixties. It was a sign of what happened in Babylon
and was contrasted by them with the better life to be had in the
community. Father Rapp himself scrawled a postscript to the
emissaries in a letter sent by Frederick exhorting them not to be
ashamed of declaring themselves devoted Harmonists.

The homesickness that you have for us as appears in your
letters makes us happy, for it says loudly enough that
you would gladly be home again with your people out
of the foreign land, &c . . . We are, in spite of everything,
blessed everywhere and the happiest people on earth, so
that already the eyes of many religious societies have
been opened and they confess the Harmonie as the only
truth in the entire world that could not be shaken by
this time, and they are right.

In 1823, the state legislature approached Harmony for a loan
of $60,000, to get it out of a mess created by the recent collapse

of the Vincennes Bank. The sum of money requested was huge and can be represented by the annual income of 3,000 Indianians: Frederick Rapp loaned it at 6 per cent over four years. He did so in the name of those who might not quite be 'the happiest people on earth' but who, if they had reservations, had long ago learned how to keep them in check. The Harmonists might be reviled by the jealous in Württemberg and patronised as browbeaten peasants in their adopted country, but they had the upper hand in both places. They were far from being misled and pathetic religious zealots living in the world on sufferance: what was this loan other than Babylon coming to them cap in hand?

SIX

The truth of those principles which I have advocated

As Owen passed into his fifties, his youthful and foxlike features softened and his face began to take on the serene, faintly vacant expression of a man who had yet to make an inventory of his shortcomings and perhaps now never would. Relationships with his wife were strained: the sons had been sent away to Switzerland for education at a Pestalozzian school, which had the unfortunate effect in the case of the second oldest, Robert Dale Owen, of his falling in love on his return with the daughter of a New Lanark worker. He was not yet twenty; the girl of his dreams was an illiterate ten-year-old. Owen had nothing to say about the matter, neither for nor against. It was a hard rule but a necessary one: any system of praise or blame in the way children were brought up was a continuation of aboriginal error.

The young man's mother thought otherwise. Two of Caroline Owen's sisters were married to evangelical parsons and she herself was a deeply religious woman: was this infatuation of her son's an example of wholly rational behaviour and superior education? She thought not. And, though she had not been present at the City of London Tavern in 1816 when her husband laid out his vision of the new moral order – the millennial moment when he had announced himself to the world – there was enough rumour to suggest that at this meeting he had made an utter fool of himself. Owen believed the contrary. In his version of events he had calmed Lord Liverpool's mind that summer in a way that no one else in Britain could have accomplished.

Caroline Owen gave her husband eight children, four boys and four girls. They had some – but only some – of the advantages that came from being children of a rich father. They knew Glasgow well and Edinburgh a little, but not London. There was no question of them going out into society where that meant the seasonal world of balls and country house parties, picnics and sketching parties. Owen loved all his children equally and raised them in a child-centred environment that would not be out of place today. He believed in supervised play and self-expression for infants, and the concept of learning by discovery. These provisions turned them into happy and self-reliant youngsters, yet it was also Owen's duty, as he saw it, to make them, when they were fully grown, disciples.

His lack of religious sentiment was the principal source of discord with his wife. Caroline Owen beseeched her son Robert to help her when the boy was hardly eleven years old, adding: 'I pray to God that He will turn your dear father from the error of his ways, and make him pious like your grandfather.' That was in 1812, when she thought her husband still capable of being led into what was for her the righteous path – a simple and modest existence as a man of property with additional and unobtrusive Christian charity. Ten years on, it was too late. He could no more change now than the moon could alter its course: what distressed Caroline Owen was not so much his lack of piety as a gathering realisation that he would never alter a single opinion about anything. He saw no need. He was the champion of truth over error, St George with his lance plunged into the neck of the serpent, no matter what the ground.

It might have helped his cause better, even with his wife, if Owen had named some of society's errors instead of lumping them all under a single abstract heading. His failure to do so leaves him open to a charge of dryness. She, after all, had grown up in a busy and expostulating family environment where specific wrongs were righted. She, more than her husband, understood that indignation was the emotional currency of the day at both ends of the political spectrum. But this was a feeling completely foreign to Owen. His father-in-law, meeting a mutilated soldier hobbling the lanes on home-made crutches, or a whore soliciting in some filthy Glasgow alley, might have stopped to talk, to ask questions and commiserate. Even Caroline and her evangelical sisters would poke their bonneted heads into some one-room hovel and donate food or a few pennies to the wretched inhabitants. War, disease, famine, injustice – none of these things interested Owen at the individual and particular level. The poor had no personal histories worth repeating: they were ciphers in the great equation he had devised. Sir Robert Peel's parliamentary committee of 1816, from which Owen cribbed some statistical evidence, included this submission from a member of the general public. Asked about conditions in a mill at Emscot, near Warwick, Theodore Price replied: 'I have four daughters, and I say upon my word of honour, that if I was put to the choice either to send them to this cotton mill for seven years, or to Warwick Bridewell, I would prefer the latter.'

Mr Price was a Warwickshire JP who had in his time dispatched felons to the jail in Warwick. The expressions of anguish made by decent men like this never crossed the threshold of Owen's interest. Had he been questioned about the case, his answer would have been no more than this: *of course* the magistrate was exercised by what he had seen. His eyes had been opened and he had discovered aboriginal error. Further details were irrelevant.

The immensely popular journalist William Cobbett was an early opponent. For him, the question was not how working men could

be changed for the better by philanthropic interventions. The
impetus for reform would flow from the bottom up once a few
stark questions were answered. Who was it that actually produced the wealth of the country if not the labouring poor? And
was it not these same unsung people from the fields and the
factories who also shouldered the country's muskets and manned
the fleet in time of war? Cobbett thought so. 'With this correct
idea of your own worth in your minds,' he encouraged those at
the bottom of the social heap, 'with what indignation must you
hear yourselves called the Populace, the Rabble, the Mob, the
Swinish Multitude?'

His own moral arithmetic depended on hammering home a
single proposition: that by their labour the mass of the people
were supporting the privileged classes, both in the countryside
and the new manufacturing towns. For Cobbett, that was the
whole problem laid bare (and in much more readable form than
ever Owen accomplished). And what was the solution? He had
no hesitation in answering with the equivalency of a sharp punch
to the guts. The poor were being kept poor not because they
were stupid, or steeped in error, or lazy. It was very much simpler
than that. 'As to the cause of our present miseries,' he thundered,
'it is the *enormous amount of the taxes*, which the government
compels us to pay for the support of its army, its placemen, its
pensioners, &c, and for the payment of the interest on its debt.'
Once this was accepted and understood, then it followed that the
only way to change society was to reform the Parliament that
made the laws and set the taxes. The king rules for all, the priest
prays for all, the soldier fights for all, and the peasant pays for
all. But, said Cobbett, not necessarily, and not for much longer.

It was the classic radical opinion. In 1816, at the very time
that Owen was circulating his *Address to New Lanark*, Cobbett
composed his *Address to the Journeymen and Labourers*, from
which the above quotations are derived. Up until that time, he

had been producing the *Political Register*, which was taxed as a newspaper. By omitting the news, Cobbett found he could sell what he had to say for two pence, which brought it within the purse of a working man. This was the first of his 'two-penny trash' pamphlets and the success it had was astounding.

Cobbett's *Address* sold 200,000 copies within a year. When sales were multiplied by readership, maybe as many as a million of the poor came under its influence. His vigorous way of expressing himself was known to hundreds of thousands who had never heard of Robert Owen. The master of New Lanark might influence the opinions of men like the Archbishop of Canterbury but Cobbett spoke to workers at their own hearthside, puzzling over the price of a loaf of bread. He was no more a revolutionary firebrand than was Owen himself – he was a self-taught sentimentalist who wanted to perpetuate the healthy and bucolic paradise he remembered from the days of his youth in Farnham. Cobbett was, in a way, John Bull personified: bluff, derisive, patriotic to a fault. He was also a superb political journalist. Part of his advice to the working man was that, even if he did not have the vote yet, he should attend the hustings and make his voice heard. 'I advise my countrymen to have nothing to do with any *Political Clubs*, any secret *Cabals*, any *Correspondencies*, but to trust to *individual exertions and open meetings.*'

In all that he wrote, there is the tang of the open air and nothing at all of the study. Owen could never have reacted as Cobbett did one day, when riding along the road north from Tetbury in Gloucestershire. He came across a fine country estate, reined in and asked a passing plumber (the detail is characteristic of his writing) who it was who lived there. The man replied vaguely that it was the residence of 'the old gentleman'. This would not do for Cobbett. He pressed, and the old gentleman in question turned out to be none other than his – and Owen's – *bête noire*, the economist David Ricardo. Mind, the plumber rambled on, it was true the old gentleman had recently died but the place was now taken up by his son and – 'God damn the old gentleman and the young gentleman, too!' Cobbett interrupted with a cheerful yell.

There were others in the movement for reform equally as charismatic. In 1776, when Owen was only five years old, Cobbett's friend John Cartwright published a pamphlet entitled *Take Your Choice*, calling for annual Parliaments and general constitutional reform. He was for the colonials in the American War of Independence and later on for the revolutionaries in France. Always called Major Cartwright in honour of his militia rank (which was stripped from him after he attended a meeting celebrating the taking of the Bastille), this sweet-natured man gave his life to reform. In his youth he had joined the navy and rose to be a lieutenant under Admiral Howe. That rank, too, was removed from him. He continued unabashed. Once, when his friend Wilberforce met him in the street and said admiringly that he hoped they would meet in a better world, Cartwright answered pointedly, though with trademark courtesy, 'I hope we shall first mend the world we are in.'

Cartwright was 60 at the turn of the century. In the troubled war years that followed he was badgered by police informers and eventually arrested and tried for sedition. Though he was found guilty, his gentlemanly rank saved him and he was let off with a £100 fine. During his long life he published 80 pamphlets, saved four people from drowning, invented improvements to naval gunnery – and stumped the country for reform of Parliament. In the winter of 1813, he set out on a 900 mile journey as far north as Newcastle upon Tyne, speaking and agitating in 36 towns. He was then 73 years old. Two years later he did the same in Scotland. These tours brought back to Parliament hundreds of petitions signed by working men. He died in London in 1824.

Owen's was a very different personality. Very early on in his career, in the Manchester days, Coleridge met him and described him as a mere 'reasoning machine'. The nickname stuck. Radicals despised him for his lack of practical engagement with the struggle for reform and many of the clergy were alarmed at his want of spirituality. The progressive education he gave his sons in Switzerland, his tireless investigations of communitarian schemes in Holland, Ireland and wherever else he heard a note that chimed with his own convictions were all of a kind. He was looking for confirmation that a new great day was dawning. When it came, Owen himself would rise swiftly through its midsts and take his rightful place as the supreme arbiter of what was to be done next and how the world should live in future, for all time.

Like many intellectuals, he had few practical abilities. He was not nimble, nor was he specially interested in how things worked at the mechanical level. He advocated the use of the spade in cultivation but had no interest in his own gardens. As a young man in Manchester he had been invited to join the hunt. Owen knew nothing of horses other than their ability to amble at five or six miles an hour from one northern town to another: he studied the challenge from a rational point of view, got up on to a more mettlesome mount than he was used to and – at any rate to his own satisfaction – proved as good as anyone else in chasing the fox. He felt no need to continue the exercise in later years.

Though he might not have a practical bent – not even enough to work in his own mill at the most menial tasks – he tirelessly searched out best practice for others: in educating children, how to design a poor man's cottage, teaching his workers what vegetables to cultivate, how they might dress, eat and interact with their betters. Did Owen himself know how to dig a well, cure bacon, set a broken arm or replace a window pane? He did not. Had he ever lived at the level where a handful of potatoes was the equivalent of coin? Of course not. And yet there was something inside him, some essential rigour that would have helped

him survive the worst shocks of poverty and despair, had he
been so placed. For all his shortcomings, he had the one great
virtue of the saint. He could not be broken and he would never
give in.

Owen's bloodless doctrine floated high above the real and
actual world. There was nothing of pity in his scheme of things,
no telling detail to make the heart bleed. He had merely shown
the world its intellectual squalor and pointed to the sole way
out. By 1819, he considered the battle already won – and for a
characteristic reason. The very silence of his critics was a demonstration of his triumph. In April of that year, he paid for the
insertion of an 'Address to the Working Classes' in two newspapers, the *Star* and, ten days later, the *Examiner*. The essay
began with Owen's habitual abruptness.

> The truly intelligent in Europe and America, by their
> silence when publicly called upon, now admit the truth
> of those principles which I have advocated as preliminary
> to the introduction of a New System for the government
> of mankind. Hitherto, no individual, either in this country
> or abroad, who possesses any knowledge of the theory
> and practice of governing men or of forming their charac-
> ter, has attempted to prove error in any one of the prin-
> ciples developed in the 'New View of Society'. On close
> examination, they are all found to be nature's laws and
> therefore unassailable.

Owen could hardly have supposed these words would be
studied by real and actual working men, such as were in that
same year bringing Stockport and Manchester to the edge of riot:
the title of his essay was a provocation, a *ruse de guerre*. Those
of the middle classes who read on had their prejudices reinforced,
for the meat of Owen's address was that the working classes
should give up their envy and hatred of the rich. 'Let me however
guard you against a mistake which exists to a great extent among

the unprivileged orders. The priviliged classes of the present day, throughout Europe, are not, as this mistake supposes, influenced so much by a desire to keep *you* down, as by an anxiety to retain the means of securing to *themselves* a comfortable and respectable enjoyment of life.'

Within four months, this ridiculous caution was put to the test. In August 1819 a huge meeting for parliamentary reform took place in Manchester. Samuel Bamford, the weaver-poet, last seen in this narrative when he was hauled before the Privy Council two years earlier, led a contingent of 3,000 men from Middleton, marching together in semi-military formation, with what he called the colours and a band of music at its head. When it reached a piece of open ground by St Peter's Church, Bamford's party was swallowed up in an immense crowd he estimated at 80,000. Police spies had warned the magistrates the night before about the scale of the demonstration and, just as the speeches were about to commence, the Manchester Yeomanry rode into the packed masses with drawn sabres, their intention to arrest the radical agitator Henry Hunt. After an hour or so of blind panic eleven people lay dead – two of them women – and another 400 were wounded with the kind of cuts normally seen only on a battlefield.

In Owen's world, it was the role of the man who possessed nothing to assist in the education of the privileged, hamstrung as they were by 'the unfortunate situation in which they have been placed by birth'. At first blush, this would seem the least helpful reading of events like Peterloo; but the day following the disaster, Bamford, who was on the run from the militia, talked to John Kay of Royley Lane and asked him whether this was not the time to rise up in revenge? Kay thought not. 'On account of this affair neither you nor I are happy, but our oppressors are wretched. We, according to the impulse of our nature, wish to avenge this outrage. Let us be quiet, it is already in the course of avengement. Those men would, even now, shrink out of existence if they were only assured of getting to heaven quietly. They are already invoking that obliviousness which will never come to their relief.'

This may even have been true of the magistrates and some of the yeoman troopers, but Lord Liverpool proved less remorseful. The government brought in swingeing legislation ('the Six Acts') to prevent another disaster of this kind. The machinery of repression ground on. In that same year, 2,606 of Liverpool's fellow citizens were transported to New South Wales and Van Diemen's Land; the following year the number rose to 3,643. The prime minister had it always in mind that at the end of the Napoleonic wars nearly a third of a million men were thrown back into civil society, to fare as best they could. Parliamentary reform was in the air but then so was fear of outright revolution. The Home Office, the department of state charged with responding to sedition, had a staff of less than twenty clerks. Intelligence gathering and even basic detective work were farmed out to police informers, with predictably inflammatory results.

What compromised Owen's theories and made them seem increasingly redundant to the central issues were two linked causes. The first of these was his ignorance of economic geography. Owen never revisited Manchester after coming north to marry Caroline Dale. Had he done so, he would have learned that the town had doubled in population since his day. So it was with Leeds, Glasgow, Liverpool, Sheffield and Birmingham. The geography of Britain was changing everywhere: hundreds of miles of new turnpike roads, a nearly complete canal system; new pits, new technologies, new towns built on old villages. Merthyr Tydfil, a little over 50 miles from Owen's birthplace, was once a comparably small community. By the 1820s four out of every ten tons of iron produced in Britain came from Merthyr and it boasted by far the largest population of any place in Wales.

Owen did not register these changes because he did not travel enough in Britain to see them. The indefatigable Major Cartwright could have told him things that would have engaged his mind with the rawness of real events. Instead, his base of operations – his searchlight on the vast changes sweeping the country – was an out of the way milltown in Lanarkshire. It was true that at New Lanark he had received the adulation of princes and bishops. All that he claimed for the community he had engineered there was likewise undeniable. But the second fault in his great plan for humankind sprang from an indifference to history itself.

Owen could have unveiled his concept of a new moral order at almost any time, independent of what was happening outside his front door. It stood apart from the political weather – indeed, the whole point of his argument was that it must ignore contemporary circumstance. By his account, the society in which he lived now was no different from that of his parents, or even his grandparents. Nor, unless he did something about it, would life alter in the experience of his future grandchildren and their children. History was the mere repetition of the same single error.

However, dramatic events were reshaping the world, whether he acknowledged them or not. By the 1820s the demand for parliamentary reform was moving ever closer to centre stage. At the very beginning of that decade Robert Peel wrote a musing letter to his crony John Wilson Croker. Both of them were inveterate Tories.

> Do you not think that the tone of England – of that great compound of folly, weakness, prejudice, wrong feeling, right feeling, obstinacy and newspaper paragraphs, which is called public opinion – is more liberal – to use an odious but intelligible phrase – than the policy of the Government? Do not you think there is a feeling, becoming daily more general and more confirmed – that is, independent of the pressure of taxation, or any immediate

cause – in favour of some undefined change in the mode
of governing the country? It seems to me a curious crisis
– when public opinion never had such influence on public
measures, and yet never was so dissatisfied with the share
which it possesses . . .

In July 1824 Owen entertained at Braxfield William Maclure, a
Scot who now lived in Philadelphia. Maclure was a merchant
who had received a classical education (leaving him, as he said,
'as ignorant as a pig of anything useful') and was the sort of man
Caroline Owen would consider a gentleman. He was 61 years old
and had lived in America as long as the Owens had been married
– that is, for 25 years. For all that he was born in Ayr, he was
now a distinguished American citizen and came to Braxfield as
president of the Academy of Natural Sciences in Philadelphia and
founding president of the American Geological Society. His visit
was balm to Owen's soul. Maclure made no bones about it: he
considered Owen 'the only man in Europe who has a proper idea
about humanity and the use he ought to make of his faculties'.

The American was a robuster version of Owen himself – hugely
opinionated, unswervingly loyal to a few fixed principles. The
chief of these was the Baconian assertion that knowledge is power:
the only way to a just society was a more egalitarian distribution
of property and the only way to achieve that was not by bashing
in the heads of the rich but expanding the minds of the poor.
He had discovered Pestalozzi long before Owen and persuaded
two of the institute's teachers to join him in Philadelphia and set
up a school there.

Never trained as a scientist, Maclure was by now his adopted
country's most distinguished geologist and a vigorous patron of
all the sciences. Like Owen, he was a rich man, but unlike his
Braxfield host, when it came to attacking the existing system, he
was more of a sharpshooter than a scatter-gun. The two men

liked each other, though each might have sensed some deeper reservations they did not put into words. Of the two, Maclure was the more worldly. He had crossed and recrossed the Alleghenies nineteen times and visited all the states of the Union to collect his geological samples, long and lonely expeditions on which he did not once feel the usual tug of the frontier. His situation, as he described it, was perfectly understandable to Owen as a replica of the best in European society, one in which men subscribed to libraries, visited museums or the opera, taught at the academies, associated with others of talent and laid out, in an atmosphere of liberty, the blueprints of a more just world. There was one crucial point of difference. For Owen, knowledge was self-awareness. For Maclure it was measurement, comparision, evaluation. What made him such an invigorating guest was that he understood, as Owen did not, that the outcome of a universal change would result in not simply nicer human beings but a radical redistribution of power.

Maclure responded warmly to the idea of a self-sustaining model village, his host's one big practical idea. In Britain the proposal was dead in the water but for the American it answered some of the questions posed by his country's westward expansion. What was better – for individual families to be lured into settlement and take their chances with nothing but an axe and rifle as their aid? Or for them to group into economic and social units from the very start – to arrive as a town, as Harmony had done? Owen's plans for a network of such model communities touched on the realities of American liberty and independence. In Europe, such a scheme would always depend on gifts of land by philanthropic individuals, for no state government could contemplate wholesale expropriation of property. But in America, the government was the custodian of untold acres. Where it had sold on to speculators, even at the rock bottom rate of $2 an acre, the land account was in debit, simply from the difficulty of retrieving the money. If anyone wanted model villages, it was surely the federal government of the United States? This was thrilling for Owen to contemplate.

A fortnight or so after Maclure's departure, a second visitor from America turned up at Braxfield. He was none other than the elderly and faintly faded Richard Flower of the English Prairie, who had a story to tell that meant more to him in the first place than it did to his host. In March, his neighbour out on the frontier, Father Rapp, had commissioned him to go to Europe and find a buyer for the second Harmony. Owen was his first port of call in Britain.

It says something that a man could cross an ocean to sell, not simply an estate or a manufacturing plant, but an entire town. Flower was gratified to know that Mr Owen had some idea of the place he was talking about from the report submitted by Blane but there was much to emphasise and underline, most especially the almost incomprehensible decision (as it seemed to Flower) to abandon one of the most successful enterprises in America. As he explained, the Harmony Society was contemplating a return to Pennsylvania, though he could not for the life of him say why. His own town of Albion would not have survived without Harmony to keep it alive and his former friend Birkbeck was even more indebted to the Rapps. The feeblest explanation he could come up with for why the Germans wished to abandon such a gold mine was that the Indiana climate did not suit them.

Flower was a good man and a gentle one, about as apt for the practicalities of frontier life as, say, Charles Lamb. He knew of Owen only by repute. He had not flown like an arrow to its mark – for three months he had been trying to find out exactly how he stood and on the very day of his departure for England he was still writing to Frederick Rapp to clarify what it was he was supposed to do and say to a potential European buyer. He had good reason. Very much against his wishes, the property was also being advertised for sale in America. Sitting talking to Owen in Braxfield, Flower knew he could well be wasting his host's time by offering a deal that had already been struck on the other side of the Atlantic.

Owen surprised him by showing keen interest, so much so that Flower turned to Robert Dale Owen at one point and asked incredulously, 'Does your father really think of giving up a position like this, with every comfort and luxury, and taking his family to the wild life of the far west?' It was a touching bewilderment. Flower was 63 and had only five more years to live. He had burnt his own boats, so far as Britain was concerned: in making his bid for something better, he had turned those dreams to ashes, too. His former partner was now his inveterate enemy, the prairie had turned out to be nothing like he imagined, the town he owned was a negligible pimple on the face of southern Illinois. In his present guise, sitting nervously in Owen's study, he was a mere messenger boy, the tool of more important men.

When he expressed surprise at Owen's interest in Harmony, he did not realise his was the second visit touching on America in a fortnight. Owen was not listening to him so much as reflecting on conversations held earlier with Maclure. Even so, he might have felt more caution to have been appropriate. His host had enough money to do exactly as Flower had tried to do on the prairie – find a virgin site that suited him and build from the foundations up. Did he need a fully fledged town in Indiana to make his dreams come true? Practically, Flower had to admit, he did not.

Leaving aside the question whether Harmony was still his to offer, it must also have crossed Flower's mind that his own noble gesture of giving up everything to join the land of the free had been, as he looked back on it, naive. Time was on Owen's side, he could absorb what had been said to him, discuss the prop-

osition with his family and perhaps plan a reconnaissance visit
to America at some time in the future. Flower knew that if an
American bought Harmony it would be strictly a money-making
business: buy the town, sell it off in lots, take the profit. He was
the British agent for the vendor and it was in his interest to press
Owen for a decision, but the pitch he made was maybe less than
wholehearted. The master of Lanark was a much more complicated figure than he had imagined. He came expecting to find a
rich man but had not reckoned on meeting quite such a fevered
ideologue.

Owen's fondness for the dramatic gesture came into play. 'Well,
Robert, what say you – New Lanark or Harmony?' he asked his
second oldest son. Robert Dale Owen did not hesitate. 'Harmony'
he replied. Suddenly, nothing would do but an immediate departure. Bags must be packed, pamphlets, files and drawings
assembled, letters fired off. America was holding the door open
in welcome to the single great idea, the creation of a new moral
order! Poor Flower. He had left Philadelphia for England in early
June. On 2 October 1824 he found himself putting out from
Liverpool in high winds, accompanying Owen and his younger
son William back across the Atlantic. Also of the party was a
vigorous young captain of Royal Engineers called Donald
MacDonald, who had been placed on half pay four days earlier.
(He continued to draw it until his death in 1872 at the ripe old
age of 89.)

MacDonald had the useful soldierly habit of keeping a diary.
He was a devotee of communitarian living and had known Robert
Owen for two years or so: it was not long before the maps and
plans of the model village came out and the Owen party was
plunged into dispute with two Church of England ministers, the
doctors Strachan and Stewart. They were watched with a mild
amusement by the more worldly elements on board, most of them
merchants on their way to America to make money. Owen had

distributed copies of his pamphlets and it was almost the duty
of the two divines to try to argue these down. Strachan objected
to Owen's views on the grounds that they destroyed the notion
of an individual conscience; that is to say, he held that men might
choose between good and evil and were not forever helpless in
the mesh of error.

This Atlantic passage captures Owen at his best. Day after day
the clergymen returned to the attack and after each lengthy
debate – on the existence of sin, the role of a man's free will in
his moral development, the intentions of a wise and benevolent
God in human affairs – they retired defeated. The mainsail split,
in the ladies' cabin a sofa collapsed in the storm, the passengers
ate with their plates secured by fiddles and (much more to Owen's
dislike than the weather) Dr Stewart instituted morning and
evening prayers. The clergymen were the first to break. Owen
was retelling his attempts to change the world in the meetings
of 1817 when Stewart interrupted testily to say that nothing
much had come of his efforts. Owen explained that what he called
the higher classes had yet to see the great advantages that would
accrue from the new moral order, not simply to the poor, but to
their own kind. Stewart capitulated.

'Then America is your place and we will support you as far
as our principles will lead us.'

That night the wind rose and a hard cold gale blew, forcing
the captain to take in all canvas. The passengers huddled in the
roundhouse, at the mercy of what MacDonald called, with his
usual sang-froid, 'the troubled elements'. The following day happened to be a Sunday and Strachan preached to the passengers
and crew as the ship skidded to leeward under a close-reefed
foresail. His theme was contentment.

Owen landed at New York on 4 November 1824. Almost the
first person he met on the dock was a prancing madman called
Edward Page, who introduced himself whimsically as the Page

of Nature, to which end he was dressed entirely in green. He greeted Owen as a friend, for he too was trying to raise funds to quit society and retire into the depths of America, there to mingle with the trees. Page had written to Harmony in 1822. 'If your government was not in an aristocratic form, as I am informed it is – but of a pure democracy – not in the priest but the people – and your elections annual, or monthly (for all new officers) then I would go to the ends of the earth and join a people so consistent as to encourage matrimony and the increase of home manufactured population.'

When he read this assurance, Frederick Reichert turned the paper over and scribbled in German, 'Phantasie!'

Page got equally short shrift from Owen, who once he was off the quay and installed in his hotel, was given the sort of welcome accorded by New York to men of distinction. His fame had preceded him. In the week that followed Owen was entertained by Charles King, editor of the *New York Evening Post*; his colleague Morse of the *New York Observer*; several learned judges; and members of the New York Athenaeum, including the venerable Samuel Latham Mitchill and Dr Hosack, president of the College of Medicine. There were only two faintly discordant notes: Dr Blachley, who was president of the Commonwealth Society, a small group of Quakers who were interested in communitarian ventures, showed Owen a cautionary letter from Thomas Jefferson, written in 1822, indicating that while private experiment of this kind was all very well, it would not do at the national level. And a Pestalozzian teacher called DuFief, who had once visited Harmony, made a very perceptive comment about the country Owen had just entered. 'The Americans,' he warned, 'will always be difficult to regulate or confine, as they are fond of roving, and might be called a migratory race.'

Nevertheless, it was a flattering first reception. Owen arrived in the United States in the last days of James Monroe's second

term of office as president. A few months after his first inauguration, in 1817, a Boston paper, the *Columbian Sentinel*, coined a
phrase that stuck: Monroe had ushered in 'the era of good feelings'. In federal and international affairs, this was perhaps more
of a wish than an accomplished fact but when the London *Times*
rather condescendingly (and inaccurately) reported New York as
the London of America, it was thinking of the kind of society
Owen moved among in that first hectic week. The people he
met exhibited those Monrovian 'good feelings' – shrewd money,
ambitious public undertakings (of which the soon to be completed
Erie Canal, connecting the seaboard with the Great Lakes, was
the outstanding example), high artistic and cultural intentions
and well-organised philanthropy. Buchanan, the British consul
in New York, occupied his private hours in schemes to 'civilise'
the native Americans.

Owen and MacDonald took a steamer trip upstate to Albany,
where they paid visits to the state governor, Stephen Van Rensselaer and his political adversary De Witt Clinton. They attended
a session of the State House of Representatives and Van Rensselaer
suggested they visit the Shakers at Watervliet, who rented land
from him on which they had built their village. MacDonald was
greatly impressed by the cleanliness and order he found, though
the community hardly numbered a hundred. (He may have under-
estimated by as much as 50 per cent: clearly Owen himself was
torn between complimenting them and disparaging the modesty
of their enterprise. At this period there were sixteen such Shaker
villages in existence, with a combined population no larger than
4,500.)

There was one incident that gave Captain MacDonald pause.
The Shakers took in families from the outside who shared their
beliefs but also accepted orphans, runaways and what we now
call 'difficult' children. It was very striking to the Scot, who had
an eye for these things, that as he was being guided round the

village he came across more than one smiling and pretty girl. He joshingly asked his host what he would do if a young Shaker woman should ever turn out sullen or unkempt. Without a moment's hesitation, the man murmured that such a person would, of course, be expelled. MacDonald was deeply shocked – this was a far cry from the Institute for the Formation of Character, in which he believed as heartily as Owen. Maybe it was all so agreeable at Watervliet because only agreeable people were permitted to stay.

Their conversation touched on a central issue. The neat Shaker houses with their polished wood furniture and pretty floor coverings, their miniature workshops in which men made things like whips and silver pens, were an apolitical expression of the good life. Even giving full weight to the zeal the Shakers possessed, it was as though the men and women of Watervliet had come to accept – as a religious insight – there was nothing they could do to transform society at large. The greater world of politics, as represented by their landlord Van Rensselaer, was irredeemable and what MacDonald (and perhaps Owen) took as a timid quietism in them was a much deeper intellectual pessimism. The larger the scale of any human society, the clearer the limitations of a purely political solution to its problems. The Shakers were simply living out their lives as they knew best. Any attempt to live in the world and change it would merely result in their being changed by it. This had implications. The number of Shaker communities in America never rose above 27: by 1925, a hundred years after Owen's visit, the total had fallen to six. (Watervliet was one of them.)

On 19 November, the two travellers set off by steam packet for Philadelphia, where they rejoined an agitated Flower. He had heard from the Rapps that two American offers had been put in for Harmony and that unless Owen made a bid before the end of the year, he would lose his chance. The proprietor of New

Lanark absorbed this information with his customary calm and
set off on a round of visits and working breakfasts with the
leading men of the city. (Flower, who could see his agent's fee
flying out of the window, was left wringing his hands.) Owen's
new friend Maclure was still in Europe, where he was trying to
promote an agrarian community of his own on the unlikely soil
of Spain. All the same, even without Maclure, there were more
than enough flattering acknowledgements of what had been
accomplished at New Lanark – Owen was moving about the
republic as an honoured guest, one whose good works were
already known. His admirers were brought up to speed on the
political implications of these achievements by the liberal distribution of his pamphlets.

New Lanark, where it was known at all in America, was seen to
be compassionate philanthropy at its best. It also doubled as that
most American of ideals, the well-run business enterprise. If there
was ever a way to organise labour into a productive unit, Owen's
mills were it. That he had accomplished this in the very maw of
tyrannical repression was further merit: in Jeffersonian terms, he
had put one over 'the Egyptian slave-masters' at the heart of their
odious empire, the British factory system. In short, his hosts were
predisposed to like him. Even his fastidious demeanour pleased
his hosts: this was a serious and sobersided man of a kind well
known to the intellectual classes of the eastern seaboard.

What the Philadelphians had not quite bargained for, touching
the pamphlets now thrust into their hands, was their unexpected
content. Owen the Redeemer, the harbinger of a new world order,
was a very different kettle of fish to 'Owen of New Lanark'.
He was, after all, talking to people who considered their own
democracy the summation of what was possible in human affairs
– not yet perfect, maybe, but perfectible. Americans were well
used to being the object of admiration and respect from foreigners
and as it happened were on a nostalgic binge that very year with

the triumphant return of General Lafayette, the ancient friend
to independence. Those who read Owen in this light were quick
to see that opinions intended to subvert the British government
and all its foul works were also aimed at America, at the very
moment of its greatest confidence in its own destiny. One could
be generous and say that Owenism was a message intended for
the whole world; but for it to include, even by implication,
America in the general catalogue of error was – at the very least
– contentious. The Duke of Saxe-Weimar Eisenach followed Owen
along the same route some six months later and was received by
many of the same people. In the book he published of his travels
he had this to say: 'In the eastern states there is a general dislike
of him . . . I heard at that time unfavourable expressions from
persons in the highest public offices against him; and one of them
gave Mr Owen to understand very plainly that he considered his
intellects rather deranged.'

Owen was not the man to pick up on this sort of thing quickly.
Since he expected (at the rational level) to be talking to men
whose minds were still clouded, his social antennae were short
and blunt. He spent three days in Philadelphia and then coasted
down to Baltimore, arriving in the middle of a cattle show. After
only a brief visit, he took the stage to Washington. Ever since
his arrival he had been pressed by well-wishing American friends
to deliver public lectures on his ideas but this he refused to do:
the capital was to be where he announced himself.

Thus, on his first morning, he sent in his card to President
Monroe, who engaged to see him the following day. He then met
John Quincy Adams, secretary of state, John Caldwell Calhoun,
secretary of war, and the attorney general, William Wirt. He
rounded the day off with a brisk interview with Mr Addington,
the British chargé d'affaires. Monroe was as good as his word
and next day – which happened to be a Saturday – Owen had
an audience with him and Adams. The president gave a cautious

and non-committal reply to Owen's explanation as to why he was there, saying only that 'this country gives more scope to improvements than any other'. As for Adams, Owen saw *him* at a difficult time. It was still not yet clear that he would receive the nomination for the sixth presidency. (In the end, the electoral college votes were inconclusive and he was elected in the House of Representatives, the decisive vote being cast by Van Rensselaer. Calhoun had already been shooed in as vice president.)

For a Welshman who had hardly been in the country a month, Owen had done well to make these face-to-face contacts. We do not know what he said to Monroe and Adams, nor they to him, though it would have been extraordinary if Adams, the real author of the 'Monroe Doctrine', enunciated a year earlier by the president in his address to Congress, had not made some allusion to it now. Under its terms, the United States would henceforth regard as a threat to its own integrity any attempt by European powers to create new colonies in the western hemisphere. Owen's writings were nothing else but a scheme for the colonisation of America – and everywhere else – by incremental means. On the other hand, Adams may have reflected, this strange man had no stake in the country as yet and owned no land. He was in the same position as Mr Page, the green-suited Page of Nature. He was a projector, a dreamer.

Before he left Washington, Owen held parley with four Choctaw Indians, who were in the capital to lobby the government. He explained that he had come 3,000 miles to meet them, from a country where they were much admired. Chief Pushmattaha thanked him and listened appreciatively as Owen promised that before he returned to Britain, he intended to 'make known to the public a way of bringing up children and reforming society, so that all persons might be trained to have whatever is good in both the Indian and European characters, and to be without all that is bad in them'. Pushmattaha indicated that this was his own opinion of the way forward. MacDonald, who was present at this meeting, thought very little of the way these native Americans dressed themselves. Their spokesman wore a military coat with gold epaulettes and one of his lieutenants a shawl made from the Stuart tartan.

Owen had come down the seaboard like a miniature cyclone but could no longer delay setting out for the interior. Without waiting for the sale of Harmony, George Rapp had shifted ground back into Pennsylvania, where he was setting up in a new town, to be called, with unsubtle irony, Economy. On Sunday, 28 November, Owen and his party set out from Washington for Pittsburgh, themselves and their baggage crammed into three stagecoaches. They reached Pittsburgh the following Friday. Rapp's new community was being established eighteen miles upstream on the banks of the Ohio and next day they went there, finding the usual signs of energetic occupancy by the advance guard.

At long last, vendor and prospective purchaser came face to face. As was customary with Owen, the proceedings kicked off with a synoptic account of his system for a new moral order, the which Father received with general though very vague expressions of sympathy and accord. Owen, of course, wanted to know why Rapp had quit Indiana. He found his answers evasive, though a possible explanation emerged a day or so later. Even before the sale of the Indiana site, Rapp had opened an account on a Pittsburgh bank and deposited the staggering sum of $150,000.

MacDonald was not much impressed either with Father or his followers. 'Mr Rapp is a stout healthy active old man of about 67. He has a steady, determined manner, but very little of that amiable mildness, which a patriarchal life and benevolent principles might be expected to produce. The people appear steady, sober, goodhumoured and plain in their manners. Their character and expression of countenance is German. They do not appear very lively or intelligent . . .'

John L. Baker was the official interpreter between Owen and Rapp and after a certain amount of discussion, suggested that the Welshman have his pamphlets translated into 'correct' German, at which point Father might be in a position to respond better. MacDonald, just as Blane had done, found the atmosphere faintly spooky. These Germans were assuming the upper hand. He thought he knew why. He confided to his diary, 'it seemed to be the impression among those who had some knowledge of their proceedings that in a very few years they would be the richest association in the U.States and wealthy enough to buy their own state'.

Owen spent only one night in Economy. On 5 December, he set out for Harmony in the steamboat *Pennsylvania*, still travelling with his entourage and a mountain of luggage, still keeping his own counsel. It was reckoned by those who knew the river that had he waited another day, the Ohio River would have frozen over. It was coming up to the tenth anniversary of Frederick Rapp's heroic dash to be with Father on Christmas Eve of 1814 to join him in prayer on the muddy building site that Harmony then was. Rapp had come down the river with flailing oars, fending off disaster with poles and boathooks. Things were different now. When Owen's steamboat cast off in a sharp frost with all the usual fuss and smoke that went with departure, there were 79 such vessels in commission on the Ohio. The Harmony Society owned two of them.

Though money-making was no part of the great scheme of regeneration envisaged by the master of New Lanark, there was that niggling image of $150,000 sleeping in a Pittsburgh bank, soon to be augmented by a further $200,000 when and if the sale of Harmony went through. Owen was enough of a capitalist to calculate that if he chose to buy, his investment would be secure beyond a doubt. Indeed, were he going down the Ohio purely as a business man, there was no saying what might befall.

SEVEN

As foretold by the sages of the past

One thing Owen learned on his brief visit to Economy was that the Society's Indiana property was for sale in the name of Frederick Rapp only, Father and the membership having surrendered power of attorney to him. However, Owen was enough of a businessman to judge that he had been speaking to the real principal. On his side, Father took it for granted that Owen was not fooled by hints and rumours about other potential buyers. They were like two men discussing the sale of a few hectares of vines in the old country. Deception and misdirection were part of the process.

Looked at another way, it was a rare and unusual confrontation. An eighteenth-century rationalist living out of his time came face to face with a quasi-mediaeval prophet; or, to put it another way, optimism broke bread with pessimism. What was in play here was a question that had bedevilled the last hundred years, one without which Harmony would never have come into existence in the first place. Was man his own master and reason his only means of interpreting the world? Or was his fate preordained by a God infinitely superior in wisdom and judgement, whose plans for His own creation included, at a time now fast approaching, its utter destruction?

Father taught – and we must suppose believed – that God had grown weary of the evil that man had wrought. The ecstatic self-hating prophecies of St John of Revelation left little in the world that was a compensating good. Faith by itself was no answer – it had to be cranked up to such a pitch that by prayer and works it positively invited the final cataclysm. Since no outsider was permitted to attend a Harmony church service and all preaching was in any case conducted in German, the bleak convictions Rapp shared with his followers were never properly understood, neither by his Indiana neighbours nor the man who had come to buy his town.

For someone of Owen's temperament, Rapp's beliefs about the doom shortly to fall on the material world could be safely ignored as error in its most hysterical form. What mattered were the accounts and these appeared to show the whole story. The store was full, the workshops always busy: things could be bought or mended, space could be leased on the boats plying between Harmony and Pittsburgh or New Orleans. The town was a haven of good money: it extended no credit and would not transact business except in coin and government bills. The practice of discounting bills from doubtful or distant banks, sometimes by as much as 50 per cent, was a thing Frederick Rapp particularly refused to do. The $60,000 loan he made to the state legislature was to cover the failure of the Vincennes Bank, which had borrowed bad money to build a steam sawmill.

Owen shared with Father the conviction that the world was out of joint. Yet he misunderstood the pessimism that seethed in Rapp and failed to trace its material consequences. He seems to have grasped that Harmony was as economically powerful as it was because it had no labour costs and enjoyed (or suffered) a complete absence of private property – after all, he had in mind a community along the same lines. But what Rapp preached in church – particularly the terror it created – was for Owen the ultimate irrationality. He failed to see that it was the motive power that made Harmony successful.

Very little of the money that came into the town was circulated within it and how these substantial sums were reinvested was a matter of indifference to its citizens. As a communitarian project, Harmony had one supreme advantage: by constant repetition of a simple and unchanging dogma, participants in the Society voluntarily gave up the idea of family, personal estate and all other worldly vanities. They had no ambition nor envy of others, no yearnings or hidden dreams. What was left was easily mistaken for a lumpen servitude. It was not often understood that their obedience was to prophecy and only thereafter to George Rapp. He had helped them search their souls but St John of Revelation was their spiritual guide. Rapp had not made Harmony. He adopted as his son a businessman of genius, but Frederick Rapp had not made Harmony either. Hundreds of fanatical believers gave the project its life; men and women steadfast to a vision of Christ the destroyer of earthly vanities. These are extracts from the letter an unknown man wrote to his children in Germany, twelve years after his arrival:

> Your letter to me I received on August 4, 1816 and saw from it that you look upon me as a faithless father because I left you and your mother as I did. This would indeed be so if I had followed my own inclinations, but, my dear children, the light of God which all human beings bear within themselves beamed forth from my innermost being and revealed to me my entire life's conduct ... Now I had to resolve to leave according to the words of our Saviour: He who does not leave father and mother, wife and children cannot be my disciple. Further Scripture says one must obey God more than man and [yet] because of that my tender paternal love for you has not been extinguished. If you were with me I would duly fulfil it. Your memory is before me whenever I see children of your age.

Associated with the letter are some scraps of manuscript on which this father scribbled his rough draft. One of these reads far more baldly and tellingly than the version he finally sent: 'You want a letter from me, you should have it, you are innocent and I will forget and forgive everything that has happened. The ways of providence are just and not to be criticised.'

To anyone from outside the Society who saw this man the day he posted his letter, he was just another dupe in a brown smock, a slave to the despotic and tyrannical Father Rapp.

Owen and his party arrived in Harmony on Thursday, 16 December 1824. That same afternoon, in the last of the light, Frederick Rapp took Owen and MacDonald to the top windows of Father's old house and they looked out on to the silent streets. MacDonald studied Frederick covertly, finding him 'a tall, raw-boned, sallow complexioned, serious and plain German'. His hair was long and untied, he wore a grey tunic and carried a broad-brimmed country hat. Just as had happened with Father at Economy, the adopted son showed no particular excitement at Owen's arrival. They parted after a short while and Owen went back to the hotel. He was invited to dine with Frederick the following day.

The mass of the Harmony Society had said its goodbyes six months earlier. Under the stairs in one of the dormitories some unknown hand had written. 'On the twenty-fourth May, 1824, we have departed. Lord, with Thy great help and goodness, in body and soul, protect us.' Thus what Owen saw from the upper storey of Father's brick house was a half-deserted town (MacDonald called it a village). It comprised two main streets running at right angles to each other, defining an area not much more than half a mile long and 400 yards or so wide. Most of the houses were empty.

The night before their arrival the prospective purchasers had lodged at Springfield, the county town; and the night before

that at Evansville. Comparisons were inevitable. Harmony was
sodden, its municipal trees were stark and bare and sheets of
water lay in the sandy roadways, but it was very recognisably
a place built by European sensibilities. The Wabash, which was
swollen to about a hundred yards wide, was soon lost in the
surrounding forests but about 3,000 acres of trees had been
cleared, giving, at that season of the year, an impression of parkland. MacDonald responded warmly. 'To a traveller just emerging
from a forest where little or no improvement has taken place,
and remembering the many days he has spent in wandering
through a thinly peopled & badly cultivated country, the view
from these hilly pastures down upon a rich plain, flourishing
village, and picturesque river winding through a magnificent
forest, is highly gratifying.'

The next day, Frederick Rapp again furnished a top-view of
the property, this time from the roof of the church, where once
the town band had played to celebrate the glory of God. It had
rained heavily during the night and the ground inspection of the
mills and workshops was a muddy affair. They looked into the
dormitories, where a party of ten women sang to them. Mac-
Donald, it seemed, was as determined as Frederick Rapp not to
get carried away. He found the living spaces hot and stuffy and
the workshops lacking in the best of new machinery. He was
coming the inspecting officer over his hosts and clearly would
have liked a bit more animation about the place, and though at
dinner he found Gertrude Rapp, John Rapp's daughter, comely
enough, his overall impression of the Rappites was one of dreary
earnestness.

There was more music on Sunday, when the visitors were
invited to the church, shorn of its mysteries now that Father was
gone. After the second service of the day, the company repaired
to Frederick's house for a dish of tea (they had taken wine, beer
and cider at the Friday dinner and found them all of excellent

quality) and here again there was music. It was provided by
Gertrude at the piano, a few flutes – and, with a violin tucked
under his chin, old Doctor Mueller, the man who had described
to John Melish the religious hysteria of 1808. Among the offerings
was a tune called 'Away with Melancholy'. Outside, there was
frost on the ground and, at the edge of the cleared land, wolves
prowled.

Owen spent only four days looking around. On Monday, he,
MacDonald and some others set out for the English Prairie, to
spend Christmas with the Flower family. They were at once back
with the commonplace of frontier towns. Albion was no more
than a few straggling cottages, the largest of which belonged to
the Flowers, father and son. However, news of Owen's arrival
spread and during the Christmas period he met many of the
families out on the prairie. The notable exception was George
Birkbeck.

Poor Birkbeck! His eldest son Richard had turned out badly
and though his father gifted him a sizeable farm, the boy spent
his days in an alcoholic stupor, broken only by drunken threats
directed at his young wife and her brother. It caused Birkbeck
huge shame. He had come to Illinois to be a gentleman and a
farmer and the prairie got to him on both counts. What was left
of his reputation locally was shredded by his heated objections
to the introduction of slavery in Illinois. In the end the state
legislature voted down the proposal put before it and as a reward
for his pamphleteering exertions Birkbeck was made secretary of
state. So great was the animus against him in southern Illinois
that he resigned within two months.

The slave question was a problem for all the English on the
prairie. George Flower made the gesture of renting land to three
black families and as a consequence put their lives in constant
danger from local rednecks. There was a tragic twist to this
particular tale. Flower had brought out the son from his first

marriage to share the American dream. One night this boy ran
out to stop the dogs barking at a gang of drunken backwoodsmen
yahooing the hated English. In the mêlée, someone threw a bone
which struck the teenager on the head. He died without regaining
consciousness. The man who killed him was acquitted, having
taken precautions to pack the jury with his friends.

The English had habits always likely to irritate their feisty
neighbours. These last, when they were not engaged in wrestling
and eye-gouging, liked nothing better than shooting at target as
a form of relaxation. Whisky was the lubricant to all their plea-
sures and they found it curious that the English lived in what
one of them described as a 'beer fog'. In Albion that Christmas
there was roast beef and plum pudding, as well as a cricket match
and hunting with greyhounds. There was chamber music – of a
kind – and country dancing. A ball was being prepared for early
in the New Year. Many of the English immigrants were from
farming backgrounds – sturdy John Bulls who gathered to revel
with their neighbours on the smallest of excuses. They were
emotional exiles, their eyes filled up with the immensities of the
west, their hearts, many of them, still at home in England. For
them, the beer fog was a comforting reminder of a very different
kind of village community, the one they had forsaken. Here, they
taught their children to kill rattlesnakes with a stick, eyed with
yeoman distaste the wild men who rode through their pastures,
and kept a loaded gun behind the door. Just before Owen's
arrival, a party of Kickapoo warriors in warpaint had appeared
out of the woods, on their way south in search of some obscure
revenge.

The settlers greeted Owen as a similarly romantic, almost fairy-
tale figure. When next would these struggling homesteaders meet
a man who was (by his own account) on intimate terms with
both the British prime minister and the American president, who
knew the great figures of the political class in Paris, Geneva and

Frankfurt, who had gone to Aix-la-Chapelle in 1818 to present to the Congress of Sovereigns memorials based on the very pamphlets they now had thrust into their hands? (Owen's particularly exalted account of this last event was that the British delegates, Lord Castlereagh and the Duke of Wellington, had assured him 'that those two memorials were considered the most important documents which had been presented to Congress during its sittings'.)

Everyone in Albion knew that association was always going to work better than independent effort; they also realised that by themselves they were unlikely to achieve it. The quarrel between the Flower family and Morris Birkbeck kept them at perpetual loggerheads but that was not the whole story, either. The English Prairie was well named. The people on it were too sentimentally attached to the old life: putting it another way, they did not know how to be ruthless. Among Richard Flower's personal acquaintance, Mr Orange and Mr Wood were cheerful and bucolic tavernkeepers, Birkett a settler from the West Indies, Lewis a London merchant who had come out west to retire. William Pickering, a Yorkshire land surveyor, was married to one of Flower's children and Hugh Ronalds, a tanner, to another. A blacksmith called Johnson was justice of the peace.

On Boxing Day, it was agreed that all those interested in Mr Owen's principles should meet in a small room in Albion. After two dozen had gathered, it was suggested that as it was a windless day, the company should adjourn outside. In the end 200 settlers arrived to hear Owen speak, which he did for two and a half hours, his listeners sitting on logs or standing in the winter sunshine with their children in their arms. Not everybody could be brought to his understanding of human nature – the Methodists chose not to come at all and there were very few Americans present – but enough listened with a wild hope in their hearts.

In his old age, George Flower reflected on 30 years spent on the English Prairie. He is worth quoting at length because the tone in which he writes retains its nervy Englishness, though he was then 62 years old and had seen as much as any man of his generation who was American-born. He was present at the open-air meeting just described.

> It is true, I neglected somewhat that shield of popularity which men of any standing in our new Western country might not at that day with impunity neglect. I rode into our little town most days to attend to any business, or speak with those to whom I had anything to say. I did not linger much, or enter grog shops, for I used neither whisky nor tobacco, their chief articles of sale ... A man to be popular in our new Western towns, and with the country people around, should be acquainted with everybody, shake hands with everybody, and wear an old coat, with at least one hole in it. A little whisky and a few squirts of tobacco juice are indispensable. From much of the former you may be excused if you treat liberally to others. If there is one fool bigger than another, defer to him, make much of him. If there is one fellow a little more greasy and dirty than another, be sure to hug him. Do all this and you have done much toward being a popular man.

When Owen laid out, in his matter of fact way, his new view of society and at the same time appeared to promise its inauguration a mere horse-ride away, at least some of the appeal was aesthetic. Who knew what fine people would be attracted to a remodelled Harmony, where reason would be made to shine like a beacon and all coats be without holes?

On 3 January 1825, Owen made an agreement to purchase Harmony from Frederick Rapp. By coincidence, it happened to be the same day that Father sent off the English translation of his philosophic musings to a Pittsburgh printer. The book was called *The Destiny of Man*, a title with a terrible and echoing irony in light of what was to follow.

Rapp was now in his late sixties and had discovered a taste for temporal grandeur. The house that was being built for him in Economy was 120 feet long and sited in a prime location – for the third time in his life he was demonstrating his mastery of the material world he so much despised. He had not understood Owen's version of man's destiny, believing him to be merely some sort of obscure Scottish Shaker.

The relationship between Rapp and his adopted son was no longer warm and intimate but they did share a complete lack of sentiment when it came to property. What happened to the painfully worked up fields and orchards, the mills and workshops in Indiana was no longer of consequence. There was just one duty left to Frederick Rapp, which he promised to discharge when he was able, which was to build a wall around a certain patch of ground. In ten years of labour by the banks of the Wabash 219 Harmonists had died and were buried there in unmarked graves.

Owen, having made up his mind (and in doing so, roused the whole locality to the wildest speculation), then took a very foolish step. He shook hands on the deal in the morning and left for the Ohio River that same afternoon. It was the worst season of the year in which to travel, his inspection of the property had been no more than cursory and he had yet to meet anyone of political importance in Indiana. Buying an entire town perhaps deserved more attention to detail. Having come so far, he had spent only eighteen days in the area, most of them in Illinois. To set off for the east again so abruptly was surely folly of the highest order.

He left his son William and Donald MacDonald in charge. They pottered about taking stock and exploring the property, much like strangers in a new house who do not like to open too many cupboards. They were right to feel uneasy. All the signs were that Owen would not lack for supporters and investors in this new venture but some huge questions remained unanswered. Was this purchase a means of inviting a community of interests into existence, a sort of Susquehanna Project on the grand scale? In which case, he could be assured of a ready response from like-minded rationalists and freethinkers, not just locally but from his admirers on the east coast. Or was it to be the full Owenite revolution, starting point for the redemption of the human race? In either case, as the commonsensical William Owen was the first to realise, there was a very narrow window of opportunity available for planning. In eight weeks' time or so, the growing season would recommence.

Owen's son remembered a strange thing that had happened over the Christmas season. Talking to a group of Albion homesteaders, his father announced that he had a bright idea, one that had only come to him that morning. Maybe, he said, he should rent accommodation and land at Harmony to such good friends as he saw around him, people prepared to labour towards a common end, etc., etc. Then a man named Clark asked the obvious question. What would happen to the farm he already had? Owen's answer was staggering. 'If the soil is wet it might be laid down in grass, if dry in cotton or farmed for the private benefit of the individuals of the society.' In other words, Mr Clark was invited to be in two places at once, wearing two different hats – the communitarian and the individual. He could pay rent to Owen to farm and turn the produce over to the common good and also – by some means not specified – keep up his original investment out on the prairie. The offhand suggestion that he might otherwise let his ploughland revert to grass must have been especially galling.

Seen in this light, Owen's abrupt departure was akin to a fit of madness. He travelled back up the Ohio and by the time he reached Pittsburgh nothing would do but that he gave an immediate public lecture announcing the purchase. It was certainly newsworthy and there was perhaps no city more interested in the fortunes of the Harmony Society than Pittsburgh. Owen intended that they saw the story his way. This was not a story about a group of elderly Württembergers, but the inauguration of the new moral order. It was a story about Owen.

When he gave his lecture, enthusiasm was said to be so great that court sessions were suspended, a report that probably originated with Owen himself but which was sent back to the *Scotsman* and duly reprinted as fact in the London *Times*. From Pittsburgh he hurried on to Philadelphia where reports of the lecture had galvanised many of the people he had met a few weeks earlier. Owen now owned one of the most valuable properties outside the eastern seaboard: what might he do with it and to what benefit for mankind? Maclure was back in the city and already being begged by friends to transfer all his scientific activity to Indiana. Troost, Speakman and Say, very influential members of the Academy of Science, undertook to do the same.

It is the time to step back and take stock. A very rich man has come to America and bought an entire town as a going concern. He has no prior knowledge of the country and has arrived on its shores in the winter months, when travel is difficult, but has already met the outgoing president and the president elect. This town he has bought is located in the most politically sensitive part of America, where the new fortunes are going to be made. His own wealth has been accumulated from the operation of a highly successful Scottish cotton mill, run along lines that seem both cost-efficient and humane. In order to fund his new investment he will (it is rumoured) put his British property on to the market and sever his links with Europe.

However, the facts can be laid out a very different way. For

nearly ten years this same man has been advocating an entirely
new form of communitarianism. He is not so much a businessman
as a visionary philanthropist. What he has done for New Lanark
he believes can be done for all mankind. Indeed, he sees no other
way out from the miseries of the world. He has not come to buy
one town in America and develop it in the energetic and rational
fashion that brought him so many admirers in Britain. He has
come to America to change everything, beginning in a small way,
but with the intention – about which he is perfectly open – of
imposing on his hosts a new moral order.

Of the two paths Owen could have taken, he unerringly chose
the one most likely to lead him into trouble. In practical terms,
the last thing he needed was an overhasty declaration of intent.
Those who wanted to believe in Owenism had already come some
way along the same road, albeit from different points of departure, and their support was all the more valuable for being rooted
in prior experience and reflection. What he had to say about the
formation of character particularly interested educationists; yet
examined piecemeal there was something for everyone in his
teachings – best agricultural practice, social engineering, constitutional reform, utopian idealism, world government.

His American admirers supposed that he would be prepared
to temper his ideals and accommodate his one great idea to circumstance. After all, the New Moral World he proclaimed was not
new in Philadelphia; it was only 40 years since Franklin, posing
as 'a farmer of plain sense', had characterised his country in an
essay written at a desk in that city, shortly after his return from
Paris.

> Whoever has travelled through the various parts of
> Europe, and observed how small is the proportion of
> people in affluence or easy circumstances there, compared
> with those in poverty and misery; the few rich and
> haughty landlords, the multitude of poor, abject, rack-

rented, tythe-paying tenants and half paid and half starved ragged labourers; and views here the happy mediocrity that so generally prevails throughout these states, where the cultivator works for himself and supports his family in decent plenty, will, methinks, see abundant reason to bless divine providence for the evident and great difference in our favour, and be convinced that no nation known to us enjoys a greater share of human felicity.

These were sentiments hard to argue with by even the most critical of American citizens in 1825: life might be more complex than Franklin made it appear but the spirit of the piece he wrote had not faded one jot. America was not perfect – or not yet – but it was beautiful. Only a fool or a scoundrel would say otherwise. There was a taste for communitarian experiment – in New York there was even a Society for Promoting Communities, a sort of clearing house and message board for various schemes. But none had as their intention the eventual overthrow of the United States. Owen's plans did – or so it seemed to those unlucky enough to have their ear bent by his frenetic propaganda.

On 25 February and again on 7 March, Owen delivered addresses in the Hall of the House of Representatives in Washington, to an audience of both houses of Congress, the Supreme Court and President Adams. He spoke for three hours. Representatives of the Franklinesque 'happy mediocrity' listened politely yet with varying degrees of irritation as he described how Harmony was to be a collecting point for the first village ever built according to Owenite principles, for which, happily, a site existed 'from two to four miles from the river and its island'. The vexation they must have felt came to a head with this ringing declaration:

> And here it is, in the heart of the United States, and almost in the centre of its unequalled internal navigation, that Power which governs the universe and every action

of man, has arranged circumstances which were far
beyond my control, and permits me to commence a new
empire of peace and good-will to men, formed on other
principles and leading to other practices than those of
present or past, which principles, in due season, and in
the allotted time, will lead to that state of virtue, intelligence and happiness which it has been foretold by the
sages of the past would at some time become the lot of
the human race.

In the printed version of Owen's 'Address' it is interesting that
such a lengthy sentence was immediately followed by another of
only nine words – 'I have, however, no wish to lead the way.'
This may have been an unscripted reaction to the mood of the
audience. It was, as he hastened to point out, for governments
to 'adopt the principles [and] encourage the practice'. However,
until that time came, what he described as 'private exertions'
would commence at New Harmony, beginning a few weeks hence
in April.

Owen attempted to answer two questions that had already
been put to him and which must have been stirring in the minds
of those present. First, what would be the local consequence
wherever 'one or more of these societies of union, co-operation
and common property should be established'? And secondly, if
they worked as well as he said they would, where would that
leave the people who were listening to him – or as he put it,
'what effect will they have upon the government of and general
prosperity of an extensive empire?'

His reply in each case was painfully naive. The answer to the
first question was simple – 'the old system of society would
soon break up'. An Owenite village would quickly undersell and
outperform its unregenerate neighbours, making it both necessary and desirable that they joined in, abandoning what Owen
called 'the miserable, anxious, individual system of opposition

and counteraction'. Then, as the new order spread, national government would be made all the easier, with the additional benefit of being cheaper – he calculated by as much as 90 per cent. There would be no more 'trouble and anxiety' for the lawmakers, such as those who sat ranged listening to him now.

Owen's speech was widely reported in the press but received only a lukewarm reception from his Washington audience. It is easy to see why. Politically, Owenism, as outlined by its author, was a nullity. The United States had just concluded the acrimonious presidential election of John Quincy Adams amid accusations of political horse-trading that would seem mild today but which opened up the ancient debate in America about the contrasting virtues of strong government and the least government possible. A year hence, Henry Clay, who had managed the election for Adams, and was by now secretary of state, fought a duel on the subject with the Virginian senator, the half-demented John Randolph. It was true, therefore, that the shape of any future United States was a subject not without heat and passion. But Owen's solution was pure fantasy. Going away into the woods to turn your back on the political process was one thing. Weak or strong, the government had a long reach and would find you out. But going away to begin the wholesale remodelling of American society was quite another enterprise. It seemed to Owen a bonus point that he would start his new system 'almost in the centre . . . of internal navigation'. It never occurred to him that the state legislatures in Indiana, Ohio, Illinois and Kentucky – if everything worked out the way he promised – might have something to say about that.

The presumption hidden in Owenism was that any rational person could see the benefits of the system and once awakened would be only too happy to subscribe. Coercion would not be necessary, any more than the model village had need of a jail. After all, in its British context, Owen's scheme was an *alternative* to jail, a way of rescuing the poor from iniquity. The villagers would have no choice but to associate and the governing class, as represented by men unwilling to pay the cost of the poor rate, would gratefully accept a problem solved. For America, Owen added in the concept of the doomed 'individual system', never able to return a dividend on happiness and prosperity, fatally flawed by its irrational and contrarian elements. He reckoned without – indeed seemed not to realise at all – the ingrained habit of mind in his audience that considered the exercise of liberty as the supreme civil right. The tree of liberty was watered by the bloody-mindedness of patriots.

Meanwhile, reports of his Washington excursion led to hundreds of enquiries. William Owen and Macdonald were being driven mad by applicants, not just from locally, but America-wide. Here was a half-empty town surrounded by 3,000 acres of farmland that presently lay fallow. It was clear, even as early as February, that the existing stock of housing would be inadequate to satisfy demand. But then a dreadful realisation came that had completely escaped them at the time of the sale. There *were* no builders' yards or timber merchants conveniently to hand, no brickworks or commercial quarries just over the next hill or in a not too distant town. William was aghast. He was a green young man from Scotland who supposed somehow that you sent out an order and a few days later the bricks, or sawn timbers, the dressed stone came rumbling in by cart. That was how it worked in Lanark – but not here. The scale of what Harmony had achieved by its own efforts finally began to sink in.

Without Owen's presence – for after all it was his money that had been invested – not a foot of land nor a single house could be rented or leased. And still the enquiries poured in. Some people wanted to come to Harmony to work for wages as craftsmen or tradesmen, some wanted to share goods in common with the great philosopher, their pittance flung in with his wealth, all against the promise of a future golden dividend. Some were attracted by the opportunity to air their own utopian schemes, cooked up in some attic and pitifully expounded in the back room of a tavern to half a dozen men and their dogs. And some – more than enough – simply saw the chance to sponge. William Owen was swamped. He was 23 and loyal to his father's wishes, yet he began to think that what was happening here was the overture to disaster.

EIGHT

Many are coming from the east

One of the unexpected features of the old Harmony was a maze, sited on a path that led down to the river. At its centre was a bench where people might sit and contemplate, or if they were otherwise minded, chat and gossip. If in Rapp's time it had a spiritual lesson to offer – the journey to the heart of the matter, the inwardness that was the beginning of a love of God – it was also a pleasant and harmless reminder of days in the old country when a man or a woman could rest an aching back and watch the sun go down. Though its secrets were soon learned, that was hardly the point – and since a maze needs to be lovingly kept up, perhaps the greater spiritual exercise to be found was in pruning its hedges and sweeping its paths.

That early spring of 1825 the buds broke unnoticed on the dripping branches and last year's leaves blew this way and that along the paths. The old community had done with its maze and the incomers hardly seemed to notice its existence. Captain MacDonald, whose diary reveals a keen eye for anomalous detail, does not mention it.

Owen arrived back in the town – now to be called New Harmony – on 13 April. The first thing he announced to those milling around him seemed almost like prophetic utterance – many were coming from the east! His elation was understandable, for from being for so long the only man in step he was now at the head of the parade. He flapped away William's anguished reports, preferring to dwell on the phenomenal publicity given to Owenism since the Washington addresses. In Cincinnati a second Owenite village community was in contemplation and he fetched two of its sponsors back with him. They happened to be Christian ministers but that did not seem to matter any more. Or not to him. Pressed later in the year, he frankly admitted 'he did not believe the old and new testaments to be the word of God, any more than he believed any other writings to be the word of God'. This had yet to dawn on the more enthusiastic of his millenarian supporters. Meanwhile, he was able to report Philadelphia in uproar and the New York press clamouring for his presence. Dispatches describing his triumphs had been sent across the Atlantic to all the leading European newspapers.

In Washington, Owen had outlined his intention to create a Preliminary Society, from which would follow the real thing, the building of the first community in its full architectural form. This was a sensible precautionary measure, taken to mean by the distracted William Owen that applications to join would be vetted and a formal undertaking made between his father and those admitted. But Owen had gone on to announce that anyone who wanted might join the experiment – and this had consequences for people who had never met this mysterious benefactor and were responding to newspaper reports and hearsay. Moving to the Wabash meant selling up and abandoning the old life altogether, yet such was the volatility of American society that many had done just that. They were already turning up in dozens, soon to become hundreds. Some were lean and rawboned people, marked by the greenish pallor that distinguished those who lived in log cabins. Others were city folks with soft hands, dressed in elegant clothes, dainty about mud and insects and the heat of the sun.

Owen addressed them all on 27 April at a meeting in Rapp's

church, renamed the Hall of New Harmony. To many present, this redirection of the use of the church was of itself a thrilling thing. Superstition and bigotry (as represented by religion) were cast out and in their place came free thought and free speech. Liberty loving Americans were entranced by Owen's opening statement. 'I am come to this country,' he declared, 'to introduce an entire new state of society; to change it from an ignorant, selfish system to an enlightened social system which shall gradually unite all interests into one and remove all causes for contest between individuals.'

He emphasised his belief that nothing could be achieved in life by praise and blame. Only care and compassion could bring about the changes he desired and there was to be no coercion in this new community. For some of those present this seemed almost a Christ-like ambition. William Pelham, an elderly man who had abandoned his old life out of deep unhappiness, was one of these. In a letter to his son, reporting the first meeting of the Preliminary Society, his description of Owen was rhapsodic. 'He is an extraordinary man, a wonderful man – such a one indeed as the world has never before seen. His wisdom, his comprehensive mind, his practical knowledge but above all, his open-ness, candour and sincerity, have no parallel in ancient or modern history.'

But as events were to prove, there were some for whom this first address was a confusion; worse still, a basic contradiction of what they believed to be an inescapable truth about life. For such as these, it seemed self-evident that not all could be alike, save in the sight of God. They wanted another chance in the here and now and that was why they had come. One of the men attracted to Harmony who did not have Mr Pelham's naked emotional needs asked Owen if he might buy a piece of land outright. When the proprietor agreed, this opportunist immediately began the construction of a second tavern. Owen was mortified. But for the new tavernkeeper it seemed a perfectly straightforward transaction and an instance of the American way of doing things.

The Preliminary Society's constitution was published on 1 May 1825. Under its terms, the proprietor himself would direct affairs in the first year. In the second, the membership would form committees to plan the final stage, which would then flourish under its final and glorious title, the Community of Equality and Independence. The publishing of the constitution answered some questions but left open some of the most practical and pressing ones, such as where to house everyone and – crucially – how to get the manufacturing side of the town working again.

Owen's promise of personal management during the setting-up period was vital, for there were questions left dangling that only he could answer. He had hinted as much in his inaugural address, stretching the point somewhat. 'Ardently as I long for the arrival of that period when there shall be no artificial inequality among the whole human race, yet, as no other individual has had the same experience as myself in the practice of the system about to be introduced, I must for some time partially take the lead in its direction . . .'

This left the impression that the most pressing practical problems had already been faced and solved elsewhere, supposedly in New Lanark. The most radical provisions in the Preliminary Society's constitution were those affecting common ownership and the abolition of private property. None of Owen's ardent new disciples realised that their leader had no more experience of this than anyone else.

He proposed some rational arrangements on this point that at least read well on paper. Members would be expected to find their own tools and furniture in return for being housed by the proprietor. Money would not change hands anywhere in the town. Instead, the labour of each individual would be measured carefully and recorded by a system of bookkeeping, and paid for in goods. If you entered New Harmony eager for its principles but without money, then if you did not work, you did not eat. This made sense and was hardly controversial. However, if you worked extremely hard, or your labour was highly specialised, you were still paid according to a scale whose gradations were, compared to the vilified 'individual system', miserly. An unskilled man might merely be grateful to find a roof over his head. A craftsman – say, a carpenter, a potter, a dye master, most valuable of all, an 'engineer' – might not feel so fairly rewarded.

Newspaper comment often reflected doubts about the feasibility of communal property. The *Daily National Intelligencer*, published in Washington, pointed out that 'however applicable to a crowded population, abounding with paupers, it was not adapted to the present condition of any part of the United States'. Support for this point of view came from an unexpected quarter. The London *Times* felt that the end of private property was in any case 'at variance with the course prescribed by Providence for the exertions and enjoyments of human beings in a state of society' but once it had got this off its chest, it moved very close to the *Intelligencer*'s position.

> There will be more industry without [Owen's] inter-
> ference than with it, because individual existence in these
> self-dependent regions can be no otherwise supported
> than by daily toil; and an establishment where labour
> and the fruits of it were to be in common, would present
> less powerful stimulants to toil, than where the father of
> a family was conscious ... that, for the preservation of
> his wife and children, he had no resource but in the
> vigour of his *own* arm.

Someone sitting at a desk in London, perhaps someone who had never had to dirty his hands with anything other than ink, had made a leap of imagination that landed not far short of the mark.

On 5 May, the last of the Rappites left, travelling aboard the steamboat *William Penn*. It was a sign of their great works and astounding faith that these penniless people, the butt of so much scorn from their neighbours, still dressed in the drab work clothes they wore to the fields, actually owned the steamer upon which they were embarking. It was their 21st year in America and apart from a few half-forgotten weeks in Philadelphia, their lives had been spent entirely within the invisible walls of their commune. Now they marched down to the river with a band at their head, singing German hymns. Owen bade them farewell in a voice that broke with emotion and a watching crowd of locals unexpectedly surged forward to shake them by the hand. One of Father's purchases had been a ceremonial gun, which had been fired only once before, when it accidently killed a bystander and maimed a child. It was fired again now and the *William Penn* cast off. MacDonald was in the crowd. 'As she went down the stream both parties continued for some time waving hats & handkerchiefs, while the band played a march. I never in my life returned home from parting with friends with so sad a feeling as that (to me) melancholy afternoon.'

Among those who bade farewell to the Harmonists that morning was George Birkbeck, partially reconciled to the Flower family but always heavy with warnings to Owen about the difficulties he faced. The day after the Harmonists left, this lonely man rode back to Wanborough with one of his sons and in crossing the Fox Creek his horse reared and trampled him. He died at the river bank and was carried back to Harmony, where he became the first outsider to be buried within the confines of the town, a funeral attended with grief by both friends and former enemies.

It was said that every state of the Union was represented in New Harmony, their numbers soon to be augmented by arrivals from most countries in northern Europe. Some of these hopefuls – it is overwhelmingly tempting to call them the faithful – were experienced tradesmen. Some lacked any skill other than the strength of their arm. Families who had never lifted anything heavier than a teaspoon turned up with their servants and domestics. Beautiful young girls persuaded their rich fathers to bring them to this supposed arcadia, along with the family pianoforte and a satchel of sheet music. There were applications from men difficult to classify at all, unless it was under the head of idealist, or even more vague, well-wisher. Bad poets and high-minded artists found in Owenism the challenge their muse had been seeking. They mingled with adventurers, opportunists and downright no-hopers. Not until the gold rush twenty years later was so volatile a group assembled in America at such short notice.

Owen now made a second grave error of judgement. Thinking things over, it seemed inescapable that some communitarians were more valuable than others – not all pigs were equal. There would have to be some Society members exempted from labour and treated differently. It did not help that these favoured few most often resembled Owen himself, that is to say intellectuals and not primary producers. But then where did this leave the community of property? Was the man who set off to the fields at dawn with a scythe over his shoulder labouring to keep his late-rising neighbour in pens and quires of paper, books and newspapers? Was a man who brought 200 or 300 sheep into the Preliminary Society exactly the same under the constitution as a raggedy shepherd with nothing but the clothes he stood up in? In another (and actual) example: could a society beauty from Philadelphia really be expected to break off from a piano recital to milk cows?

The new Harmony was soon as noisy and argumentative as the old one had been quiet. Captain MacDonald had drunk his fill of the incessant badgering and it was his soldierly opinion that Owen would do well to consider cutting the knot by bringing out the entire population of New Lanark, ordering them what to do and then making sure they got on with it. He reckoned without the sea change an Atlantic crossing had wrought in his hero.

At home, the British could hardly find a good word to say about Owen's ideas. Waving him off to his new life in 1824, one newspaper commented breezily that 'this system of living will answer better among the savages of America than the enlightened people of England'. Here in America, despite some misgivings, he was honoured as a seer and a prophet. It did not help his cause that one of his admirers described New Harmony as 'the focus of enlightened atheism' but the immediate and electric response to his teachings, as he saw them, disposed him to lower his guard. Once an aloof and wary man, he began to trust other people according to the strength of their adulation. Much to his liking, he had become a celebrity.

From Owen's leave-taking on 3 January to his return in April was a period of exactly 100 days. In that time the valve that had kept his emotions in lifelong check finally blew. The 'reasoning machine' began to disintegrate, to be replaced by a sentimentalist who believed that things would happen simply because he wanted them to happen. William Owen was especially amazed. He had never seen his father drunk but the effects were not much different. The wrangling going on in Harmony's streets would have galvanised the old Owen, the one that set about the New Lanark rabble in 1799. A quarter of a century on, he gazed about him with just a little too much beaming geniality. Normally a stickler for detail, he was letting things pass that were certain to spell trouble later on.

William's prior view of his father was that he was inalterable: painfully, he was forced to come to terms with the fact that what he saw now was a changed man, almost a stranger. The man who set out to describe a world filled from end to end with error had discovered pockets of extraordinary common sense – that is to say, people who agreed with him. These were not the great and the good, pondering his words in a study or committee room, but ordinary men and women. Every day, they came up to him

and shook his hand. It was a new experience – and it was exhil-
arating.

In his autobiography, written in extreme old age, Owen never
spares us the compliments paid to him by others. Though he
spoke no French, his visit to Paris in 1817 was especially fondly
remembered. His guide was the Swiss-born Professor Pictet,
through whom he met Von Humboldt, Cuvier and LaPlace, but
also the Duc d'Orléans and other notables. 'With such a friend,
guide and interpreter, our visits were always to men and women
of high standing for some eminent qualities, and our conversations were therefore always on the investigation of some important knowledge worth the time and trouble of interpreting. And,
from one cause or another, I was made during this period, through
the Professor's means and others, the lion of Paris.'

Maybe so, but then Owen always had at the back of his mind
that he was a prophet without honour in his own country.
America changed that. He no longer *had* a country: what he was
about now was universal citizenry. In the past he had gone
home to Scotland to an uncomprehending wife and the incessant
reminder of factory clatter to bring him back to his real business,
which was to be a cotton manufacturer with partners to satisfy
and a workforce to chasten. Now the woods and empty skies of
Indiana, the endless plucking at his sleeve by well-wishers, acted
on him like a psychedelic drug. Perhaps for the first time in his
life he felt free.

It made him reckless. There was very little growing in the
ground and the workshops were at a standstill, yet every day
brought new arrivals, walking up from the river, some with
umbrellas and monogrammed leather luggage, some toting their
entire wealth in a sack flung across their back. Owen let it all
swirl round him. To William's dismay, he did not buckle down
to bringing some order to the situation but set out from Harmony
again on 5 June, accompanied by the phlegmatic MacDonald. He

was going back to Scotland. There was the disposal of his shares in New Lanark to be arranged, but also the fate of his marriage. He had already decided that his wife was to play no part in the great experiment.

Caroline Owen died in 1831, not before seeing her husband, all four sons and one of her daughters desert her for America. It was an unkind end to a life that had started out in such high romance. It was she who first introduced Owen to the New Lanark Mills, when she was only nineteen years old. It was summer when they met. As well as inspecting the spinning sheds, for which she was a very inexpert guide, they walked the banks of the Clyde together. At that time he had yet to meet her father and knew nothing of the family other than what she told him – and that was unpromising.

Caroline's mother died when she was twelve, since when she had kept house for the family. In talking about David Dale to Owen she emphasised his deep religious convictions, making clear she wholeheartedly shared them. She could hardly have mistaken their absence in the gloomy young Welshman. There has to be an explanation for how this mismatch of beliefs and ideas was overcome and in his autobiography, written so late in life, Owen has one: Caroline was besotted with him. His account makes her confide romantic but humiliating feelings. 'Before she parted from me at New Lanark, she said she would never marry against her father's consent, but she had made up her mind that she would remain unmarried unless he could be induced to accept me for his son-in-law.'

Comfortably, then, Owen was led to marriage by a woman's passion. Dale's manner continued 'cold and distant' for a while but gradually he thawed. The marriage took place in the parlour of the family house in Charlotte Street, Glasgow, and was offici- ated by a Mr Balfour, 'a member of the regular Scotch Church'. The service was suspiciously unchallenging. The Reverend

Rappites they had displaced, more prone to exploration. On their forays to meet the neighbours, they came across people who had never drunk tea or owned a watch, yet for whom, luckily, whisky was a staple of existence. The old Harmonists might have been unpopular but one thing they were not was importunate. The new crowd talked up their town a great deal but were never averse to cadging a meal or a night's drinking outside it. It did nothing to add to their popularity.

Though roughly the same number of people occupied Harmony as in Rapp's day, the town was overcrowded. This was because private families had replaced the strict separation of the sexes — the communal activities were popular simply because for the rest of the week people were living on top of one another, sometimes with complaining and ungrateful newcomers lodging behind a curtain. The Sunday sermons that many sought as a solace were often grudge matches between the rationalists and visiting clergy. The Reverend Mr Jennings, one of Owen's friends from Cincinnati, took a special pleasure in confounding Baptists, Shakers, and anyone else unwary enough to stray into his sights. William Owen, trying to keep the peace, used his regular sermons to read aloud from his father's printed works, which he did in an uninspiring monotone. It was more fun to watch Jennings rip into organised religion, as represented by some unlucky visiting preacher. Everybody who liked the sound of their own voice found Harmony a ready megaphone.

The civic niceties began to disappear. Rapp's people had famously kept up fenced gardens and vegetable plots. The fences broke down or disappeared for firewood and soon the hogs ran wild, eating up whatever they could find. The new Harmonists who came from farms or homesteads expected nothing much of pigs by way of manners — pigs commonly pushed their way in wherever they could eat. In Mr Jennings's home town, Cincinnati, there were so many about in the streets that the place was often called Porkopolis. In Harmony, they ate gardens that for ten years previously had been filled with beans and cucumbers, swaggering about the place like aggressive vagrants. High-minded thinkers and gentlemen from the east coast who had never kicked a pig before now found it a rational necessity.

'The hogs have been our Lords and Masters this year in field and garden,' complained the mild-mannered Thomas Pears. 'We are now, as we have been, without vegetables except what we buy, and I believe we shall go without potatoes, turnips or cabbages this winter, unless they are purchased.'

The only crop under cultivation was barley. Those unused to agriculture who enquired why this was so had it explained to them that from barley came beer. Without beer the winter would be wretched indeed. Pears's wife tried to look on the bright side but as the summer lengthened, she wrote to a friend these bleak words, dragged out of her by a long chapter of disappointments: 'We are beyond Humanity's reach . . .' Maybe most of the difficulties that upset the Pears could be put down to teething problems. There was no shortage of good ideas, many of them impractical, but the general tone was earnest rather than despairing. After all, Mr Owen was surely about to return from Scotland and direct affairs for the good of the whole: the pioneers were only caretakers, muddling along as best they could against the promise of that great day.

The town published a newspaper, the *New Harmony Gazette*, and William Owen contributed articles to the first two editions. They were intended to describe the manufacturing potential of the community but told instead a gloomy story. In every workshop and mill, production was almost at a standstill for want of skilled labour. It seemed that cottage industries like candle-making, cobbling or the making of hats were operating well enough and for an obvious reason: labour spent on these traditional occupations could be turned into food at the store. But the dye house was deserted, not enough lumber was being cut at the sawmill, nobody was making pots and the state-of-the-art cotton spinning machinery was either idle, or being experimented on by unskilled hands. No saddler or harness maker was willing to come forward to offer his services, any more than a coppersmith, a glazier or half a dozen other trades. Hidden in the report was the alarming fact that only 36 of the community of 900 described themselves as farmers or field hands.

William Owen, the son of a rich man, was too young and inexperienced to guess why there was a reluctance for skilled workers to come forward. In Rapp's day, they did it for love of God and as an unconscious expression of peasant virtue. The people who came along in their place were not less skilled but more conflicted personally. They came to Harmony because they saw in it the possibility of something better and grander altogether than wage labour. Of course there were sawyers and millers in the town but they were there expressly to be changed from their prior existence. If they did not exactly know how this was to come about, there were more than enough theorists to tell them. What was making the hogs run wild in the streets was not too few fences but too much politics.

The masthead of the *Gazette* read, 'If we cannot reconcile all opinions, let us endeavour to unite all hearts.' There were almost as many opinions as there were people to express them and it was remarkable that the political temperature did not rise to boiling point. A truly dedicated communitarian had the answer to that, which he expressed in a letter to a friend. 'There is no such thing, under the new system, as an insult; every man speaks according to the impression which dictates his words, and all impressions are made upon him by the exercise of faculties over which he has no control.' So, you might call a neighbour a fool or a scoundrel and he was obliged to forgive you, since by Owenite doctrine, you were speaking from an ancient stock of error. If the man *was* a scoundrel, his behaviour was likewise conditioned by his past experience and so must be seen as blameless. If your hammer (or your wife) ended up in his house and not yours, this was a situation that could only be resolved by rational discourse. If that proved impossible, the *Gazette* had a view that did not answer all cases but strove to be reassuring. 'Popular opinion being now decidedly opposed to indolence and vice, the idle member must become industrious, and the vicious become more virtuous, or they cannot rest contentedly in the bosom of our community.'

Owen recrossed the Atlantic on 1 October, sailing from Liverpool with MacDonald and a new acquisition, the London architect, Stedman Whitwell. It happened to be the same passage as that taken by the musical Garcia family, on their way to found an opera house in New York. MacDonald did not like the look of the father but found his seventeen-year-old daughter, Maria Felicita, well worth a second glance. She had a baby sister called Michelle Ferdinande Pauline. Without realising it, MacDonald had met two girls destined to be the most famous sopranos of the nineteenth century, known by their married names as Malibran and Pauline Viardot. Someone wrote a poem that grumpy old Garcia set to music. On a certain day it was given a concert performance on the deck of the ship.

> Land of the West we fly to thee,
> Sick of the Old World's sophistry
> Haste then across the dark blue sea,
> Land of the West we rush to thee.

Metaphorically, that is. Owen landed on Sunday, 6 November, part of his luggage a six-foot square architectural model of the ideal community, built for him by Whitwell. This was not destined for the hungry and bewildered in the Land of the West but was sent down to Washington for the approbation of the president. Owen himself stayed in Philadelphia. He did not finally arrive back in New Harmony until 12 January 1826. The weather had been unseasonably warm and the Wabash was in spate, flooding the land round the town, which had now become an island. A hundred or so schoolchildren and many adults waded through the floodwaters along the road to Mount Vernon and when they saw his mud-spattered horses and carriage lurching towards them, burst out with chants saying 'All will be well now!' and 'He has come back to us!'

The great Redeemer was alone in the carriage save for a mysterious woman called Mrs Fisher, someone he had picked up in New York. After a great deal of splashing he regained firm ground, said hello to his son William and ordered the rearrangement of that night's entertainment. The Hall of New Harmony was packed out to hear what the great man had in store for them. Of all the things he might have announced, the last thing anyone expected was the news that soon – very soon indeed – a boat would come down the Ohio filled to the gunwhales with the greatest company of intellectuals ever assembled for the benefits of mankind. Maclure and the Philadelphians had thrown in their lot with the great experiment.

It was clear that Owen thought this a very good thing but it may not have entranced his listeners. The town was filled to bursting, nothing much had been accomplished in his absence and almost as soon as he finished speaking the temperature began to fall. In the next few days the Wabash froze and ice gripped the little town like a fist. It was hard to see what a party of intellectuals could do about that, no matter how many were coming.

NINE

A boatload of knowledge

William Owen and his brother Robert were educated by the Pestalozzian system, which held that a child was not to be hammered into adult shape like a flat sheet of metal attacked by a tinsmith, but nurtured and husbanded. Pestalozzi believed that the purpose of education was the discovery and development of individuated personality, wherever that led and at whatever cost. In this way education was subversive of old forms – and that was its true nature.

It is hard for us to realise today that this was as radical an idea as ever came out of the eighteenth century. As a man, Pestalozzi was quite as eccentric as any of those who plagued William Owen's existence in New Harmony, but his methods, particularly when applied to poor children and orphans, were widely admired. His final school at Yverdon, opened in his old age, attracted men of a liberal tendency from all over Europe who wished to prepare their children for the new age dawning.

William and Robert Dale Owen were educated at Hofwyl, near Berne, by a disciple of Pestalozzi's called Fellenberg. It was a little like sending coals to Newcastle, for Fellenberg and the boys' father were so much of the same mind that Robert Dale Owen confessed that he was hardly conscious of a change when he crossed Europe to go to school there. Fellenberg was as cautious as Owen about disturbing the social order. He believed that the upper classes of society should be made more aware of their responsibility to it and the labouring class educated to bear their impoverished role in it with dignity. He drew his pupils from each extremity of the social order and boarded them under identical conditions. This was hardly revolutionary in itself but the importance placed on manual labour as a component of his teaching led to one startling and unexpected consequence: the school was self-supporting. If mutual dependence was as successful as Fellenberg's account books demonstrated, then Hofwyl functioned both as an educational establishment and a communitarian model. The rich youth and the son of a birdscarer stood on equal terms and the outcome was harmony.

If, like Owen senior, you believed that all life was error, then early education was the only way out – it was hardly too fanciful to say that doctrinally children would be much better off without parents at all. For many of his contemporaries, the visionary in Owen only came into focus when he was talking about education. It was the most approachable of his ideas and the one most easily verified by investigation. Many of the distinguished visitors who came to New Lanark over the years were much more interested in the school than they were in the operation of the mill. Without exception, they were struck by the sheer joy they found inside its walls. The sentimental found it tender and touching to witness such romping infant bedlam but more reflective minds made the connection Owen intended. The search for justice and humanity in the world could only start among the very young.

There was certainly much ground to make up. Traditional classroom learning was a matter of rote and lessons were often enforced by the sort of discipline more common among animal trainers. In a Pestalozzian school things were very different. It was better, for example, to hold a turnip or a mouse in the hand and learn by exploration rather than recite the signifier 'turnip' and be made to spell it over and over. Pestalozzi's gift as a teacher

was an uncommon one for his age: he loved children. When
Owen sent two of his sons to be educated in Switzerland, he had
a ready and fairly recent local example of the alternative. The
little farm boy Robert MacQueen grew up to become the awesome
Lord Braxfield by having his knuckles rapped and his ears boxed
as a pupil in the Lanark grammar school: in time, the law claimed
him as a list-gatherer and rote learner of distinction. Braxfield
knew a lot of things and had a prodigious (and vindictive)
memory but in his adult life was about as reactionary as it was
possible to be. Unconsciously or not, he was steeped in error,
and had been since his earliest years. In Owen's view, the longer
his 'education' continued, the more lost to reason he became.

The New Lanark infant school was a dramatic rebuttal of existing practice. It was run by a rough and ready man of no education
himself, a former cottage weaver called James Buchanan, who
was assisted in his work by Molly Young, an illiterate young
mill girl of seventeen. The school was the darling of Owen's heart
and the curriculum he devised for it was strikingly simple. The
children should enjoy themselves and by doing so learn the beginnings of communitarian life from each other. There were no toys,
no books and very little equipment. No punishment was ever
inflicted, nor was good behaviour rewarded by prizes or commen-
dations. Buchanan's task was to find things for the children to
study according to their own interests. In time Owen installed a
magic lantern that projected images of objects and places that
might stimulate the imagination and there were maps of the four
quarters of the globe hung on the walls. But the main instrument
of their education was the infinitely patient Buchanan. Owen
claimed that he was specially apt for this role because his wife
had spent a lifetime henpecking him. Accordingly, he knew how
to keep his temper.

When admirers spoke of Owen as an educationist, then, it was
the startling freedom of the children under his care at New Lanark

they most wanted to indicate. 'We saw them romping and playing in great spirits,' one observer reported. 'The noise was prodigious but it was the full chorus of mirth and kindliness.' Sometimes as many as 70 delighted guests at a time would crowd into the schoolroom to witness the children at play. They marched, they sang, they danced – not just ring-a-ring o' roses but 'all the major dances of Europe, with so little direction from their master that the strangers would be unconscious that there was a dancing master in the room'.

It left most visitors filled with wonder and admiration. But not all: in 1817 a grumpy young Thomas Carlyle, himself a teacher at the time, visited New Lanark in the course of a walking tour with his friend Edward Irving. 'We called to see Robert Owen, the then incipient Arch-Gomeril's "model school", and thought it and him, whom we did not see and knew only by his pamphlets, a thing of wind, not worth considering farther . . .'

There was, of course, another way of interpreting the spectacle, apart from dismissing it altogether like Carlyle. These children, who seemed to be so artlessly romping, were being empowered in such a way that would one day bring about the alteration of existing adult society. Proponents of religious education were especially alarmed at the freedoms being granted to children so young. Mr Owen's pride in his infants was all very well but what he was really about was trying to turn the world upside down. (Carlyle had only ever been turned upside down to have his backside tanned: the school in *Sartor Resartus* is called in bad German the Hinterschlag Academy, and has some resemblances to the Annan Academy as remembered by its most distinguished pupil.)

It is in this context that the imminent arrival of a contingent of learned men to New Harmony has to be seen. William Owen may have wished his father to concentrate on bread and butter issues of much greater urgency but he could hardly deprecate the coming of what everyone soon learned to call 'a boatload of knowledge'. Education was the central plank of every reformer's platform and only the most scallywag members of the Society could fail to recognise in this exodus from Philadelphia a sudden and sensational endorsement of Owen's project. Men and women known only by their reputation, learned and distinguished savants hitherto at their ease behind their ivory walls, were now coming to share with the simple and homely on the basis of equal shares.

Almost a full year of occupancy had left the pioneers scratting about in the mud and ice, no further forward in the grand design. In that time, no natural leaders had come to the fore, nobody had risen from the ruck, smilingly or otherwise, to say that enough was enough. It was hoped, therefore, that these new men and women on their way west to join the great adventure were coming as a task force of experts to help mop up the mess. A hundred thousand bricks or a running mile or two of sawn timber might have been more welcome to William Owen but here was an earnest of good intentions that could only lead to rapid actual improvements.

It was a misreading of the community's problems but an understandable one. What New Harmony lacked was not good intentions but good government. It was proving difficult to be decisive and fully communitarian at the same time. There was a reason for that; the citizens were ill-assorted, as had become very clear, but shared one thing in common – a distaste for authority, all too easily rendered by them as tyranny. There was a paradox here: it seemed the land of liberty was not the best place to found a libertarian commune. The New Harmonists were like pilgrims sailing to a promised land, each one of them cast in the role of navigator. Without an imposed authority, weeks and then months passed in discussion about directions and bearings, ignoring meanwhile the very evident hole in the boat.

The weakest or most venal did not respond to moral exhortation as easily as the constitution of the Preliminary Society supposed they would. 'Oh,' cried the good-natured Mrs Pears in the privacy of a letter to her friend, 'if you could see some of the rough uncouth creatures here, I think you would find it hard to look upon them exactly in the light of brothers and sisters.' Her husband had been a successful manufacturer in his time and might have taken a lead now by knocking heads together. Instead, he was constrained to uncomfortable silence. The language of brotherly love was not so easy to speak as he had supposed and was woefully short of imperatives.

There was an example of how cumbersome rational baggage could be at the very popular weekly dances. It occurred to some overzealous ideologue that the normal enthusiastic choosing of partners for dancing went against the grain of egalitarianism. It would be better – it would be more in the spirit of the constitution – to draw names from a hat. This led to absurd mismatches and some very long faces yet nobody came straight out and labelled this sort of thing illiberal nonsense. Meanwhile, in November 1825, the template for the new world order based on community of property founded its first secret society, the New Harmony Philanthropic Lodge of Masons. It began to seem that the boatload of knowledge could not come too soon.

The key figure coming down the icy Ohio was William Maclure – the richest of these savant-saviours and the most forceful in personality. Maclure had discovered Pestalozzi's work by accident as early as 1805 and had kept in touch with the movement ever since. 'From this 30 years I have considered ignorance as a cause of all the miseries and errors of mankind and have used all my endeavours to reduce the quantity of that truly diabolical evil. My experience soon convinced me that it was impossible to give any real information to men and that the only possible means of giving useful knowledge to the world was by the education of children.'

To this end he founded two Pestalozzian schools in Paris, one conducted by Guillaume Phiquepal d' Arusmont, who was an unsuccessful provincial dentist when Maclure first met him, and the other (for girls) by Marie Duclos Fretageot. In time he brought both these teachers to Philadelphia and it was Madame Fretageot who did most now to persuade him to throw in his lot with Owen. (When the Welshman first met her he took both her hands in his and kissed her, saying she was the woman he had been longing to meet. The lady was utterly bowled over.) Maclure knew that what New Harmony needed most was money; he came prepared to invest $125,000 in the scheme, with the proviso that his public liability should not exceed $10,000. The rather gushing Madame Fretageot considered the Welshman a genius: Maclure admired him but was more sanguine.

He was also a good deal more radical. The link between education and communitarianism was common ground between the two men, but Maclure was the more thoroughgoing libertarian. It was his belief that 'the equal division of property gives vigour to the great mass, and facilitates the acquiring of knowledge, which must be the foundation of all power'. In practical terms, this meant that the non-productive class, which was also the governing class, had to be stripped of its unequal share of the world's goods, which meant in turn that the grip of national government on the individual would inevitably be loosened. About the political dangers to America inherent in this policy, he had a very simple rebuttal. 'Under the management of the majority of the inhabitants of a township six miles square, all radical reforms comporting with their interest might be tried, without the risk of hurting, in the case of failure, anyone but themselves – a losing game they would very soon tire of.'

In other words, he was the very man to wrench New Harmony back from the brink: he had money, was an out and out libertarian by instinct, and believed that, left alone, men and women would

have the sense to adjust their behaviour to circumstance. If drawing for dance partners did not work, then abandon the idea. In
theory, at any rate, the solution to all problems would rise from
the bottom up – in the particular case of New Harmony by stark
necessity. Money was needed to set the project up and for that
the communards must call on the two men who could afford to
offer it. But afterwards the answer to their problems was in their
own hands. It was tough love and on the face of it just what was
needed.

Had Maclure come alone in the guise of a troubleshooter, his
brusque common sense might have prevailed. But he came as the
leader of an intellectual community of interests, with himself
cast as distinguished geologist and elder statesman of American
science. The highly volatile Madame Fretageot accompanied him,
as well as her compatriot Phiquepal. They had with them several
pupils from their respective schools. Two members of the
Academy of Sciences, the naturalists Thomas Say and Charles
LeSueur, had also taken passage. (Their colleagues Gerard Troost
and John Speakman were already in New Harmony.)

Owen and Mrs Fisher had set out from Pittsburgh with the
main party but grew impatient when the boatload of knowledge
was trapped in the ice for a month. Maclure also left the little
argosy with Marie Fretageot and continued overland. The imper-
turbable Captain MacDonald was left on board, as was Robert
Dale Owen, the first of the Owen children to take up their father's
offer of a new life. They shared their mess with the architect
Stedman Whitwell, the travelling companion from hell.

There were altogether 40 sailing on the keelboat *Philanthropist*.
It had been specially purchased for the exodus, its accommodation
divided along rationalist principles into four, a quarter for the
crew and the rest for the travellers. The ladies were given a
quarter to themselves, gallantly named Paradise. It was bitterly
cold weather, set off by stoves below deck that were stoked to

cherry red heat, though during the period when the vessel was locked in by ice, Say and Lesueur took away a little of the cosiness in the main living quarters by occupying themselves in stuffing specimen fish, some birds and a brown fox. There was seldom an idle moment. MacDonald mentions Mr Symmes, a man who came on board to demonstrate his theory of the polar extremities to the most distinguished audience he had ever met. The poles were actually saucer shaped, as could be proved once the ice was removed. He passed round a double-dented ball of clay to illustrate the point. His name may have been familiar to some from a satirical poem published that month in the *Philadelphia Gazette*. It began:

> The devil at length scrambled out of the hole
> Discovered by Symmes at the freezing North Pole;
> He mounted an iceberg, spread his wings for a sail,
> And started for earth with his long barbed tail.
>
> He heard that a number of people were going
> To live on the Wabash with great Mr Owen:
> He said to himself, 'I must now have a care,
> Circumstances require that myself should be there.'

The devil foresaw there would be much work for him in Indiana – in his view Owenism represented the greatest assistance offered to the forces of darkness since Adam ate the apple. After gleefully reviewing the situation, he hurried home with instructions for his fell imps at the North Pole. They must widen the hole.

Whitwell also had a bee in his bonnet. It struck him how many times Washington, Springfield, Jefferson, Franklin and so on had been used in the naming of American towns, as well as absurd examples from the Ohio Valley like Horsetail, Dead Man, Custard, Brindle and Racoon. This was clearly an area a rational mind could make tidy and Whitwell came up with a means of substituting the letters of the alphabet for numerals. It was but a short step from there to name places by their latitude and longitude, expressed in words and not figures. Thus his birthplace, London, became Lafa Vovutu; New York, where he first set foot in America, Otke Notive; and Pittsburgh, which he had just left, Otfu Veitoup. The president lived in Feili Neivul, not to be confused with where Whitwell was headed, New Harmony, or Feiba Peveli. It is easy to picture Captain MacDonald listening to all this with a cigar clenched between his teeth, while Say and Lesueur cut up specimens a few feet away and the stove roared.

When they all arrived in New Harmony, the situation was assessed by fresh eyes. Not many more than 200 Harmonists were actually at work on community projects – the rest had opened parlour shops or set aside a bit of their already cramped living space to install a workbench. The only crop grown in the previous year had been those 200 acres of barley. Where once the neighbours had ridden in to buy produce cheaper than they could grow it themselves, now most food was imported, the bill for which was running at $30,000 annually. The money came from Owen's pocket. For him the outlook was bleak. Once he had paid over the last instalment of the purchase price to the Rapps, the drain on his remaining resources would leave him bankrupt by the end of 1826.

There were 140 children at school, funded by the Society, but the passbook system, which put food in their bellies, was pedantically slow in operation and had utterly failed to encourage enterprise. It was clear that scores of people had no business to be in the Preliminary Society at all and were freeloading. Signs of disaffection were already beginning to stir among the emigrants from the English Prairie; and the Methodists, all of whom came from backwood farms and smallholdings, were smouldering at what they perceived as godlessness and worldly vanity.

On the other hand, it was intoxicating for the newcomers to

breathe the sharp clean air of liberty. Maclure and his party elbowed their way into temporary accommodation and walked about the town much more impressed with its potential than the actual. It was after all the dead season of the year and so the appropriate period for forward planning. The past year of misery was not such a very long time (if you had not endured it yourself) and had to be set against the enormity of the task engaged upon. Meanwhile, nobody was actually starving, morale was high generally, and the people were hungry for knowledge. Debates about the politics of common property could be heard over every hearth and public meetings were crammed to the doors.

On these first impressions, then, Maclure was by no means disheartened. The probationary character of the Preliminary Society could be invoked to get rid of scrimshankers and then, as he believed, rational debate would do the rest. It was not in people's nature deliberately to harm themselves. He felt encouraged. William Owen, the caretaker proprietor, was a credit to the Fellenberg system and his brother Robert Dale Owen was if anything even more intelligent.

Maclure was not a farmer but a man most at home among his books. If he generally saw the world from a study window, his travels in America had nevertheless inured him to some terrible inns and taverns and he had pitched up in towns with much more meagre benefits than the one he was in now. In material terms – location, housing stock, general amenities – New Harmony was as good as it got. As for the Society it housed, all that was needed to knock that into shape was time and patience.

He reckoned without Owen. Only thirteen days after his arrival, the Welshman concluded a series of excited harangues and addresses by proposing this resolution to a general meeting: 'that a Community be formed as soon as practicable out of the present Society & that from the formation of this community the Preliminary Society do cease'. With that, time and patience went out of the window, along with all common sense. It was a staggeringly inept move. There was to be no more halfway house, no three year plan – the commune would jump from where it was now direct to the ultimate goal, the Community of Equality. No room for hesitation or equivocation: this was it, all or nothing at all.

If Owen was looking for a way of electrifying his listeners, nothing could have succeeded better. Those looking for decisive action thought they had found it now. The resolution was adopted by acclaim and then people waited for the next big idea. Instead, some of those present immediately called for a constitutional convention. Next day, Dr Price – one of the newcomers – was elected president of the convention and Thomas Pears its secretary. A committee of seven was then chosen to frame a draft constitution. They included both Owen brothers and Captain MacDonald. Owen senior and Maclure excused themselves from the task.

It is very difficult to see why Owen forced the pace in this way. Later on in life he said that such progress had already been made that the old timetable could be thrown out as redundant: this was patently nonsense, as his bank book showed. He had bought New Harmony as a going concern, one which turned over a profit of $20,000 a year. It was now costing him his lifetime accumulation of wealth to sustain the town at even its present broken-winged level – and that was after only one year. The gross imbalance of labour between farmers and others would have been enough to stay the hand of the old Owen, master of New Lanark. Then, the living machinery had been dumb and to some extent blind and was led from its misery by coercion. The present community was not the surly workforce of millhands that Owen inherited from his father-in-law and transformed. These were men and women he believed had drunk at the same well as himself.

There followed twelve days of enthusiastic drafting. Captain

MacDonald was the big surprise, emerging as the committee member who wanted least government of all. He called instead for practical measures 'unencumbered either by Creeds or Codes'. The former soldier was beginning to lose his faith in the Owens. If he had found William Owen hesitant and insecure when the two of them were left to fend off prospective members back in the spring of 1825, he now found Robert Dale Owen far too ingenious, too bunged-full with bright ideas. Meanwhile, Owen senior was working in the background with plans to introduce clauses to the new constitution designed to provide a *daily* audit of how hard each member worked. MacDonald was not impressed. He favoured what he called an 'open family assembly' which presumably included provisions for a clout round the ear to its backsliding members. He called a meeting of his own to canvass support: it failed, possibly because his vision of Harmony was considered too naive. The general feeling was that what was being drafted here was something able to be written in stone and passed down to all posterity.

On 5 February, the new constitution was presented and unanimously adopted. It began, like the Jeffersonian model, with a declaration: 'Our object is that of all sentient beings, happiness.' There were some principles by which this might be achieved and some 'self-evident' truths:

> That man is uniformly actuated by a desire of happiness.
>
> That no member of the human family is born with rights either of possession or exemption superior to those of his fellows.
>
> That freedom in the sincere expression of every sentiment and opinion, and in the direction of every action, is the inalienable right of each human being, and cannot justly be limited except by his own consent.
>
> That the preservation of life, in its most perfect state, is the first of all practical considerations.

There was more in this vein, but the main planks of the constitution were to be found in the clauses providing for a community
of property; the forgoing of all money or credit transactions; and
what was called 'cooperative union in the business and amuse-
ments of life'. Some attempt was made to impose the realities of
government on these wishful thoughts. The community was to
be divided into six departments: agriculture, manufactures and
mechanics, literature, science and mechanics, domestic economy,
general economy and commerce. This was intended as a way of
separating out the occupations and creating a reporting mechan-
ism that would answer to an executive council, charged with
balancing the books weekly. The assembly – the general membership – was charged with giving its opinion of the executive
council each week, and at the same meeting the executive was
also required to say what it thought of the assembly.

America had never been short of schemes of improvement.
The words liberty and freedom had acquired an almost sacred
significance and the most cursed epithet to apply to an enemy
was that he was tyrannical. The constitution of the Community
of Equality as framed was no different in kind. Why should any
random group of people come together and attempt to live not
just in a community of interests but in root and branch rejection
of property, both real and personal? The answer was common
to everyone who signed the document. 'The departure from
the principle of man's equal rights, which is exhibited in the
arrangement of individual property, we have seen succeeded by
competition and opposition, by jealousy and dissension, by
extravagance and poverty, by tyranny and slavery.'

All through the final draft constitution, what we might call
aboriginal Owenism is seen through the enlarging (and distorting)
glass of other minds. He himself could have written 'Man's
character is not of his own formation and reason teaches us that
to a being of such nature, artificial rewards and punishments are

equally inapplicable; kindness is the only consistent mode of treatment, and courtesy the only rational species of deportment.' Elsewhere, he might have baulked at passages like this:

> As to the first and most important knowledge, we desire to know ourselves. But we search for this knowledge in vain if our fellow creatures do not express to us openly and unreservedly what they feel and think. Our know-ledge remains imperfect, therefore, without sincerity. We have seen misery produced by the great leading principles which prevail over the world; therefore we have not adopted them. We have always found truth productive of happiness and error of misery; truth, therefore, leads to our object, and we agree to follow truth only.

Three days later came an instance of just how disagreeable the truth can be. The Preliminary Society, as part of its winding up, produced a report on how much labour had actually been expended in its brief existence. The figures were disastrous. Thomas Pears explained why. 'They have not by their Valuation List of labour, allowed me and the children who work, enough to pay the board of the family according to the low rates of board established by the Committee themselves.' This cost was set at a mere 64 cents a week and yet it appeared that even the secretary of the Community of Equality, after a year's service to the town, was in net debt. It was a colossal blow to the new constitution and the mood plunged from elation to despair in a day.

It was clear that the productivity of the commune was going to be the key point in its survival and not what it thought about truth or justice. There had been a proposal that in the change to the fully-fledged Community of Equality, some sort of probation-ary membership should be introduced. This was thrown out as being contrary to the spirit of the new constitution. The effect was to leave in place unproductive members who had no more intention of working at manual tasks than the grandest duke in

Britain, or the most reactionary foreign prince. Their idleness forced down the value of labour expended by the rest. As an economic enterprise, New Harmony was dead in the water and it would take not months but years to set things right.

The community was in the position of having organised a great feast, attended with the headiest wines, only to find it could not pay the bill. Confidence in Owen collapsed. Ten days after the new constitution was unanimously approved, 80 of the members changed their mind in the most dramatic way possible. They asked Owen to lease them uncleared land two miles from New Harmony, packed their bags and left.

TEN

Let every herring hang by its own head

The defection of 80 people from a total of 1,000 was not economically significant but had a disproportionate psychological effect. On windless days, the renegades' axes could be clearly heard – cutting timber for nine log cabins, girdling the bigger trees to stop the flow of sap and so kill them that way, improvising fences to guard their sowings of Indian corn. Righteousness and indignation gave them strength – even with next to no material assets they found time to plunder their stock of candles and write a constitution in outright contradiction of the one they had just abandoned. Although Owen referred to them with heroic calm as Community No. II, they preferred to call their miserable little clearing Macluria.

The majority of the Maclurians were native-born backwoodsmen, hardbitten Methodists for whom their former leader's want of religion was offensive (though if they had known Maclure better they would have found him no less atheistical). It may also have been the case that east coast manners stuck in their craw. Long before the boatload of knowledge hove into view, New Harmony began to exhibit a fault line between the educated and the plain spoken. It was in a way a battle between the axe and the pen. Maybe the families who left to found Macluria – and they included many of those previously listed as farmers – had grown tired of what seemed to them cultured indolence. We

know the weekly cotillions and concerts of music that gave so
much pleasure to the many seemed disgustingly sybaritic to the
few. A battered fiddle or a military fife was perhaps permissible;
anything else was contrary to the true spirit of the west. But
neither principle nor religion was the main reason for the
Maclurians' declaration of independence. They had to eat and
they thought they could do better on their own. Though
Methodist infighting undid them in the end, that summer they
triumphantly sold their food surplus to the New Harmony store.

Less than a month after their departure, 40 of the English
farmers who had been so star-struck by Owen in 1824, the same
men who had gathered round him in the open air and heard him
promise them heaven on earth, also made up their mind to leave.
Owen leased them the same amount of land he had given
Macluria. Uncertain what to call themselves (though 'Disgusted
of New Harmony' would have met their mood) they allowed
Stedman Whitwell his head and with British phlegm set up in a
hole in the woods named Feiba Peveli. Unabashed, Owen referred
to them as Community No. III.

There was even a Community No. IV in contemplation, this
time to be led by Owen's two sons. Far from seeing this as the
ultimate challenge to his authority, their father tried to turn the
growing wave of panic to his advantage. He was after all in
the position of distinguished author of the grand scheme, while
the men who wrote the constitution of 5 February were already
reviled and discredited. That particular hotchpotch of high flown
sentiments and lofty aspirations was in tatters. The assembly that
had endorsed it with such unanimous warmth now came to Owen
and asked him to run New Harmony himself, under any system
he chose.

Once again, he fluffed a political opportunity, not from timidity
but what was becoming a fatal inclination always to look on the
bright side. Instead of knocking heads together he tried to rally

his troops. There *was* no weakness in the constitution. He managed to persuade the assembly that it had always been in his mind that a confederated community of interests would result from the January deliberations. After all, the Community of Equality was supposed to replicate itself the world over and the chips that flew now were no disgrace but a healthy sign of its capacity to redivide. (As for his sons, Owen was quite clever about that: he gave them his blessing to go and cut down as many trees as they liked. They thought it over and stayed put.)

This new predilection for looking on the bright side was one explanation of Owen's lack of control; but there was another. At root, Owen was a solitary. Captain MacDonald was a companion and nothing more: his sons were an extension – he hoped – of his own personality. The one thing Owen did not understand was the tug of inertia on human events. The seasoned soldier in MacDonald might have told him not to expect too much of any given plan but instead Owen was in the position of a rocketeer who has done everything but calculate the forces acting against his creation.

The situation, as Owen saw it, was volatile, but not impossible. If, like many Harmonists, you were losing touch with the real world in the constant blizzard of letters, pamphlets, editorials and public meetings, through the murk there were some hazy outlines of solid ground still to be seen. Owen still controlled the *New Harmony Gazette*, that sturdy megaphone of propaganda; his gift for loquacious and extempore sermonising had not deserted him; and in an atmosphere heavy with moral fervour his unshakeable self-belief commanded awed respect. He dressed like a poor man, took his coffee in the tavern like the lowliest Rappite before him and yet, when he looked out of the grimy windows, saw visions. The mud and the endlessly chuntering hogs disappeared and in their place were palaces of reason, temples of culture.

There was also the matter of his money. Under the community of property, nobody owned anything. The more honest communitarians were forced to admit that though Owen – shamefully in their eyes – actually owned the entire town, he was also liable for all its debts. Sound men like Mr Pelham and Mr Pears who saw him at his seat in the tavern, so quiet and unassuming, recognised a battered hero. They understood money. Every week that passed whittled away at the Owen fortune and though people generally thought him much richer than he was, without his subsidies the economy would collapse in a month.

The reason was perfectly simple: the town was not producing enough by its own efforts. Having to buy food from outside when 3,000 acres lay cleared was a recipe for disaster. From the point of view of a single worker, however, the exchange of labour for money resulted in what seemed like niggardly and insulting returns. Joseph Walters came to New Harmony in October 1825 and went to work in the tanyard. In February of the following year he had suffered enough and asked for his account to be made up, for he was leaving. The committee calculated that he had worked 15¾ weeks at a rate of $130 a year. This gave him an income of $39.37. However, he had drawn $32.23 for his food and board. There was a further charge on his labour for compulsory contributions to the school and medical funds and these deductions came to $6.69. When the final balance was struck, Joseph Walters had come to New Harmony to work at one of the dirtiest trades and left with 45 cents in his pocket. He was angry enough to walk to the *Illinois Gazette* offices in Shawnee-Town and spill the beans. The details of his service and its rewards were printed under the motto ''Tis here but yet confused – knavery's plain face is never seen till us'd.'

Some elements of the general situation worked in Owen's favour. The embittered backwoodsmen who left to found Macluria were among the most rough and ready Harmonists and were secretly considered no great loss by the rest. Many people found the arrogance and chauvinism of the departed English just as offensive. The Reverend Jennings, who so delighted in putting down visiting preachers on Sunday, overplayed his hand and was sharply censured for holding up the Society itself to ridicule. He left in April. Captain MacDonald, the diarist who had seen Owen at his most manic, had also gone, setting off down the Mississippi for New Orleans and a passage to Cuba. (MacDonald never wrote one word of criticism about his mentor, even though his disillusion was complete.) Finally and most importantly, Maclure, living in the same house as Madame Fretageot, was holding his tongue. He might be biding his time, but as yet the two men had not quarrelled.

Robert Dale Owen's idea of dividing the community into occupation-based departments was also showing some slight returns. It was the one piece of the February constitution that had an immediate outcome, for it forced members to say, not who they were and what they wanted, but what they could do. It also opened up a very necessary debate about the value of labour. Obviously, a girl raised on a farm could milk a cow much faster than a city girl from Philadelphia, yet if the city girl had a willing heart, who was to say she should be paid less for her efforts? Again, some carpenters did more in an hour than some others who were just as skilful: it was the way craftmanship operated. Who was to say which man was the more productive? A barn built by a slow moving fellow was still at the end of the day a finished barn.

There was practical urgency to these questions. Owen had bought Harmony for $125,000 and then let out his property at absurdly low rates. At some point soon – not to help him especi- ally but as a matter of principle – there would have to be a valuation exercise and his tenants (as, of course, they were under the old and despised 'individual system') must free themselves of obligation to their landlord and buy. It was the one unavoidable issue for Harmonists of conscience. If there was a single unifying motive that had brought all these men and women to the west in the first place, it was to call no man master. The constitution, intended to point the way down the ages, entirely omitted the uncomfortable fact that all its signatories were in effect Owen's pensioners. Could they be free and in debt to him at the same time? Sharpening the point: unless Owen was bought out in some way, could a true community of property ever come into existence, at least among men of honest mind?

It was now that Maclure struck. He had brought himself and his colleagues from the east to live and work as scholars and educationists, not ditchdiggers or cowherds. His invaluable collections – and those of his friends like Say and LeSueur – were being transferred from Philadelphia on an almost daily basis. Whether his neighbours understood him or not, he was laying down something of permanent intellectual value, for which he needed buildings, funding and – to an extent not yet realised by Owen – independence. Maclure was a man with a perfectly clear agenda, about which he was prepared to be ruthless. More than that, he left had Philadelphia with this need for ruthlessness already fixed in his mind.

The real 'Macluria' was located not out in the dripping woods but inside the town boundaries and described an aristocracy of talents that could never be properly recompensed by the existing system. Someone recently – some crazed enthusiast – had invented a Harmonist uniform based on rational principles, a sort of fanciful (and unisex) trouser suit, tied off at the ankles with tape. Most people found it ridiculous and impractical but Maclure's circle wore it with pride. It emblematised their difference.

The question their leader put was very simple: were distinguished scholars making the best use of their time by participating in the general corvée, milking cows, pushing wheelbarrows and tending sheep? Maclure thought not. Reading a book or examining a geological specimen might not be immediately to the general good but it was no danger to the overarching principle. New Harmony must accept that 'those who work with their heads, or mental labour, are as productive as those who work with their hands'. Under a properly balanced economy and with the community in surplus, this might have led to an instructive debate at one of the evening meetings. Maclure brought it forward at a time when it was certain to provoke outrage.

Not all those who did work with their hands to save Harmony were accustomed to such menial and back-breaking tasks. Many thought their labours could have been better directed. If men with soft hands like Thomas Pears could make the sacrifice, then why not men like William Maclure? It seemed suddenly that not only were all pigs not equal, but even some of those more equal than others wanted additional special privileges. The Literati, as they were called, wandering about in their rational pantaloons, became deeply unpopular. It looked as though everyone was making sacrifices except these newcomers.

Maclure did not waver. He proved an exceedingly tough-minded man who knew how to get what he wanted. He pressed, and on 28 May, the third revision of the original constitution was made. He was its sole author. The town was now to be divided into three independent communities – a School and Education Society, an Agricultural and Pastoral Society and a Manufacturing Society. Each would be represented on a Board of Union. It was, as Maclure put it, in a reversion to the language of his Scottish childhood, a system designed 'to let every herring hang by its own head'. Let the agriculturalists have the fields and the mechanics the workshops and do with them what they will. He would take possession of the three largest buildings – the granary, Rapp's old meeting house and the deconsecrated church. What was more, he would buy them outright.

It was a shockingly brutal move, like a scythe through dandelion heads, and it left Owen completely outflanked. Though he owned every other building that stood and was subsidising their rents to an impossible degree, the founder and first begetter was driven back on control of the store and the tavern. By the logic of Maclure's argument, there was nothing else left. The cruellest of Owen's detractors at once claimed he had assumed 'the characters of a retailer and tavern keeper, to save by ninepenny and four-pence-half-penny gains, after the manner of pedlars, the money which he had lost'.

Maclure's redivision of the community proposed that each Society run its business its own way and find its own method of paying for labour. There would be a free exchange of goods and services but the financial obligation of the individual member would be limited to the Society he chose to join and not to the assembly as a whole. There would be no more fine words about the future of mankind, no more visionary expostulations. A man's duty would be in the first instance to his companions in the Society. If he performed well there, the greater common good would be served. As Maclure was very ready to point out, the number of children in school, which was now under his direct care, had doubled to nearly 400 since his arrival. Was not that a clear example of how the system might work?

The community as a whole was ready to accept just about anything that would get them out of their miseries. There were some truly absurd conflicts: two rationalist sisters in search of the sincerity advocated in the original constitution set about each other with fists; a plot of early cabbages rotted on the stalk because it could not be decided whose job it was to cut them. On days when lightning threatened, an elderly man called Greenwood patrolled the streets with a twelve-foot iron rod. He was tired of life in New Harmony but could not bring himself to end it by his own hand. The rational solution was to save someone else's life at the cost of his own. In the school one day, children provoked one of their teachers, the superwet Monsieur Balthazar, into a duel with a colleague. Both pistols were charged with powder only, but when Balthazar's opponent obligingly feigned death for the sake of the joke, the poor man suffered a nervous breakdown and took himself off back to Europe.

Also flitting about the streets was a Thersitical figure, in the shape of Paul Brown. Brown was a recent arrival who claimed to have heard about the great adventure when a guest of friends in Tennessee. He at once set off for Indiana with all speed. Brown was a Quaker with a couple of books to his name, unmarried, unloved and bristling with indignation. Maybe he came to New Harmony to have his feathers smoothed but, once installed, he found ample opportunity to exhibit the cantankerous side of his nature. The book he wrote about his experiences was published after the death of New Harmony and in it he spares his subject nothing. 'The individual suffering from the privations and embarrassments arising out of the continual shifting of arrangements, as well as by the circumscription of subsistence, deadened the wonted sympathy of many ingenuous souls. Money was in higher repute than in any other town, and became almost an object of worship.'

This last sentence was grotesquely unfair. If Brown had any friends at all in the town, they were drawn from the ranks of those who thought it Owen's duty to put his hand in his pocket down to the last cent, while they wrestled with nobler ideas and aspirations. Brown had experienced dark secondary consequences to this love of money. 'The sexes fought like cats and dogs about individual marriages, there was no politeness between the single persons of the two sexes, but a dark, sullen, cold, suspicious temper, and a most intolerable, miserly allusion to individual property as the standard of worth.'

Brown was one of the most vociferous critics of luxury. It

appalled him to think of all those candles burning to stubs while girls he fancied for himself danced the night away with more agreeable partners. The search for pleasure shocked him deeply, or so he said. He discovered people playing cards and that set him in a tizzy. A Punch and Judy show in the school drew down magnificent wrath. He was not getting his points across as he would wish, and not just in the ballroom. The out and out communist was having trouble with his linen. 'The single men of the town were generally obliged to make their own beds, carry their clothes to wash and recover them when they could, as much as if they had belonged to an army. Everyone was for himself, as the saying is.'

Brown was an example not unknown in present times of an educated man drawn to politics out of sheer hatred of other people. He had a madman's energy – calling meetings, writing tedious and tendentious letters to the *Gazette*, printing handbills which he nailed to doors and trees.

'What can a person lose, as an individual? He can lose what he owns. How much does one own? That which makes him comfortable and nothing more . . . if he has more than this, it does not belong to him . . . All that this man, then, would have lost as an individual would be his comfortable living in a community for the present moment.'

Which described him to the letter, a single man with not much more than the clothes he stood up in. Maclure was probably thinking of zealots like Brown when a good-hearted Harmonist said that after all the trials and tribulations of that summer of 1826, all the leave-takings and desertions, only a quarter of those remaining could be described as 'good for nothing'. Maclure fixed him with a glare and replied that he thought the truer figure was between three-quarters and nine-tenths.

The community was in its death throes. There was a fourth revision of the constitution and then a fifth but the details hardly matter. It comes to the point where it is easier not to think of New Harmony as a tangle of high ideals and wishful thinking, lost opportunities or mistaken ideals but instead to walk away from the town out into the fields. There the peach and apple orchards gave way to fields reaching to a wall of aboriginal forest. There was a silence here far more melancholy than any to be found in the fevered babble taking place in the streets. For two years no crop of any significance had been grown. There were Rappite vineyards gone to ruin and orchards where the fruit rotted in the ground – altogether almost 3,000 acres lay fallow. What had seemed to Captain MacDonald like parkland when he first clapped eyes on it in the winter of 1824 was reverting to scrub.

MacDonald had been specifically attracted to communitarianism because of its close connections to the land and the dignity a poor man could recover by working the soil and providing for his own. Stripped of his rank and the xenophobia that came as naturally to him as the air he breathed, life under the Rapps might have satisfied him more than life with their successors. But then, if Owen had thought clearly about the delegation of duties, he could have harnessed the captain's unimaginative stolidity and turned it to better use. As an army officer, MacDonald knew only too well that things were quite as likely to go wrong as succeed. Moreover, in the end, everything went wrong. The soldier's duty was to stand his ground and take the consequences. It was the difference between the parade ground and the battle-field: the future of Harmony lay in these forsaken acres. As it was, nothing but the ghost of Father's mocking smile hung over them.

Maclure's temper was shortening. He found the summer climate enervating – he was a stout and not very healthy man in his sixties – but the real reason for his growing irritation was Owen. He wrote to Madame Fretageot, 'My experience at Harmony has given me such a horror for the reformation of grown persons that I shudder when I reflect having so many of my friends so near such a desperate undertaking.' For the word friends, he meant her to read herself, of course, but also all the other Literati. Gadflys like Brown he could ignore, as he did the saintly Mr Greenwood wandering round with his lightning rod. There was only one cause of error: Owen was incapable of administering his great idea. Maclure put the case in a single muddy but devastating sentence. If Madame Fretageot had to read it twice to sort out the syntax, the underlying meaning was inescapable. 'I must repeat that the cooperative system has rose in my esteem and strong conviction of its utility, in exact proportion as the positive conviction of Mr O's mode being the ruin of it for some time in this country, and that he has been working hard to defeat his own views.'

Poor Owen. In August 1826 he inaugurated a system of 'social education' to be held three times a week and attended by all adults and their children. Maclure had gone south for a few months to seek a better climate, otherwise he might have stopped this project in its tracks. What Owen was trying to do was little more than browbeating, such as had produced results in New Lanark among men who after all owed him their livelihood. If the town had no sense of citizenship, then he would teach it some. The scheme 'requires no more than an honest endeavour on your part to attend regularly, take your seats quietly, and listen attentively. By this simple process, you will acquire a better education and more valuable knowledge than has been given by any system of instruction heretofore put into practice.' Heckled, contradicted, broken up by repeated interruptions about money matters, Owen's lectures lasted only a few weeks.

The full horror of his position was that to make use of the hall for these meetings and moreover to demand the presence of the schoolchildren at them, he was trespassing not metaphorically but actually on land now owned by Maclure. He assumed Maclure saw himself as a partner and that what was done in Owen's name would inevitably be endorsed. He was wrong, Maclure had a very ready store of invective for others less gifted than himself but had never before used it on Owen. His contempt was all the more wounding now for being silently expressed. It had become clear to everyone in the community except Owen himself that he was sidelined. Neither Maclure nor any member of the Literati would lift a finger to help him.

In February 1827, the curtain went up on the final act. Frederick Rapp arrived from Economy to claim the last instalment of the purchase price. One glance round the town and its familiar streets was sufficient to prepare him for Owen's news: he could not pay. Rapp was offered semi-coherent accounts of 1,000-year leases of land the Rappites themselves had cleared, now put out to tender.

Rapp stood his ground. The balance due was $20,000, a sum that in his day Father could have paid in coin drawn from under the prophet's bed. Maybe Frederick Rapp knew – there were plenty to tell him – that Owen had wasted $200,000 turning a money-making concern into the shambles that New Harmony now was. If he did know this, he was not going to let it cloud his judgement. Sympathy had no part to play in business with the devil and what Rapp saw in his casual inspection of the property, all that he heard from the clamouring unbelievers who crowded the tavern, was a clear demonstration of Babylon.

The only man who could pay the debt was William Maclure. As soon as he was Owen's creditor, the rest of the story was inevitable. The 1,000-year leases were shown to be fantasies – Paul Brown reporting the real situation with sadistic glee. In one corner of the 3,000-acre estate he found four backwoods families occupying a single cabin. The only other smoke rising anywhere in Owen's fields came from the chimneys of 'three or four poor families of German immigrants, just arrived in the country'. A little further afield, Feiba Peveli staggered on with typical British obstinacy. The Methodists in Macluria had vanished and their cabins were deserted. As for New Harmony, far too late in the day, undesirables and freeloaders were evicted. Egged on by Brown, they asked for their travel expenses to be paid. At God knows what cost to his emotions, Owen agreed.

In May, about the time of his 56th birthday, he finally gave up. Characteristically, he delivered not one but two farewell addresses, lengthy and rhapsodic celebrations of the new age ushered in. There was not a single word of reproach in what he said, neither did anyone plead with him to stay. Maclure ignored him, his sons were grief-stricken but helpless. On 1 June 1827, he left.

He was alone, there were no bands of music playing and nor was the rusting cannon in the riverside weeds fired in his honour. He quitted the town dry-eyed and with his chin up, for it was still in his nature to believe that he was always right. If he had repeatedly misplayed his hand with the argumentative rabble attracted to New Harmony, he remained the ardent advocate of co-operation and communitarianism. Nothing could extinguish that, any more than the total conviction that he had laid down a marker for history.

As he sailed back up the Ohio River, for once without the imperative call of pen and ink to send him down below deck, he could look out on the river bank and be certain he had played for the highest stakes there were. Travelling with him were men with nothing much more on their mind than business in Louisville; or soldiers and their ladies on the way to Pittsburgh. He could be civil to them – in manners he was always more accomplished than his erstwhile partner Mr William Maclure – but what was their existence but the continuation of error, constantly thrashed up like the water churning inside the paddle boxes of the steamer they travelled on? Owen could look with a special regard at the ministers of religion on board. For the time being his taste for controversy was exhausted, but if challenged, he could say with some pride that a saddler's son from Montgomeryshire had – and would never fully relinquish – a benevolence not always found in organised religion.

On the shuddering and complaining deck, beset with cinders and woodsmoke, he was nothing but a passenger like all the rest. That much was true. But open his heart and look inside and there could be found, bloody but still faintly legible, Robert Owen's plan to beat the devil. What other use for reason was there?

ELEVEN

It was not the end. Owen lived another 31 clamorous years and died in harness while scheming to reorganise the education of parish children in his Welsh birthplace, Newtown. By his own request he had been carried there to see out the final week or so of his life, which he spent propped up in bed in the house next door to the one in which he had been born. It may have given him some last satisfaction that the church in which his parents were married and to which their own coffins had been carried was now in ruins: all the same he arranged to be buried beside them.

The brief life and agonised death of the Community of Equality was not even the last of his American adventures, though his subsequent visits to the United States were never so dramatic again. Where before presidents had listened to him with grave faces, their ears bent by the one great rational explanation of all their woes, in the latter days his audiences were half-attentive and easily distracted Congressmen. Five of his eight children now lived in America; his wife and two of his remaining daughters in Britain were dead. He was on his own, as befits a prophet.

The supreme 'one idea' man of his generation carried his tattered banner through the battlefields surrounding the Reform Act, Chartist agitation, and the rise of a formidable Victorian meritocracy that only half remembered him. No prime minister after Lord Liverpool received him and the Prince Consort, irritated by the petitions and memorials with which his wife was being deluged, replied with unfriendly tartness by the hand of his secretary: 'You must be aware that the only constitutional method of addressing the Sovereign upon matters relating to the Government of this Country, is through the advisers of the Crown, who are responsible for the administration of the Government.'

Rail transport, gas lighting, the telegraph, iron ships, mass circulation books and penny newspapers, the rise of political unions on the one hand and the incorporation of the professions on the other, above all the huge leap in population, in which the new victims of society appeared to acquiesce in their own servitude, rose inexorably to mock Owen. He never learned how to be a Victorian: that is to say he never accepted that events so awful to him could be interpreted as progress by others.

For example, George Hudson was originally an apprentice linen-draper in York, just as the young Owen had been in Stamford. Owen had been offered a future partnership after the expiry of his apprenticeship and declined: Hudson accepted the same with alacrity and then, with the additional advantage of a handsome legacy, put his money and his energies into railways. The Railway King ended badly but in the days of his pomp created thousands, possibly tens of thousands of jobs, and was fêted by kings and princes. He was just one among many Victorian entrepreneurs of the same kind. The age of progress depended in the first instance on seeing the world as it was and not as it should be.

Owen's domain shrank to small rented rooms and meeting halls, struggling newspapers, wishful thinkers and (often exasperated) fellow-travellers from the radical left. Even so, he did great things, but always in a contrarian spirit. In 1839, the Owenite London Institution celebrated 'Good Friday in the Christian calendar' with a determinedly secular dance, interspersed with scientific lectures.

> The philosophical experiments, under the management of Mr Thorne, were of a superior description. Amongst some of the experiments were oxy-hydrogen and Bude lights, the last new invention of Mr Gurney for lighthouses; decomposition of various chemical compounds, as sugar, potass, etc; and with a good electrical machine we were able to electrify nearly all present at one time.

The evening concluded with a demonstration of laughing gas. In July, Chartist riots began in Birmingham.

No man gave more of his time and energy to a cause. Whatever was happening in the world of real events, Owen held fast to a single superseding idea: that what was waiting just around the corner was a giant leap into an alternative existence, where the clocks ran suddenly backwards and all the counters were set to zero. The search for Year One transformed even the most unpromising evidence into signs of imminent change.

'The thick clouds are everywhere dispersing,' he wrote once from Barnsley, in the South Yorkshire coalfield. 'The real producers of wealth are beginning everywhere to discover their true position and are preparing to act upon it.'

Owen's convictions were unshakeable and since they were the principal part of him, he was proof against ridicule and despair right to the very end. Nor did he suffer the indignity of losing his mind – extreme old age left him with his faculties intact. George Holyoake was present at his last public appearance, in Liverpool. He was carried into a meeting of the National Association for the Promotion of Social Science, chaired by Lord Brougham. Four policemen managed to get him out of his litter, described by Holyoake as a sedan chair, and he was bundled up on stage a frail old man of 86. After just one sentence of his

address, Brougham, who was also in his eighties, interrupted him
by clapping heartily, saying 'Capital, very good: can't be bettered, Mr Owen. There, that will do.' And then he muttered to
a bystander in a choked undertone, 'Convey the old gentleman
back to his bed.' Three weeks later, Owen was dead.

What Owen was in the last three decades of his life falls outside
the scope of this story. He easily outlived Maclure, who was
driven from Harmony for a different reason – failing health. He
died in retirement in Mexico in 1840. Maclure left New Harmony
two long-lasting legacies: the school, and the quite separate
academy of scientific enquiry it had always been his purpose to
create. The Community of Equality may have collapsed like the
bag of wind it was but the town on which it was founded continued to be famous long after as the birthplace of important
educational innovation.

For those who persevered with Maclure after Owen had gone,
it was very much better to be an educated Philadelphian than it
was to be a child. Under the provisions of the Education Society,
children were taken from their parents at the age of two and
looked after by a good-natured Württemberg woman. She had
not come to America with Rapp, but by a far more romantic
route. Madame Neef's husband was an officer of Napoleon's army
who turned to fatherhood and education after a ball was lodged
in his skull during the Italian campaign. Maclure took him up
in Paris and fetched him first to Philadelphia and then to New
Harmony, where the former soldier stamped and cursed his way
through the education of the younger boys. His wife cared for a
hundred children of nursery school age, who slept at night in
wooden cots suspended from the ceiling, like so many tiny sailors.

The story of New Harmony's educational experiments is almost
as tangled as the search for a perfect constitution. Some of
Maclure's essential heartlessness shines through, for he was as
stubborn as Owen, without the compensations of having had

children or a family life himself. So, in the School of Industry he set up, pupils woke at five in the morning and worked at lessons and practical tasks until eight at night. Seven of their fifteen waking hours were given over to labour. He was forced to acknowledge slow progress. 'The basis of the institution is that the scholars repay their expenses from the proceeds of their seven hours' labour, but to effect this will require several years more.'

Luckily, the scheme collapsed before it could maim and demoralise too many children but in general Maclure believed with a passion in a spartan way of life for the young, who became under his care orphans in all but name. According to him, it was kinder than leaving them in the doubtful care of their mothers and fathers and had the extra advantage of giving parents ample time to reflect on their own stupidity. There is an account left us by one young girl who, though they lived a hundred yards or so away, did not see her parents more than twice in two years.

It is easier to honour Maclure as the dean of the adult faculty, in which his own talents and those of his friends shone. A scholarly library of 2,000 books was gathered in New Harmony, as well as important collections of geology and natural history that would otherwise have stayed on the eastern seaboard. In the very year of Owen's departure, the School Press, nominally under the aegis of the School of Industry, published the first five plates of LeSueur's *American Ichthyology*. These were hand-coloured by children. The headquarters of the United States Geological Survey was sited at New Harmony until 1856, when all the materials were transferred to the Smithsonian Institute in Washington. Another huge gift of New Harmony collections went to Indiana State University and a third to the American Museum of Natural History in New York's Central Park.

After Maclure's departure, his interests were looked after by Marie Fretageot, that pugnaciously shrill and argumentative woman who was always having to fend off accusations that she was her patron's lover. Her child Achille was said to be his, though Maclure found it difficult to feel in the slightest way fatherly towards him. The lad was hyperactive and (mordantly) 'deficient in the foundation of intellectual cogitation'. Even when little Achille had the beginnings of a moustache, he could not tell the difference between the poles and the equator on any globe presented to him and though he spoke English, could not read or write it. He was a wild child with his mother's gallic temper and – apparently – not an ounce of common sense.

Madame Fretageot was probably the most outrageous of the Literati, though her fellow countryman Phiquepal (who taught the rambunctious Achille) ran her close. Guillaume Phiquepal d' Arusmont was only eight years younger than Owen and in his thirties had come to Paris, where Maclure discovered him. It was his proud boast that he could master any mechanical operation simply by studying how others did it. So, anybody could be a carpenter, a tinsmith, or any other kind of tradesman. His contributions to primary and secondary education included the trigonometer, a device by which 'the most useful properties of Euclid are to be reduced to the comprehension of a child five or six years old'. There were other fanciful aids, other ways of impressing on children his unconscious contempt for the world of ideas. Marie Fretageot died suddenly in 1837, on her way to join Maclure in Mexico. But Phiquepal has a part to play in the fate of two more of the characters in this story.

In 1824, when Owen first arrived in America, he followed in the tracks of General Lafayette. Lafayette himself was being stalked by two sisters, Frances and Camilla Wright, originally from Dundee. They had been to America once before, travelling as unaccompanied women barely out of their teens. There was, of course, a book in it, written by Fanny, and this brought her to the attention of Lafayette. He expressed the amiable desire to meet her. She was a striking figure – tall, dark-haired, faintly masculine in appearance and as the old soldier and diplomat soon discovered drunk on hero worship. Lafayette was no slouch in the matter of flirtation but even he found Fanny a little too insinuating, a little too eager to play at daddy's-little-girl. In 1825, at Washington, he disentangled himself from a relationship that was false on both sides and returned alone to France.

If there was one place in America that suited Fanny's loftier aspirations, it was Harmony. She had hit on the idea of forming a small community of freed slaves where the black man and the white could live together on terms of equality, up to and including intermarriage of the races. She was in the audience when Owen made his Washington address to the president and Congress and seems to have followed him down the Ohio. She was certainly in Harmony the day the last of the Rappites left to tears and cannon-smoke. Almost every kind of communitarian searched out the town in those first heady months and Fanny and her sister Camilla were for the moment just faces in the crowd. But those who got to know her learned that she was very ambitious, extremely well connected, and when it came to an impractical idea, unstoppable. And was there anyone of the high-minded swanning about who particularly caught her eye? There was one – George Flower.

Flower had a credential guaranteed to warm Fanny's heart. In 1823, he kitted out six families of freed slaves from southern Illinois with tools, clothing and provisions and bought them tickets to Haiti. It was true that they were flung in jail the moment they got as far as New Orleans but their benefactor stumped up $360 in court fees (nearly twice the annual income of a working white man) to have them released and sent on their way. This created a bond of sympathy with Fanny Wright and there may have been more to it – much more – than that. In the autumn of 1825, he and Fanny sailed alone down the Mississippi to Memphis, leaving Camilla Wright to lodge with Eliza Julia, who was nursing her fourth surviving baby, a boy archly named Camillus.

Much ink has been spilt over whether the relationship between George and Fanny was sexual. It may have been infatuation on his side and skilful manipulation on hers; if it was love, it was never declared in public. However, Fanny Trollope, the mother of the novelist, met them both in Tennessee and reported to a friend 'it is said without scruple that she has had a connection with George Flower'. It seems plausible. Otherwise, trying to make some sense of Fanny Wright's disastrous investment in emancipation politics was a very strange thing for Flower to be doing, in light of the convulsions already taking place under his nose in Harmony, likely to touch his future far more directly.

He and his father Richard gave financial help in the purchase of some not very promising land at Nashoba, on the Wolf River, about fourteen miles from Memphis. As he might have guessed, Fanny, who wore the flimsy (some scandalised contemporaries said see-through) dress of the Literati as she strode about the ugly little clearing, was of no great practical help. Flower went back to Albion in December but it was not to see his wife and family. He came to fetch more provisions and set off again before Christmas. He got 50 miles downriver to a place called Flims when he was pole-axed by a raging fever. Friends only found him by accident, after he had been fleeced of everything he possessed by the semi-savage locals.

Nursing mother or not, Eliza Jane hitched up a wagon and drove to rescue him. The wagon overturned, she was carried the rest of the way and found her husband in a filthy cabin, half starved and gnawing his finger ends. He had narrowly avoided being eaten by hogs. This would have been enough adventure for most couples, the entrancing Wright sisters or not, but in February 1826 Eliza Julia dutifully went south with her husband and made an effort to establish Nashoba on a proper footing.

The sisters, so amiable over the teacups, so ready to talk up a good cause for the betterment of humanity, found the practical details of community building tedious in the extreme. Their black heroes (the bewildered slaves they had purchased) were a disappointment to them. Soon enough, Fanny and her sister deserted the Flowers in this fever-ridden hell-hole to go back to New Harmony for the summer. And at that Eliza put her foot down. She had seen quite enough of these preposterous women and in October 1827 persuaded her husband to take her back to Albion, this time for good. Camilla Wright wrote of them: 'He is a very amiable man & his society a great loss . . . Our anticipations with regard to his wife have not been so fully realised – she is not in any way suited to fill any station in this establishment nor does she possess a mind calculated to enter into the views connected with it.'

Not to be found worthy of the Nashoba project can be considered as a badge of honour, given the way it turned out. George and Eliza Flower did well to extricate themselves and they leave the story with some dignity. The years rolled on and they died of ripe old age on the same day in January 1862, she in the morning, he in the afternoon. The nineteen-year-old girl who had refused Morris Birkbeck in order to make a bigamous marriage gave her husband thirteen children, the youngest of whom was killed fighting on the Union side in the Civil War.

Fanny Wright was not easily discouraged. Rejected by Flower, she turned to Robert Dale Owen for her solace and in 1828 we find her with him in New York (a much better address) living *en commune* with Phiquepal, Camilla and a newly ensnared husband. There they were joined by two more of Robert Owen's children, Richard and David Dale. (The long-suffering William was once again left behind in New Harmony.) Another complicated chapter of high-minded flirtation and intellectual irresponsibility began, only ended when Fanny decamped to France with the elderly

Phiquepal, whom she married and who, of course, ruined her. In 1830, the *New York Courier*, believing her to be quitting America for ever, wrote a premature epitaph couched in fizzing doggerel.

> She beat Jemima Wilkinson,
> Joanna Southcott quite,
> E'en Mother Lee was nothing to
> Our little Fanny Wright.
> For she had gold within her purse,
> And brass upon her face;
> And talent indescribable
> To give old thoughts new grace.
> And if you want to raise the wind,
> Or breed a moral storm
> You must have one bold lady-man
> To preach about reform.

Fanny Wright did come back to America and died in Cincinnati in December 1852, after dragging herself round with a broken hip got while falling on some ice the previous winter. Her sister Camilla was long dead. The highly unpleasant Phiquepal, who had divorced his tempestuous wife out of exasperation with her ideas, outlived her by five years and died forgotten in Paris.

In the aftermath to the Community of Equality, a story gradually emerges in which the children of Robert Owen are left as guardians of the great idea, much altered by the one obstacle to which he himself paid little heed – the saving ability that human beings can muster for compromise. Much of the town was still owned by their father, though the return made on capital was derisory. As the original Rappite buildings grew older, they sagged a little and in general the crisp outline of the original town softened. Among academics, or at Washington, the address was as well known as any in America but locally the economic force it once had been departed for ever.

Of all the Owen children, Robert Dale inherited his father's owlishness most. After the scandal of the Fanny Wright connection he married a plain and sensible New York girl of nineteen who gave him six children. In the story of Harmony, Mary Jane Owen touches hands with the equally unassuming Mrs Thomas Pears, who left in 1828: the emptiness and coarseness of Indiana frontier life oppressed her but like the older woman she made the best of it. Robert Dale became a Congressman and kept up bachelor arrangements in Washington: Mary Jane grew vegetables in New Harmony, a little crookback figure who rose at five and walked uncomplainingly out into the fields.

The long-suffering William at last got something out of his struggles with the Preliminary Society. In 1835 he married a girl whose parents had come to New Harmony in that first heady rush ten years earlier. It was a triple wedding: in the same ceremony William's two younger brothers were married to daughters of Joseph Neef. It brings some welcome sunshine and happiness to the story. David Dale Owen was a qualified doctor who was also a distinguished geologist. In 1837, he was commissioned to survey first Indiana and then Minnesota, Wisconsin and Iowa. He took with him as assistant on his field explorations his brother Richard, who in time became state geologist of Indiana and professor of natural sciences. (He also served as a colonel of infantry on the Union side in the Civil War.)

Richard Owen was the youngest of the children who followed their father to America and he outlived all the rest. He died in New Harmony in 1890, a month or so after the inauguration of the president, Benjamin Harrison, the grandson of Indiana's famed William Henry Harrison, the man who led the wild tracts of Indiana to statehood in the now forgotten days of log cabins and hard cider.

These brief histories – and that of Owen himself in his later years – point up a feature of human existence the architect of the Community of Equality too easily overlooked. What Owen described as error is not a quantity but a quality: in human affairs, arithmetic solves nothing and the capacity to rub along is not merely the greater part of human history, but its one real story line. The endless abrasion sometimes produces sparks, sometimes outright conflagration but never a single searing consequence. The failure of Harmony affected hundreds, the failure of Soviet communism millions upon millions. In both cases, what was missing from the equation was the ineradicable modesty of human wishes.

Ralph Waldo Emerson met the great agitator in 1845 and overheard what sounds at first like a startlingly frank admission. 'He was then seventy years old, and being asked "Well, Mr Owen, who is your disciple? How many men are there possessed of your views who will remain after you are gone to put them into practice?" he replied "Not one."'

Emerson was intrigued, for he admired the benevolence in Owen and the apparently charitable construction he put on human nature and its possibilities. He saw him as a saintlike figure but may also have sensed the egotism of the saint, for whom the truth is always at heart personal and individual. Emerson's own life experience was one of loss and disillusion; he was an unhappy man who had taught himself to come to terms with circumstance. After meeting Owen, he put the problem with an elegant and moving simplicity. 'One feels that these philosophers have skipped no fact but one, namely life.'

There remains to be told what happened to Rapp's Harmony Society after its return to Pennsylvania. The miracle of hard work given freely as the expression of faith continued. Economy was soon the admiration of all Beaver County. As time went by, steamboat excursions from Pittsburgh were promoted to inspect the beauties of the extensive estates. The Society, ageing noticeably and by now with only a distant memory of its Württemberg origins, continued its patient cultivation of the fields and the manufacture of high-quality goods. From the deck of an excursion steamer the faithful could be observed moving about their tasks with quiet unhurried tread.

The serenity on offer at Economy, the subject of dozens of pencil sketches and poems, was for many a metaphor for how to live in the world, rather than how to escape it. How strange it was that the creeping brown clad figures in the landscape had seen Pittsburgh only once or twice in their lifetimes and had no idea – and no interest in – how it had turned from the muddy river port they remembered into Steel City. It was a sobering thought, too, that these frail men and women had, if they ever cared to exercise it, economic power almost beyond imagining. If the accumulated wealth of the Society was at some time put to work, it could almost literally move mountains. If it were ever realised as individual shares, the sums involved would make every person in view as rich as any man in Pennsylvania.

Benjamin Franklin would have understood: Owen never. Economy was the third and final draft of the City on the Hill and the triumph of some very American virtues – hard work, determination and a certain cold-blooded ruthlessness. The Day of Judgment had not fallen on the world as Rapp had promised: on the other hand the intellectual contempt heaped on the Society in its earliest days had turned to wonder. 'Divine Providence,' Franklin once said of the quarrel between America and Great Britain, 'first infatuates the power it designs to ruin.' Providence dealt far more kindly with the Harmony Society. Blessings had showered down on it.

The greatest surprise to the faithful was Frederick Rapp's unexpected death in 1843. But by now habits of obedience were so deeply ingrained that this calamity made no great difference to the rank and file. They worked, they worshipped, they slept. Father, by now a very old man (he had been born in the time of the Seven Years' War) died in 1847, the year Marx and Engels began writing the *Communist Manifesto*.

The membership of the Society had dwindled to 280 survivors, who appointed in place of the beloved George Rapp a Board of Elders, under whose direction they set out to weather the future. Before his death Father had made a last address which contained this injunction: 'Never let the fire on the altar go out!' And this they honoured in their own way. Since no one had ever owned personal property, there was no such thing as a will or testament. Harmony's great wealth remained indivisible. It struck the Elders that the thing to do was to invest the accumulated funds that had been garnered over 50 years in railway stocks, a bridge company and oil. It was hardly throwing the money away – the Society inexorably became super-rich. The membership grew if anything even more devout, rationalising their new income as gifts laid before Christ in earnest of their fidelity.

Just as Victorian England swallowed up Owenism, at any rate in its original form, so America found a way of assimilating the Rappites. For some years the principal trustee of Harmony was the gentle celibate Jacob Henrici, who joined the Society in 1826. After his death, it was revealed he had harboured an impossible love for John Rapp's daughter Gertrude, whose piano playing had so entranced Captain MacDonald. Henrici lived in George Rapp's house as his spiritual successor, where the walls were decorated with prints showing the disastrous consequences of carnal knowledge, beginning with Adam and Eve. This saintly oddity controlled a fortune worth billions of dollars in today's terms. Though he refused to be photographed out of spiritual modesty, there is a stolen picture of him leaving his house, a little old man in a black suit and a beaver hat, for all the world like a Wall Street banker hiding in a monastery. He died on Christmas Day 1892 and the stage was set for the era of John Duss.

Duss was born in Cincinnati in 1860. When he was a year old, his father seems to have deserted the family to go to New Orleans, a move that resulted in him being recruited into the Confederate forces during the Civil War. At the Battle of Bull Run, Duss senior ran away from the rebel lines and enlisted – or was dragooned – into the Union army. His luck ran out at Gettysburg. He died of wounds in a military hospital in 1863, twenty days after the battle.

Duss and his formidable mother Susie had fitful connections to Economy over the years but the son did not come to live there full-time until 1890. Within two years he was made sole trustee. Of all the things that Duss might have done with the money, his choice was the most bizarre that imagination can supply. In the 30 years of his life before he found Economy, Duss had been a homesteader, a horse-wrangler, a tailor and a schoolteacher. The huge wealth he now controlled gave him the idea that what he really wanted from life was to own and conduct a symphony orchestra. In the summer of 1902, the *New York Herald Tribune* ran this headline. MILLIONAIRE MAKES HIS DEBUT WITH BAND. DUSS, OWNER OF THE TOWN OF ECONOMY, IS ORIGINAL, AND HIS MUSICIANS MAKE LOTS OF NOISE.

The following year, Duss resigned from the Society and was paid off with a $500,000 'departing gift'. He was not finished with music – he had barely started – but the 'fame' he had brought to Economy by his assault on Broadway brought a hundred years of history to a close. The Harmony Society sank into that most American of all fates – extensive litigation and a hunt for the missing millions.

So, the quarrel between reason and religion that led to the foundation of Harmony in the first place and was dramatised by Owen's purchase of its Indiana base played itself out. George Rapp had not the slightest intellectual interest in what later Americans characterised as Progress and, for different reasons, neither did Owen. They were each locked into conflicting views of human nature, which though poles apart, shared one thing in common. For either man to be justified, history would have to be seen to stop in its tracks, either by Christ's intervention, or in Owen's case, the substitution of a new moral order altogether.

Perhaps the devil's plan is to cover human history in dust, not whipped up by satanic storms but laid down mote by mote, an almost insensible thickening and blurring of outline that every successive generation assumes to be the true shape of the world. Only the exceptional have eyesight keen enough to notice this, or the will to do something about it. George Rapp and Robert Owen were two such radicals, insisting from opposite ends of the political spectrum that the rest of us were being beguiled or betrayed by the devil's fiendish tricks. For most people, however, revelation is a price too high to pay. The dust, after all, is never so thick as to threaten our survival and the perceived value of a salary or a love affair, family life or the national interest, even our personal salvation, may be approximate but is nevertheless sufficient. We are not unconscious of the dust but explain its presence with a long suffering quietude. What else, we say, are we to expect? Nothing lasts for ever.

At which, the devil smiles.

BOOKS CONSULTED

No student of George Rapp and the Harmony movement can fail to acknowledge the monumental contributions of Karl J. R. Arndt. Dr Arndt compiled and edited twenty years of the correspondence of the Rappite Harmony, published in two volumes in 1975 and 1978 (*A Documentary History of the Indiana Decades of the Harmony Society*, Indiana Historical Society). He followed Rapp from Iptingen to his death in *George Rapp's Harmony Society, 1785–1847* and completed his work with *George Rapp's Successors and Material Heirs, 1847–1916*. His energy and scholarship have been a major guide to understanding a remarkable life.

Robert Owen is better known in Britain and has attracted a wide range of commentary. His autobiography, *The Life of Robert Owen*, was written in the last years of his life and takes the story only as far as 1820. The most complete biography is Frank Podmore's two-volume *Robert Owen* (Hutchinson, 1906). Podmore was the first to describe Owen as a prophet and the most helpful examination of that claim is entitled *Robert Owen, Prophet of the Poor: Essays in Honour of the Two-hundredth Anniversary of his Birth*, edited by Sidney Pollard and John Salt (Macmillan, 1971).

Owen's reputation has suffered a long and not altogether ungraceful declension. The best short biography is *Robert Owen of New Lanark* by Margaret Cole (Batchworth, 1953). Mrs Cole was then at the heart of studies promoting Owen as a socialist and seer. Her little book is the exemplum of wry common sense.

Other books consulted:

Bailyn, Bernard, *The Peopling of British North America: An Introduction*, I. B. Tauris, 1986

Becker, C. L., *The Heavenly City of the Eighteenth Century Philosophers*, Yale University Press, paperback edn, 1970

Bestor, A. E., *Backwoods Utopias*, University of Pennsylvania Press, 1950

Boewe, C., *Prairie Albion*, Southern Illinois University Press, 1962

Boorstin, D. J., *The Americans – The National Experience*, Random House, 1965

Buley, R. Carlyle, *The Old North West*, 2 vols., Indiana University Press, 1950

Carmony, D. F. and Elliot, J. M., *New Harmony, Indiana: Robert Owen's Seedbed for Utopia*, Indiana Magazine of History, vol. 76, 1980

Cohn, C., *The Pursuit of the Millennium*, Oxford University Press, paperback edn, 1970

Dunckley, H. (ed.), *Bamford's Passages in the Life of a Radical*, 2 vols., Fisher Unwin, 1893

Duss, John S., *The Harmonists*, Pennsylvania Book Service, 1943

Harrison, J. F. C., *Robert Owen and the Owenites in America*, Routledge and Kegan Paul, 1969

Lockwood, G. B., *The New Harmony Movement*, Dover, 1971

MacDonald, Donald, *The Diaries of Donald MacDonald, 1824–1826*. Indiana Historical Society Publications, vol. 14, no. 2, 1942

Melish, J., *A Geographical Description of the United States, etc*, Philadelphia, 1816, reprinted by the Gazetteer Press, 1972

Pitzer, D. E. and Elliott, J. M., *New Harmony's First Utopians*, Indiana Magazine of History, vol. 75, 1979

Pollard, S. and Salt, J. (eds.), *Robert Owen, Prophet of the Poor*, Macmillan, 1971

Prentice, A., *Historical Sketches and Personal Recollections of Manchester*, 1851, reprinted Cass, 1969

Stein, S. J., *The Shaker Experience in America*, Yale, 1992

Taylor, A., *Visions of Harmony*, Oxford University Press, 1987

Veitch, G. S., *The Genesis of Parliamentary Reform*, Constable, reprinted 1965

Walker, J. R. and Burkhardt, R. W. (eds.) *Eliza Julia Flower, Letters of an English Gentlewoman, etc*, Ball State University, 1991

Waterman, W. R., *Frances Wright*, AMS Press reprint, 1967, of *Studies in History, Economics and Public Law*, vol. 115, no. 1, 1924

Wilson, W. E., *The Angel and the Serpent*, Indiana University Press, 1964

Wood, Ralph (ed.), *The Pennsylvanian Germans*, Princeton University Press, 1942

INDEX

Adams, John Quincy 151–2, 168, 170
Addington, Mr (British diplomat) 151
Albert, Prince Consort 222
Albion, Illinois 113, 127, 143, 144,
  160–2, 229
Allen, Elizabeth 88
Allen, Mary 92
Allen, William 87–8, 91, 92, 100
American Geological Society 141
American War of Independence 8–9,
  26, 135
Anabaptists 52–4
Andrews, Eliza Julia, *see* Flower, E. J.
Arkwright, Richard 25
Arndt, Karl 123
Aubry, Thérèse-Angelique 99

Baker, John L. 82, 154
Balfour, Revd 182–3
Balthazar, Monsieur 214
Bamford, Samuel 105–6, 138
Basse-Mueller (German diplomat) 62
Beissel (founder of Ephrata) 59
Bell, Andrew 96
Bentham, Jeremy 88, 89
Bethlehem, Pennsylvania 59
Birkbeck, Morris 123; appearance 109;
  background 112; character 110–11;
  death 178; family of 160; and
  Harmony 113, 127, 143; journey to
  Illinois 107–10; publications 111;
  quarrel with Flower family 111, 113,
  144, 162, 178; and religion 108, 112;
  reputation in Illinois 160; at
  Wanborough 113, 115
Birkbeck, Richard 160
Blachley, Dr 147
Blane, William Newham 126–7, 143, 154
Bockelson, Jan 53
Bourne, William Sturges 103

Braxfield, Lord (Robert MacQueen) 18,
  22, 23, 24–5, 41, 192
Braxfield House, Lanarkshire 18, 22, 23,
  141, 183–4
Britain 15–17, 28, 139, 221–2; anti-
  slavery movement 26–7, 92; cotton
  19–20, 25, 35–7, 100–2; enclosure
  acts 27–8; parliamentary reform 135,
  138–9, 140; population increase
  85–6, 139, 222; poverty 7–8, 21,
  26–8, 86, 133; public hangings 6–7;
  social reform 89–92, 100–3, 132–3;
  unemployment 86, 101
British Army 90
Brothers, Richard 98
Brougham, Lord 223–4
Brown, Paul 214–15, 217, 218, 219
Buchanan (British consul) 148
Buchanan, James 192
Butler County, Pennsylvania 42, 43, 74
Buxton, Hannah Fowell 92
Buxton, Sir Thomas Fowell 92

Calhoun, John Caldwell 151, 152
Cambridge Intelligencer 109
Cambridge University 26
Cane Ridge 73
Carlyle, Thomas 193
Cartwright, Major John 135, 140
Castlereagh, Lord 162
Chartists 221, 223
Chicago, Illinois 124
'Church and King' movement 20–1, 24
Cincinnati 174, 185
City of London Tavern 101, 130
Clapham Sect 27, 88
Clarkson, Thomas 26–7, 88
Clay, Henry 170
Clayton, John and Mary 109
Clinton, De Witt 148